WHAT HAVE WE DONE

WHAT HAVE WE DONE

THE MORAL INJURY OF OUR LONGEST WARS

DAVID WOOD

Little, Brown and Company
New York   Boston   London

Little, Brown and Company
Hachette Book Group
1290 Avenue of the Americas, New York, NY 10104
littlebrown.com

First edition: November 2016

Little, Brown and Company is a division of Hachette Book Group, Inc. The Little, Brown name and logo are trademarks of Hachette Book Group, Inc.

The Hachette Speakers Bureau provides a wide range of authors for speaking events. To find out more, go to hachettespeakersbureau.com or call (866) 376-6591.

ISBN 978-0-316-26415-0
LCCN 2016932416

10 9 8 7 6 5 4 3 2 1

LSC-C

Printed in the United States of America

For the storytellers in my life,
my mother, Elizabeth Smedley Wood,
and my wife, Elizabeth Moore Frerking

If you've ever been to war, seen what it's really like, you never want to go to war again.

—General Ray Odierno, former Chief of Staff, U.S. Army, five years as a combat commander in Iraq

Contents

Contents

Author's Note

This book is about the Americans we sent to war in Iraq and Afghanistan and the moral injuries they sustained there. In those conflicts, civilians also were caught up in the fighting, as willing or unwilling participants or as bystanders. Even as our wars were getting under way in 2002, most Afghans and Iraqis were already enduring high levels of anxiety, depression, fear, grief, bitterness, and hopelessness from past conflict and repression. The years that followed must have deepened their physical and psychological trauma to levels of pain we can scarcely imagine. The moral injuries of the Afghan and Iraqi people are beyond the scope of this book but not, I trust, out of our thoughts.

WHAT HAVE
WE DONE

The Baptismal Font

For a moment, the chaplain wondered if this improvised ceremony might violate some obscure canon of Christian liturgy. But using the baptismal font for this purpose felt appropriate. After all, the symbolic cleansing of warriors after battle was an ancient ritual familiar to the Greeks, the Crusaders, Native Americans, and many others. And the liturgical rite of baptism, older than Christianity itself, was a ceremonial washing away of sin and the receiving of God's forgiveness. The chaplain's soldiers, he knew, needed both.

It was 2006, a soft May evening in Iraq, and the fierce heat had eased a bit. An orange moon rode the dusty horizon, and there was just enough wind to rustle the palm-tree fronds outside the blast walls of the American compound at Habbaniyah. Inside the small chapel, soldiers sat hunched on white plastic chairs, scrawling on the three-by-five index cards the chaplain had passed around. He had asked them to jot down a few words about their twelve months in combat, now coming to an end. When they were done, the chaplain had told them to bring the cards forward and place them in the baptismal font, the dry stone bowl recovered from the weeds where the Iraqis had thrown it years ago when this former British army chapel was converted into a mosque. Now, at least for a time, this was an American base. The stone bowl rested on a plywood stand, and one by one the soldiers approached, dropping in one, two, even three cards.

It had been a hard time for them all. The fighting there, just outside Falluja, had been brutal. Sniper shots and bomb explosions ripped through their ranks. Suicide bombers blasted their convoys, and rockets and mortars rained down on their camp, once spraying the stone-block chapel itself with shrapnel. Fifteen of their own soldiers, their closest friends, had gone home in flag-draped coffins. Many more were wounded, in body and spirit. They had fought back, killing or capturing when they could. Local civilians, women and children, had died in front of them by errant or careless gunshots or blast fragments. The soldiers had witnessed inexplicable hatreds among Iraqis: prisoners and innocents of the wrong sect tortured by insurgents and shot or beheaded, their gruesome remains left for the dogs.

None of it fit with the prior life experiences of this Pennsylvania National Guard battalion, men and women from pleasant, uneventful small-town and suburban American life. They were still reeling from the recent deaths of five friends, killed when a convoy took a wrong turn and a Humvee rolled over a makeshift bomb, bursting into flames. The turret gunner was killed instantly, and the other soldiers tumbled out on fire, their dying screams seared into the souls of the living.

At the chaplain's request, the soldiers committed what they could of this to paper. Write down what you want to leave behind, he had told them in his soothing, sonorous voice. Things you have done or left undone…things you have seen. They wrote fast, words of sorrow and anger, regret, shame, guilt, grief. Words inadequate, perhaps, but still too poisonous to carry home. Write down, the chaplain said, what is troubling you.

The chaplain himself, a man whose smooth, boyish face belied the pain and suffering in his eyes, put his own card in last. Every inch of it was filled. He had held dying soldiers in his bloody arms, had said memorial services too many times. He had struggled to protect, strengthen, and comfort his soldiers. Yet, he had once written home in a despairing note, "I can read it in their eyes. They think my answers are shallow and hollow." The chaplain's wounds were deep, and now he was nearly spent.

He had read somewhere of the formal cleansing rituals some African villages held for returning child warriors guilty of astonishing cruelties. The young killers were accepted home, but only after ceremonies of healing and forgiveness. He knew, of course, the Old Testament instructions for the purification of warriors returning from battle before they could enter camp. Something like that was needed here, he believed. He was afraid that he and his soldiers were contaminated by war trauma; that, unless they began the cleansing now, once they got home their moral wounds would suppurate, perhaps for decades, until the pain finally would erupt.

It was the best he could do. As the soldiers stood, he struck a match. The pile of cards caught and flared. Wisps of smoke and red embers rose, and they watched in silence until it was all gone, and then they walked out into the night.

CHAPTER 1

It's Wrong, but You Have No Choice

The Army needs its Soldiers to kill without thinking too much about the moral implications before or after pulling the trigger.
                    —Paul D. Fritts, Major and Chaplain, U.S. Army

Broad shouldered and lean at six foot two, Nikki Rudolph, an affable sandy-haired Californian, was twenty-two years old when he was sent as a marine infantryman to Afghanistan, where he shot and killed a young boy. This was not uncommon in the murderous confusion of our recent wars, where farmers and mothers and young kids might seize a weapon and shape-shift in a moment into a combatant and back again to an innocent civilian, and young Americans peering into the murk would have a moment to decide: kill or not. This time, an exhausting firefight with Taliban insurgents had dragged on for hours across the superheated desert wastes and tree-lined irrigation canals of Helmand Province. Late that afternoon, Nik saw from the corner of his eye someone darting around the corner of an adobe wall, spraying bullets from an assault rifle held against his small hips. Nik swiveled his M4 carbine, tightened his finger on the trigger, and saw that it was a boy of maybe twelve or thirteen. Then he fired.

According to the military's exacting legal principles and rules, it was a justifiable kill, even laudable, an action taken against an enemy combatant in defense of Nik himself and his fellow marines. But now Nik is back home in civilian life, where killing a child violates the bedrock moral ideals we all hold. His action that day, righteous in combat, nonetheless is a bruise on his soul, a painful violation of the simple understanding of right and wrong that he and all of us carry subconsciously through life.

Those two emotions, pride in having prevailed in a firefight and the dark shadow of wrongdoing, together illustrate the baffling and sometimes cruel paradox that so often dominates the lives of those we send into war. Duty and honor, and self-preservation, define Nik's decision to pull the trigger. At home, strangers thank him for his service, and politicians celebrate him and other combat veterans as heroes. And Nik carries on his conscience a child's death.

Americans who have served in Iraq and Afghanistan are coming to understand Nik's lingering pain as a *moral injury,* a trauma as real as a flesh wound. In its most simple and profound sense, moral injury is a jagged disconnect from our understanding of who we are and what we and others ought to do and ought not to do. Experiences that are common in war—inflicting purposeful violence, witnessing the sudden violent maiming of a loved buddy, the suffering of civilians—challenge and often shatter our understanding of the world as a good place where good things should happen to us, the foundational beliefs we learn as infants. The broader loss of trust, loss of faith, loss of innocence, can have enduring psychological, spiritual, social, and behavioral impact.

Each of us, of course, has experienced at least a twinge of moral regret and sometimes deeper and lasting moral injury. History is marked by immense human calamities and periods of unspeakable moral violation. Yet the moral jeopardy of war, especially in the wars the United States began and fought in Iraq and Afghanistan, is different. These wars demanded the intense and prolonged participation of a tiny fraction of the nation's youth in sustained campaigns built on the intentional violation of the ancient sanctions against killing. Those who returned did so without the healing rituals of cleansing and forgiveness practiced by past generations. Threads of anger and betrayal run through their stories: violations of their sense of "what's right" by the Afghan and Iraqi civilians who turned violently against them, by an American public that turned its back on the war, and by the lack of clear victories in Iraq and Afghanistan that might have justified their sacrifices.

In my experience, to be in war is to be exposed to moral injury. Almost all return with some sense of unease about what we've seen and done, about how well we and others have lived up to our own standards. Most of us are unprepared to disentangle the emotions of anger, sorrow, shame, or remorse that can result. It is common, researchers say, for those who have experienced a moral wound to react with cynicism or bitterness; to distrust authority; to be more prone to anxiety, depression; perhaps to seek comfort in isolation or the self-medication of drugs, alcohol, or overwork. Most common, to never talk about the war.

Trauma experts such as Brett Litz, a psychologist who is pioneering moral injury research at Boston University and the U.S. Department of Veterans Affairs (VA) Boston Healthcare System, also reference as symptoms of moral injury terms with which I was unfamiliar—dysphoria (severe distress), for one, and anhedonia (the inability to experience pleasure). But despite impressive advances in the understanding of moral injury and some breakthrough therapies that hold the promise of helping those most afflicted, my sense is that many veterans, like Nik, carry their regret and sorrow and heartache on into life and rarely speak of it. In that sense, moral injury is the enduring if hidden signature wound of our most recent, and longest, wars.

It is important to understand that while some veterans cannot find peace after a moral injury, most of those who have felt morally injured are not disabled, are not broken or dangerous, do not fit the insulting stereotype of combat vets as lunatic unemployed, homeless, drug-addled criminals.

Nor does moral injury necessarily describe legal wrongdoing. Moral injury does not imply that an atrocity or a war crime has been committed, simply that an individual's ethos has been violated. "War is vile. There are some things that are more vile, and that's why we fight, but that vileness affects you down to your core," David Sutherland once told me. A soldier for thirty years, Sutherland commanded the twelve thousand men and women of the Third Brigade Combat Team task force of the First Cavalry Division. For fifteen months in 2006 and 2007 in Iraq, they fought day and night. Sutherland had vowed to personally honor every one of his badly wounded and dead troops, and he did that, visiting hospitals and morgues, putting his hand on the body bag or head of each one and praying. It nearly broke him. "Guilt, shame, sorrow, bereavement [are] normal human reactions, but as commander I couldn't shut down. I was in a battle every single day. I'd wake up to an IED [improvised explosive device] exploding and go to bed with an IED exploding."

Staff Sergeant Donnie D. Dixon was part of Sutherland's security detail as they traveled the battlefields, and on September 29, 2007, Dixon was shot and killed. He was thirty-seven and left a wife and four children. "When Sergeant Dixon was killed, that affected all seventeen members of my security detachment, and some of us more than others: we were standing right by him when it happened," Sutherland told me. "How do you not believe this is a moral injury?"

★   ★   ★

For many of us, such war-related moral injuries are invisible because we are so disconnected from the lives of the men and women who serve in the military. Almost two million of them are home from Iraq or Afghanistan, proud of their difficult and demanding service and profoundly affected by their experiences at war. Most of it was lived in vivid extremes far removed from the ordinary: there were dazzling highs and depressing, boring, and sometimes despairing lows; the burning devotion of small-unit brotherhood, the adrenaline rush of danger. The pride of service, the thrill of raw power. The brutal ecstasy of life on the edge and the deep grief of loss. Nik Rudolph thinks of it as "the worst, best experience of my life."

But war is an alternate moral universe where many of the rules and values we grew up with are revoked. Do unto others, suspended. An alien world in which complex moral puzzles, like confronting a child combatant, demand instant decisions by those who are least fit to make them, for reasons of incomplete neuro-logical development and life experience. An environment for which the United States has trained its warriors exhaustively in physical fitness and military tactics but left them psychologically and spiritually unprepared. An environment from which they return to find their new understanding of the world and who they have become fits awkwardly or not at all into their old lives in peacetime America. They return to a civilian public whose spo-radic attention to veterans largely fails to comprehend or acknowl-edge the experiences they have absorbed on our behalf.

This is the dark truth of war, a secret we are all complicit in keeping. We know, though we rarely acknowledge it, that war imposes terrible costs on human beings and that, while some are strengthened by the experience, others buckle. We understand at some level why combat veterans shrink from sharing their stories: we don't want to know them. In our sometimes-frenzied veneration of war heroes, we are too eager to rush past the shad-owed doorway where lurks what the poet Peter Marin calls "the terrible and demanding wisdom" of war. In the lofty discussions about putting "boots on the ground" among Washington's strate-gists and national security experts, those in government service or awaiting their turn in the city's comfortable think tanks, there is little room for considering the inevitable cost, the well-being of those men and women we will send next.

But out there, it will get worse. The brutal new conflicts that tempt American intervention as we move deeper into the twenty-first century pose intense new moral challenges. The old signposts of morally acceptable behavior, the laws of war, the Geneva Conventions, the just war doctrine, seem increasingly irrelevant in a world of drone killings, the beheading of hostages, and the deliberate massacre of schoolchildren by Islamist extrem-ists. Traditional ideas about "victory" over these groups are obso-lete, battered relics of a bygone age, given their ability to inspire disaffected youth and the wildfire spread of weapons technology that has enabled them to armor their utter ruthlessness with the killing power once reserved for nations. Moral challenges face us as well back home as we continue to recruit, train, and dispatch a tiny number of our youth for military actions about which we are deeply skeptical and for battlefield risks we ourselves are not will-ing to take.

What we know of this latest generation of veterans, and what we fear of the future, demand that we finally pay urgent attention to the moral dimension of war. As we consider committing more young Americans to twenty-first-century warfare, we must do so with full knowledge and acceptance of the price they will pay on our behalf.

I crossed paths with Lance Corporal Nik Rudolph and his fellow marines when I deployed to Afghanistan as an embedded journalist with his unit, the First Battalion, Sixth Marine Regiment, or One-Six. Nik is the kind of marine who always wanted to be a marine. His dad was a marine, an artillery spotter and a recon scout. As a toddler Nik wore the Marine Corps T-shirts his dad would bring home after being away on long field exercises. Nik graduated to playing with GI Joe action figures and building forts. After high school he studied auto mechanics, but there were no jobs in the downturn of 2008; even car dealerships were closing. So Nik did what he'd always yearned to do: he enlisted and was soon on his way to boot camp at Parris Island, South Carolina.

I spent months with the marines of One-Six on their first tour in Afghanistan. But it would be a few years before we could sit down and sort through all that had gone on during their second deployment, in 2010, and in particular on the February day when the marines of One-Six and the Taliban were locked in that firefight, a fury of reckless rage and exhaustion that went on for nine hours. The battle had erupted, as the marines later understood it, after Taliban insurgents castrated a young boy in a nearby village, knowing his family would summon marines for help and the marines would come, walking into a deadly ambush that would ignite the firefight. Then there comes that instant, an eternity Nik has replayed over and over in his mind, when he has to choose to kill or not. He squeezes the trigger, and the boy's body spasms and hits the ground. Now what? "We just collected up that weapon and kept moving," Nik explained. "Going from compound to compound, trying to find them [the insurgents]. Eventually they hopped in a car and drove off into the desert."

There was a long silence after Nik finished the story. He's lived with it for years, yet the telling still catches in his throat. Eventually, he sighed. "He was just a kid. But I'm sorry, I'm trying not to get shot and I don't want any of my brothers getting hurt, so when you are put in that kind of situation... it's shitty

that you have to, like…shoot him. You know it's wrong. But…
you have no choice.

"Thank God he didn't know how to fuckin' aim," he added
morosely.

Nik is not crushed by this experience. He has a quick laugh and
a life he enjoys. He dresses carefully and is polite and deferential.
The regret, confusion, and sorrow he brought back from Afghanistan remain beneath his skin. But they break the surface now and
again, at first leading him into heavy drinking and an effort to see a
civilian therapist. He knows his demons are there. I asked him once
if he found that moral injuries like killing a child heal over time,
the bruise eventually fading. No, he said. "It will all be there."

Two years after Nik Rudolph came home from Afghanistan,
Shira Maguen, a clinical psychologist at the San Francisco VA
Health Care System and a professor at the University of California, San Francisco, published another in a series of research papers
on the psychological impact of wartime killing. In her study of
Afghanistan and Iraq veterans who had killed in combat, just over
half had killed only enemy combatants; the rest had killed both
enemy combatants and at least one noncombatant, a male civilian,
a woman or child, or an elder. All those who had killed were
twice as likely to develop frequent and severe psychological symptoms as those who had not. Those who had killed a noncombatant, she found, were the most likely to carry home the depression,
anger, shame, and guilt of moral injury.

You don't have to go to war, of course, to feel depressed, anxious, or regretful. All of us carry the nicks and bruises of everyday
experiences, and some, the deeper wounds of sorrow, grief, and
guilt. But the raw, toxic violence of war can wound the soul more
deeply, in ways that combat veterans know and rarely can describe
to outsiders. Many have felt the crushing weight of helplessness as
they are thrust into situations where they seem to have no moral
agency, and any decision will feel wrong.

In recent years, we have begun to recognize that the psychological damage suffered in war far exceeds physical injury. That many of those who were caught up in war struggle during and after their service with the mysterious, troubling emotional storms that often afflict them. We have come to group all these psychological injuries under the label "PTSD." That's wrong.

Post-traumatic stress disorder is biology. It is the body's involuntary physical reaction as we relive the intense fear of a life-threatening event and the scalding emotional responses that follow: terror and a debilitating sense of helplessness. Our response to threats, to danger, is a primitive involuntary mechanism developed for survival by earth's earliest life forms. For us, fear triggers an alarm system set deep in the amygdala, in the oldest part of our brain. The alarm causes adrenaline and the steroid cortisol to spurt into the bloodstream, making us hyperalert, breathing hard with muscles tensed, eyes wide, pulse racing, ready for "fight or flight." That's a necessary response to danger, whether it's an imminent head-on collision or a battlefield ambush, and in war, people can experience it repeatedly. What's not appropriate is when that response is triggered by a false alarm. The amygdala picks up what it identifies as a sign of danger and goes into action, not knowing it's no longer in Afghanistan, and a veteran suddenly is cowering from fireworks or a car alarm. Understandably, he or she will try to avoid situations that might trigger those reactions, an effort that can lead to isolation. But avoidance isn't always possible. A vet may be sauntering happily into Walmart and involuntarily recoil from the sudden onrush of chaos and noise and light in the vast bustling space. Instantly and involuntarily, he is in a full-blown danger response. He flushes bright red, sweat runs down his back, and gasping for breath he runs out of Walmart and smacks his fist into a fence post and yells at his kids. He's depressed for the rest of the day—*What's happening to me?*—and sleepless and anxious at night lest the nightmares come. Next day he's irritable at work because he hasn't slept, then snaps at his wife because he can't explain what's wrong. Even he doesn't understand it.

Clinically, this is described as "fear-circuitry dysregulation," but mental health professionals themselves disagree on the causes and precise parameters of PTSD. The official definition, written and sanctified by the American Psychiatric Association (APA) in its *Diagnostic and Statistical Manual of Mental Disorders* (*DSM*), has shifted four times since it was first adopted in 1980. PTSD is real, and I have seen it among the combat vets of Iraq and Afghanistan and previous wars. The mechanism of PTSD is well understood: perceived threat and automatic response. It's simple enough that the VA has hired IBM to set up a computerized "clinical reasoning" database to assist physicians in making faster diagnoses of PTSD and to accelerate the process of selecting the right treatment plan.

Although battlefield PTSD and moral injury can occur together, Nik Rudolph doesn't have PTSD. What Nik struggles with is not the involuntary recurrence of fear. He's okay with the crowds at Walmart. He doesn't startle at loud noises. In contrast with veterans who've experienced PTSD, Nik didn't feel the pain of his moral injury at the moment of the incident. It was only later, well after he'd pulled the trigger, that the implications of what he'd done began to weigh on him. Moral injury occurs "when a person has time to reflect on a traumatic experience," Major Paul D. Fritts wrote in a paper at Yale Divinity School, which he attended after serving two army combat tours in Iraq.

That's Nik. He is bothered with the memory of that Afghan boy and with questions about what he did that day. Like all of us, Nik had always thought of himself as a good person. But does a good person kill a child? Follow that line of thinking, and it quickly becomes *No, a good person doesn't kill a child, therefore I must be a bad person. And think of all the other bad things I've done.* Left unattended, a moral injury that began as a bruise on the soul can continue to disrupt life. *If I killed a child, could I ever be a trustworthy father?* The symptoms can be similar to those of PTSD: anxiety, depression, sleeplessness, anger. But sorrow, remorse, grief, shame, bitterness, and moral confusion—*What is right?*—signal moral injury, while flashbacks, loss of memory, fear, and a startle complex seem to characterize PTSD.

Most of us, like Nik, have a firm and deeply personal understanding of life's moral rules, of justice and injustice, right and wrong. That sense, our inner compass, is built on beliefs we begin to acquire as infants. Being fed and cared for and loved, the psychologist Ronnie Janoff-Bulman wrote, teaches us that the world is a benevolent and meaningful place, that we can expect good things to happen. Infants begin to develop a sense of self-worth and trust—*I'm being cuddled and fed and kept warm, so I must be a good person to deserve this.* That dawning awareness is what the philosopher and psychologist William James called "our more or less dumb sense of what life honestly and deeply means." These earliest learned beliefs are extremely powerful, buttressed by later experience into a sense of cautious optimism "that things will work out as well as can reasonably be expected," as psychologist Aaron Antonovsky has written. Most of us, through experience and over time, modify that sunny view. The world is not always benevolent; some people are jerks; some leaders are despicable.

Still, I think most of us like to believe that we act in good faith. We know we should follow the Golden Rule even if most of the time we don't, and we get angry when others treat us ill. Against evidence to the contrary, I still hope that our leaders are somewhat competent and honest and act in our best interest. Like most people, I want my life to go well. We all want the best for those we love, spouse or child or battle buddy. If bad things happen, we hope they won't happen to us.

But war, by its very nature, tends to suddenly and violently upend these remaining moral beliefs. Things don't go well in war, whose very purpose demands death and destruction. Innocents and those we love will suffer and die; some leaders will make bad decisions that put ourselves and our friends in peril. *Thou shalt not kill* hardly applies when your job is to kill people. Army Lieutenant Colonel Doug Etter says it most simply. He is a National Guard chaplain with two combat tours in Iraq. It was Etter, a Presbyterian minister, who led the ceremony of the burning of regrets in the stone baptismal font in Habbaniyah. War, Etter said, "is a sin."

PTSD has little to do with sin. It is a psychological wound caused by something done to you. Someone with PTSD is a victim. A moral injury is a self-accusation, prompted by something you did, something you failed to do, as well as something done to you. Combat veterans may feel a moral injury from being unintentionally responsible for the death of a civilian. Some may feel regret and sorrow for not having spotted the sniper who wounded a buddy. A flight medic may feel guilt and shame for failing to save a mortally wounded soldier; a young woman who enlisted to help Iraqis build a new country and found only destruction and death may feel bitter and betrayed by her leaders and may become deeply cynical about public service. Military families, too, absorb moral injury, living with loneliness and fear and perhaps emotions of anger and betrayal along with their pride of service and sacrifice.

The loss of a warrior's moral guideposts can be as devastating as a hiker losing the trail in a blizzard. Where so much is wrong, discovering and holding on to your own morally comfortable bearings can be difficult. Stress, exhaustion, loneliness, and the peer pressure of small units at war can make such reflection impossible. Guilt, the recognition that *I did a bad thing* or *I failed,* can harden into shame: *I'm a bad person.* Mild or severe depression and anxiety can follow, along with anger and bitterness. Alcohol and drugs can seem like an easy way to ease the pain. Shame can lead to risky acts of indiscipline, such as drunk driving, brawling, or mouthing off to superiors. That's behavior that could result in a bad-conduct discharge, which bars a veteran from receiving the services of the VA, a growing problem among Iraq and Afghanistan War veterans.

The moral pain of warfighters is reason enough for us to pay close attention, but there are practical considerations as well. Disillusioned, angry, or bitter soldiers can become a military-readiness issue by dropping out or underperforming. Once out of the service, veterans may find it difficult to reconcile their wartime actions with the moral standards and expectations of home. Unable or unwilling to share the emotions of moral injury, some veterans choose isolation, depriving their families, colleagues, and communities of their presence, their skills, and their insights—a loss for all of us.

The U.S. involvement in Vietnam was a watershed in our understanding of war trauma, and even though it took almost a decade for the mental health profession to officially recognize PTSD, tens of thousands of combat veterans eventually found some relief through psychotherapy. But because several of the indicators of PTSD—anxiety, depression, anger, isolation, insomnia, self-medication—are shared with moral injury, it took time for therapists and researchers to unbraid the two. Jonathan Shay, a former staff psychiatrist at the VA medical center in Boston, worked for years with Vietnam combat veterans diagnosed with PTSD before he could see the scope of the war trauma he described in his breakthrough 1994 book, *Achilles in Vietnam*. To fully capture that facet of war trauma he felt was not PTSD, Shay coined the phrase "moral injury." Cleanly differentiating it from PTSD, Shay wrote: "Moral injury is an essential part of any combat trauma that leads to lifelong psychological injury. Veterans can usually recover from horror, fear, and grief once they return to civilian life, so long as 'what's right' has not also been violated." Despite such leaps in understanding war trauma, the U.S. government's response to moral injury is light-years behind its ability to recruit, arm, and deploy young men and women into combat. "In the military and the VA, moral injury is a uniquely and significantly unaddressed war zone harm," says psychologist Litz.

Litz's colleague William Nash also has explored this wartime clash of moral values as his lifework. Nash is a combat psychiatrist, a groundbreaking researcher whose academic work is enriched by his battlefield experience: he was awarded a Bronze Star in combat with marines in Falluja. He holds a medical degree from the University of Illinois College of Medicine and did his residency in psychiatry at the Naval Medical Center San Diego. During thirty years' active duty in the navy, he established programs on combat stress and trauma and produced a long list of academic research papers—all aimed at understanding war trauma and moral injury and helping young warriors cope. In 2015 he was named director of mental health for the Marine Corps.

Nash is one of a growing circle of researchers and mental health practitioners who are defining the scope of moral injury and experimenting with promising new forms of therapy. Among these experts are Litz, Shira Maguen, and Amy Amidon at the Naval Medical Center San Diego, where the therapy group is the only government-sanctioned treatment for moral injury that I have found.

Over hours of conversation, Nash asserted that the moral values we learn early in life, and those that are reinforced in basic military training, represent the best of humanity's ideals. "It's these values that give you some chance of doing something good in a war and limiting collateral damage," he told me. "The problem is that war will break these values.

"There's an inherent contradiction between the warrior code, how these guys define themselves, what they expect of themselves—to be heroes, the selfless servants who fight for the rest of us—and the impossibility in war of ever living up to those ideals. It cannot be done. Not by anybody there," Nash told me one day. "So how do they forgive themselves, forgive others, for failing to live up to the ideals without abandoning the ideals?" Not easily. When they come home, he said, "something is damaged, broken. They wonder, in their little sphere of influence, How well did I or didn't I live up to those ideals? Very often, the answer is what kills them. They feel betrayed; they don't trust in these values and ideals anymore."

A military chaplain, Army Captain Bryan Coggins, once told me of a soldier who had come to him in great mental anguish. Months earlier he had been in a firefight and had his rifle sight trained on an insurgent, but instead of firing at the man's chest—the "center of mass" that troops are taught to aim for—he consciously lowered his weapon and shot him in the stomach, knowing that would cause a lingering and painful death. As an army medic worked to save the man, the soldier and his squad members gathered around and watched the man die in agony. "Then the guilt rushed in, about the reality of what he'd done and the decision he had made," Coggins said. "He had killed before—he was infantry—he never told me the exact number he had killed, but none of the others had been issues for him. Until he realized, 'I'm not just killing because I have to, but because I want this to be a suffering,'" and he knew that to be wrong. A painful violation of his own moral values. Coggins counseled him at a VA medical center where the soldier was a mental health patient being treated for drug addiction. "The drugs were a coping mechanism," Coggins said. "His heart wasn't as dark as his action in that moment when he shot. He didn't set out that day to make someone suffer. He just made the decision in an instant. And he was seeking forgiveness."

As the soldier was talking about it, Coggins asked him, What if the insurgent had survived? What if the medic was able to save him? What would you say to him? Let me be him, Coggins said. Talk to me as if I were this man. And he did. "A lot of it was an apology, and there was a level of self-forgiveness to it," Coggins said. "He wasn't religious, but he was spiritual enough so that he felt some concept of God forgiving him for this."

But in American society and especially within the military, there is no ready mechanism for acknowledgment of moral injury or forgiveness, and even self-forgiveness can be a hard concept to nail down. Nik Rudolph came home to Camp Lejeune, North Carolina, in January 2012 after three deployments, a total of sixteen months in combat, and he was sinking in a downward spiral. Drinking so heavily that he picked up a DUI and got busted a rank, losing his prized position as a squad leader. Seeking help, he sneaked off post to see a civilian therapist. When I asked him what prompted him to do that, he shrugged. "Not being able to …not make sense of things in my head, like, feeling bad about certain things that happened and things that I couldn't prevent. I didn't want to do this on a marine base," he said. "They've got group sessions and you'd get all these angry fuckin' marines in one room, they're like 'Take a number,' and I just didn't want it to be a pissing contest. I wanted to talk to somebody one-on-one." The therapist prescribed sleeping pills, and Nik slept through morning formation twice, getting slapped with two charges of unauthorized absence. All these demerits added up to what the Marine Corps considers a "pattern of misconduct."

At war, Nik had been exposed to IED blasts six times and shot once, while he was manning a machine gun in a firefight. He'd risked his life, led men he loved in combat, and seen some of them brutally killed. And now that he'd come home sick at heart, the Marine Corps, which he also loved, meant to kick him out. And it did, handing him an honorable discharge in return for Nik's promise to leave immediately. He signed the papers, hopped gleefully into his '68 Ford-100 pickup, and accelerated to sixty miles per hour down Holcomb Boulevard, so fast that his hubcap popped off as he tore around the curve just after the Burger King. Fuck it, he thought to himself, Lejeune can have it.

He lived for a time with a marine buddy in Philadelphia and worked as a bodyguard for a security firm. Then he headed back to California, where he studied to be a firefighter and EMT. The physical wounds he collected in Afghanistan have healed. But he can't leave the war behind. Like many veterans, Nik has found the routine of civilian life flat after the adrenaline rush and urgency of war. And the child he shot weighs on his mind. The images break his concentration and disturb his sleep; he's often mildly depressed. It's hard to see the point of anything, he said. He trusts no one except his marine buddies. "It's just everything I've seen, things I had to do," he tried to explain. Now twenty-seven, Nik is likable and, at least outwardly, seems content. His manner is careful and deliberate. He jokes that he's accident-prone and places his feet precisely when he walks. He speaks the same way, choosing his words guardedly, and when he comes back around to the child-shooting incident, his speech slows. "I really didn't hesitate. I knew it had to be done, so I just turned, pivoted…fuckin'…I *had* to shoot him."

Small wonder that combat veterans are reluctant to try to explain all this to civilians. Especially when they are called heroes and celebrated as a new Greatest Generation. One of Nik Rudolph's marine buddies from Afghanistan is Stephen Canty. When he was growing up near Charlottesville, Virginia, Stephen would occasionally ask his grandfather about his combat experiences. But Grandpa, a marine who fought in the Pacific in World War II, rarely talked about what he'd seen and done. Stephen was a thoughtful and articulate kid. He read widely, attracted girls with his mop of brown hair and lopsided smile, and whizzed through the advanced academics of the elite Blue Ridge Governor's School.

"He was born carrying a briefcase and an encyclopedia," his mother, Micheline, proudly told me.

But Stephen itched to go to war. One day he came home and announced he was enlisting in the marines and going to Afghanistan. He was seventeen at the time and had never realized there was pain behind Grandpa's grumpy refusal to talk about his wartime service. Never realized why Grandpa had other unexplained personality quirks. One was his outright refusal to eat pork chops. At his grandfather's funeral recently, Stephen finally heard the story from one of Grandpa's war buddies. Grandpa Canty and another scout-sniper had gotten trapped behind Japanese lines and concealed themselves in an abandoned foxhole beneath the bodies of Japanese dead. They could hear Japanese soldiers prowling around, probing for the two Americans, and every so often they'd get up and sprint, ducking fusillades of fire. Running and hiding, they lasted for thirty days scavenging for food and water but finally made their way back to friendly lines, where Grandpa Canty, having shrunk to ninety-nine pounds, devoured stacks of pork chops. Afterward, he could never eat another one. And he never mentioned the trauma of hiding beneath enemy bodies or his terror of being suddenly bayoneted.

Now his grandson was intent on signing up for war, too. "Don't do it," he pleaded. "You're too goddamn smart, boy."

But Stephen went.

Like the soldiers of the Pennsylvania National Guard who burned their secrets and regrets in Habbaniyah before they returned home, Canty was struggling to become a civilian again when I caught up with him. After we'd talked several times, he invited me to meet with some of his marine buddies. Stephen was learning to make documentaries and had been meeting methodically with the marines of Charlie Company, One-Six, men who'd fought together during two tours in Afghanistan. Canty was asking them to talk on videotape about their experiences in Afghanistan and their awkward and painful transitions back to civilian life. Canty and Nik Rudolph and others met with me several times, in hotel rooms in Philadelphia and New Jersey. I set out beer and my tape recorder, and for hours they talked, we drank, and I listened.

A lot of killing had taken place during their deployments, Afghans the marines killed and marines who were killed there. Canty was a SAW gunner, carrying the squad automatic weapon, a light (twenty-one pounds, with a two-hundred-round magazine) machine gun. That second deployment was spent almost entirely in the Helmand Province town of Marjah, where the marines in 2010 met unexpectedly stiff resistance from Taliban fighters. Canty and several other marines were living in an abandoned dirt-floored shop front, trying one day to rig a tarp for shade when semiautomatic rifle shots kicked up dust in the street outside and an Afghan policeman and a six-year-old boy fell. More shots followed as several children and another Afghan cop scurried for shelter. The marines sprinted out to help, past the child lying facedown in the dirt, Canty lugging his combat first-aid kit—he'd had a weeklong course in trauma first aid—and into a stifling room where he found one of the wounded policemen writhing on a blanket, moaning and bleeding, the smell of blood and sweat overpowering.

Canty yanked out his latex gloves, but they'd melted together in the summer heat. Throwing them aside, he tore open a tourniquet and leaned in and strapped it around the man's upper thigh, above the bullet hole from which blood was pumping. Cinched it tight. The man gasped in pain. "I encouraged him to pray, and began it for him in broken Arabic," Canty wrote later, in an essay he called "A Sunny Afternoon."

The man nodded, but the gesture made him again writhe in pain. He begged for water, and someone brought it in a cup.

When Canty straightened up, he noticed the three terrified children huddled in a corner of the room. He asked a policeman to get them water, then handed one of the children a string of prayer beads he kept in his pocket. To reassure the children, he wrote, "I smiled a tired smile."

Outside the firefight had intensified, marines and Afghan police exchanging shots from doorways and windows. With his SAW, Canty "fired bursts at anything that seemed appropriate, like ominous doorways and bushes." Then he remembered the boy who'd been shot. "Peering out into the street from around a corner, I saw the boy in a pool of blood, his face caked in mud... the boy was shot through the back of the head, his eye blown out." An Afghan policeman named Khan ran and retrieved the body and brought him inside. "I checked his radial pulse, the hole in his head not registering. His pulse was weak, and for some reason I thought he might have a chance." Canty lifted the child and cradled him in his arms and ran with Khan toward an open patch of land where the medevac helicopters would land. They loped past a white van stopped in the street; the driver, an elderly man dressed in white, cried out and began sobbing when he saw the mangled face of his son. Canty knelt and rechecked the boy's pulse. He found it, but it was very weak. By the time they got to the landing zone, the boy was dead.

The firefight died away as dusk settled. The old man came to get the body of his son. Canty trudged back to his room and collapsed beside another marine on an old wooden bed they used as a couch. "I took off my helmet and ran a hand through my matted, sweaty hair," he wrote. "Someone gave me a cigarette. We were mostly quiet, the comedown from the adrenaline hitting us and exhaustion setting in. We had seen truly innocent people, even kids, get hurt before, but it is a hard callus to form. I still remember the smell of that stale tobacco and the coppery, almost-metallic, tang of blood."

There's never time in war to absorb experiences like that. Not long afterward came another firefight. This time, Canty told me, "I hit this guy a couple of times with the SAW, and one of the bullets bounced off his spinal cord and came out his eyeball." Canty wasn't boasting; he seemed slightly puzzled that such a thing had really happened. The man was brought into the marines' outpost in a wheelbarrow, still breathing. "He's laying there like, you know, clinging to the last seconds of his life looking up at me with one of his eyes and just like pulp in the other, and I was like twenty years old at the time."

It's a terrible image. But Canty said he's just numb to it, insisting that he felt nothing. "I just stared at him. And just walked away. And I never felt anything about that. I literally just don't care whatsoever," he said.

For a guy who claims never to feel anything about killing, Canty constantly monitors and analyzes his feelings about war, rubbing together his thoughts about duty and murder and morality like worry beads. It turned out later that the man he'd killed might not have been a Taliban after all, maybe just a local farmer. But he'd been acting suspiciously, seemingly signaling to the Taliban when the marines came and went from their base. "My thought was, You did what you had to. But did I really? I saw him running and I lit him up. It's the right thing to do in war, but in every other circumstance it's the most wrong thing you could do," he said. "Once you go to war you realize you do what you have to do to survive, when you wouldn't have done that before. Once you learn to push past immoral behavior, it becomes easier.

"Moral injury is a learned behavior, learning to accept the things you know are wrong."

But what kind of person, he wondered, would have no qualms about killing? "Are you some kind of sociopath that you can just look at a dude you shot three or four times and just kind of walk away? I think I even smiled, not in an evil way, but just like *What*

a fucked-up world we live in: you're a forty-year-old dude and you proba-
bly got kids at home and stuff, and you just got smoked by some dumb
twenty-year-old."

Canty once had a dream that children were being held in cages by an evil headmaster, and Canty shot him in the face, a tiny hole appearing in his cheek, and then shot him again, in the forehead. "I could feel it, smell it...and you wake up and realize you *have* done things like that.

"You learn to kill, and you kill people, and it's like I don't care. I've seen people get shot, I've seen little kids get shot. You see a kid and his father sitting together and he gets shot and I give a zero fuck. And once you're able to do that, what is morally right anymore? How good is your value system if you train people to kill another human being, the one thing we are taught not to do? When you create an organization based around the one taboo that all societies have?"

Hard questions, but ones that the young men and women we recruit for war must act on in a heartbeat and whose answers they must live with for the rest of their lives. Yet we know that many of them, barely out of their teens, are insufficiently prepared for high-stress, critical decision-making because adolescents' brains are not fully developed. Not until teens reach their midtwenties do their brains reach full maturity. Until then, as parents of teenagers are well aware, they tend to be excitable, easily swayed by peer pressure, and not so good at anticipating the consequences of their actions.

But that's who we send. In 2005, with American troops in desperate fights across Afghanistan and Iraq, 29 percent of enlisted marines on active duty hadn't yet celebrated their twenty-first birthdays. Include those who just turned twenty-one, and the share of the young rises to 43 percent in the Marine Corps and 24 percent in the army. By 2007, with the wars demanding more manpower, the military services enlisted 7,558 seventeen-year-olds, including Stephen Canty. The Pentagon's total intake of seventeen- to twenty-year-olds that year was 86,072—more than half of all the men and women it recruited. And they finish at a young age: in 2010, for instance, half of marines and a quarter of army troops completed their enlistment term after serving four years. As under-twenty-five-year-olds with no experience as adult civilians, they returned to face daunting problems that would frustrate anyone with decades more wisdom and maturity: how to fit in, how to form stable relationships, how to find a career, how to manage the psychological and moral demons that returned with them.

Canty was twenty when he killed that Afghan, who was a farmer or a Taliban or both, with the SAW. Nik Rudolph was twenty-two when he confronted the boy with an assault rifle. Darren Doss also enlisted at age seventeen, served two combat tours in Afghanistan with Nik and Stephen Canty in One-Six, and was back home in Schenectady, New York, at age twenty-two, morally bruised and aged far beyond his high-school pals.

The experiences of these marines were in some ways not unlike those of the young Americans who fought in past wars. As Eric T. Dean Jr. writes in *Shook Over Hell,* Civil War veterans suffered widely from "elements of depression, anxiety, social numbing, reexperiencing, fear, dread of calamity, and cognitive disorders." Along with their families, they "often lived in a kind of private hell involving physical pain, the torment of fear, and memories of killing and death."

The World War II GIs of Easy Company of the 101st Airborne are portrayed in the TV series *Band of Brothers* as the combat heroes they were. Less well known are their postwar struggles with alcoholism, nightmares, and family abuse, chronicled in the book *A Company of Heroes,* based on interviews with the surviving family members of those soldiers.

But the moral injuries of our longest wars, in Iraq and Afghanistan, are on the whole different, perhaps deeper and more profound, than in past wars. These were our first major conflicts fought entirely with an "all-volunteer" military, which was born of the widespread antidraft movement during the Vietnam War. Richard Nixon's decision to replace the draft with an expensive professional force in 1973 had far-reaching effects unforeseen at the time. Exchanging a citizen army for a hired professional military meant that those who chose to stay home mostly remained ignorant of who served and why and were prone to ricochet between lazy indifference to the warfighting and overwrought hero-worship of returning troops. At a dinner party among liberal elites during the 1990s, I was describing some rugged army training I'd attended, and a woman asked with disdain, "Why in the world would the army train for war?" General ignorance of the military extended into Congress and the White House, where politicians tended to exaggerate what the military could accomplish and at what cost. Brent Scowcroft, a retired air force officer, senior White House adviser, and éminence grise of Washington's national security community, once told me how few people at high levels of power understood the risks of military action: "Only if you've served in the military," he said, "can you understand how quickly things can get screwed up." As the war years ground on, the gap between military and civilian seemed to widen. One evening at a remote combat outpost in northern Afghanistan, an army captain told me he'd recently gone home during a brief leave from the war. As they drove to a dinner party, his wife asked him please not to talk about the war; nobody really wanted to hear about it. "I don't have anything else to talk about," he told her sadly.

The few who did choose to join the military sometimes grew

to resent the stay-behinds. "There are times I think about all my [marine] friends who got killed and that sucks; it makes me bitter and sad," Darren Doss, the slender, black-haired young man who served with Stephen Canty and Nik Rudolph, once told me. "I understand the fact that people [at home] don't give a shit, I can't change that, but sometimes it makes me really fucking mad. It's one thing if they don't care. But they don't even realize the shit that goes on over there."

Others turned resentment into a kind of superiority. In early 2006, then major Doug Etter, the Army National Guard chaplain, gave a memorial tribute to his best friend, Lieutenant Colonel Michael McLaughlin, who had been killed in combat in Iraq. "We are a band of brothers," he said, referring to his fellow troopers of the Pennsylvania National Guard, then fighting in Iraq. "And those who are in their beds, those who chose not to fight this fight, should, if they have a drop of courage, a pint of common sense, they should think themselves lesser men." An air force fighter pilot once boasted to me, as he stood beside the bullet-riddled A-10 attack jet he had nursed home to Kuwait after a mission over Iraq, "You can't do what I do." In western Afghanistan, an army colonel commanding a helicopter regiment told me that he sees "a tremendous amount of guilt in civilian society for not having participated in this war. People thank us, but there is an awkwardness that has increased over time; they don't really know what we do." As he pondered the growing rift he saw between the military and civilian Americans, he added, "There are two kinds of people: those who serve, and those who expect to be served. Those who serve," he said, "are pretty noble."

Chuck Newton, one of the marines of One-Six, felt his service in Afghanistan with Nik Rudolph and Stephen Canty and Darren Doss had gained him membership in an elite and ancient brotherhood of arms. After a couple of beers late one night, he told me, "I always feel that me and the other guys would have been Spartans marching from Thermopylae knowing they were gonna die. We would have been in World War One, World War Two, it's just the same kind of people. We would have been in the Civil War: all my friends in Florida would have been fighting against the Union."

And, I said, you all would have paid the price for what you did. "Yeah," Chuck said. "Everybody does."

The cost of raising and sustaining this professional military, including salaries, health care, and decent housing for military families, meant the Pentagon in the 1990s couldn't afford the hundreds of thousands of troops that strategists said would be required for two wars. A smaller military was the result. When after 9/11 the two wars did come, young men and women were sent on long deployments—and then sent again and again, separated by a few months at home, time that the generals warned was too short for an adequate physical and mental recovery. "We are not big enough today to meet the demand on a sustained basis," General George Casey, then army chief of staff, told reporters in 2010. "We've done studies that show you really need two to three years to fully recover from a combat deployment." At the time, the army was sending soldiers back to battle after eighteen months at home. Badly needed specialists were sent at an even more relentless pace. A marine bomb–disposal technician told me he was injured in an IED blast in September 2004, and by another blast the following January that lodged shrapnel in his eye socket and the back of his head. Although he was awarded two Purple Hearts for combat wounds, he was sent back a year later, in 2006, with shrapnel still in his head. But he was deployed again, then once more in 2007. Finally, he was diagnosed with traumatic brain injury (TBI) in 2009 and, incredibly, sent back to war one more time, in 2010.

Beyond this demanding operational tempo were other factors that made these wars such fertile ground for moral injury. For the first time, a slight majority of those we sent were married, many with children. Young soldiers not only had to face their own anxieties of another battlefield deployment but had to deliver a morally troubling message to their families: *I'm going away for a year and I might never come back, because what I do over there is more important than being with you.* With the active-duty force struggling to meet the wartime demand for troops, the Pentagon mobilized National Guard soldiers and airmen from small towns across the country, ordering part-time troops to leave families and jobs for full-time combat roles few had expected.

And unlike previous American wars, the U.S. missions in Iraq and Afghanistan quickly morphed from pure warfighting of the kind that Alexander the Great or George Patton would instantly recognize into a disorienting mix of killing and altruistic campaigns to protect civilians and help them raise strong democracies. ("As the Iraqis stand up, we will stand down," as President George W. Bush memorably envisioned it.) Before the marines of One-Six went to Afghanistan for their second tour, they were lectured by General David Petraeus and even President Obama on the counterinsurgency (COIN) concept of protecting the civilian population and helping them build a better future rather than simply chasing down and killing the enemy. It didn't go down well. "I know how to put a rocket in a window from two hundred fifty meters," Chuck Newton remembers thinking, "and these guys are telling me I'm going there to hand out MREs [meals ready to eat]? Something is not lining up. And we get there, we start killing people, and our friends die...I'm not seeing this whole COIN thing."

Nor were local civilians always grateful for American counterinsurgency missions. Resentment at the presence of foreign combat troops often spawned local resistance. In one minor case, I once accompanied army troops in eastern Afghanistan attempting to meet village elders to ask what help they needed. Instead we retreated from a confrontation with an angry rock-throwing mob fearful that American soldiers would search their homes for weapons. Local resentment sometimes turned to treachery, with civilians helping plant IEDs and tipping off insurgents to approaching American patrols.

The effect of the new emphasis on counterinsurgency was magnified for younger troops by a shift in military doctrine that pushed responsibility for tactical decision-making down to the lowest possible levels, enabling small units to operate more or less autonomously. Far more than in our previous counterinsurgency war in Vietnam, it was common in Iraq and Afghanistan for convoys or foot patrols to be planned and led by lieutenants or sergeants well short of their twenty-fifth birthdays.

As Rebecca Johnson, dean of the Marine Corps War College, has pointed out, that meant these young leaders were required to "calculate the second- and third-order effects of their mission." Would the justifiable search of a villager's home for weapons breed ill will and perhaps turn civilians against them? What are the tactical and moral repercussions of continuing a firefight with insurgents, given the increasing probability of civilian casualties? Better to protect civilians and risk that the insurgents who got away will later kill one of your marines? For the first time, Johnson wrote, junior leaders on deployment after deployment had to make "sophisticated tactical judgments that carry complex moral ramifications," moral decision-making that is "not supported by current military training and educational initiatives."

The unpleasant reality of death, anger, and destruction, the killing, the sense that their leaders had betrayed them, all made it more difficult for some troops to justify leaving their families. But they went. Even at the peak of the fighting, in 2007, the rate of desertion was remarkably low: less than 1 percent, compared with about 5 percent between 1969 and 1971 during the Vietnam War.

These realities, and stories like Stephen Canty's, raise troubling questions for those of us outside the military as well, about wartime morality and about our rationale for killing in "just" wars and about our own responsibility for war's moral injury. What is the accountability of those who engineered the wars? Of the politicians who pushed for and funded the fighting year after year? Of those of us who silently accepted the rationales for war, voted for those in power, and paid our taxes?

Just as those returning from combat often suppress the emotional pain of their experiences, so do we all draw the cover of collective amnesia over our part in war. Perhaps we are morally injured as well and, like so many combat veterans, are reluctant to peer into that darkness. The SUPPORT OUR TROOPS stickers that blossomed as the battle casualties mounted hinted at a deeper disquiet. Too easily we have forgiven ourselves for neither taking part in the wars nor demanding an end to them. We have turned our eyes from the realities of war. To those veterans who return troubled, we assign the term "PTSD" and criticize the VA for not moving quickly enough to help.

But we have not acknowledged what we know to be true about war. We have not acknowledged our regrets, nor burned them in a makeshift battlefield baptismal font.

CHAPTER 2

Regardless of the Cost

The horrors make the fascination.
　　　　　—Henry James, "The Moral Equivalent of War"

In the dusty Ethiopian village of Jijiga, I once watched a man die
from his combat wounds, and I did nothing to help him. It was
my own very minor but personal introduction to moral injury
and might have informed my reporting on war and warriors over
the following decades. It should have been the seed of this book.
But for too long I let it go unexamined, not even having a name
for this most common but largely unrecognized injury of war.

As a *Time* magazine foreign correspondent, I was covering my
first battle, in a sporadically vicious war in 1977 fought between
Somalis and Ethiopians. Somali warriors had swarmed in from
the desert behind a couple of World War II Russian-built tanks
and after a bloody battle had sent the Ethiopian garrison fleeing.
While the Somalis were celebrating, three fighter-bombers of the
Ethiopian air force showed up. Two American-built F-5 jets and
an ancient but effective British Canberra bomber each made three

shrieking passes with bombs and rockets and then raked the survivors with 20-millimeter cannon fire. I was unwounded but stunned, terrified in the bone-rattling thunder of the jets at tree-top level, at the concussion of the bombs, the blizzards of steel shrapnel, and the pounding of cannon fire, and when the pilots finally relented, they left behind the crackle of burning wreckage and the cries of the wounded rising with columns of dirty smoke into a brilliant blue sky.

I had crawled to a place of relative safety, a low stone wall beneath a stunted tree, where I huddled in terror, dreading the return of the planes and unable to move. Near me, a man sprawled semiconscious on an olive-drab stretcher. He had been a patient at the local medical clinic that was badly damaged. Its pale-green walls of sheet metal were peppered with shell holes, and two bodies lay crumpled in a pool of blood in the doorway. The man in front of me had been wounded again in the air strikes and now lay partially covered with a blanket darkening with blood, his head swathed in bandages and his chest a mangle of flesh. Blood dribbled across his chin. He mouthed a word, then again: *Maji*. Water. I knew he wanted a drink. I also knew I was too scared to go find water. I was not going to risk my life to ease his suffering. I sat still, looking away, and a few minutes later he coughed and died and flies landed on his face.

For me, a flicker of guilt and shame has stayed with me, an event that subtly altered my view of myself as a good person. It should have given me an early insight into the far more troubling experiences of those we recruit and send into war. It should have awakened me to the cruel moral choices they must often make and to the moral injuries they bring home. But like most of us, I looked away.

I grew up in a Quaker family in a comfortable, leafy suburb of New York, far from any military base. My mother and father were the gentlest people I have ever known. They worshipped in a plain meetinghouse built in 1812, tucked away behind high walls. As a child I fidgeted through hour-long silent meeting on Sundays, dreaming of far-off adventures and swinging my legs beneath the hard wooden bench until Mom put a quieting hand on my knee. Gunplay and the imagined glory of war were an important part of my childhood, as for most kids in the neighborhood. We spent hours, long-division homework abandoned, shooting our toy cap pistols at imaginary enemies and perfecting the art of toppling over in romantic, immaculate death. I was ten when my family began hosting a young Japanese woman who had been badly burned and disfigured in the atomic blast in Hiroshima in 1945, one of the "Hiroshima maidens." They had been schoolgirls at the time, and a decade later Quakers brought them to the United States for reconstructive surgery. It was she, not a heroic soldier in a splendid uniform, who was the first person I met with direct experience of war. I had to steel myself not to stare at her sticklike arms from which flesh had been burned and to meet the eyes in her heavily scarred face.

At Quaker gatherings, we studied Gandhi and nonviolent resistance, a way to force social change that seemed like an obviously good alternative to incinerating schoolgirls. As I reached high-school age, I came to appreciate silent meeting as a respite of peace, the silence deepened on lazy summer mornings by the sleepy drone of bees and swish of distant traffic. When I turned eighteen I was required to register for the draft. I signed as a conscientious objector. With the clarity of youth, I told my draft board that I wanted to serve my country but that killing was morally wrong and I would not take part in it. I did two years of civilian service with an international Quaker relief agency and then became a journalist. In 1977, *Time* magazine assigned me to Africa; the editors wanted up-front coverage of the guerrilla wars, civil conflicts, and violent coups that were racking the continent in the late 1970s. And with no special training or preparation, I went.

Out in the blasted wastelands of Somalia, the bloody terrors of Mozambique and Ethiopia, and among the scowling young killers of Uganda and Congo, I was often scared. I was stunned by the carnage and waste of war, the casual killing, the scale of human suffering. The dead-of-night dread, cowering as detonating mortar rounds and heavy machine-gun fire crept closer, turning my guts to liquid; the drunken, murderous young soldiers at checkpoints; the empty dirt road that held either land mines and death—or a good story. The air seemed always scented with burning tires and lush bougainvillea, rotting fruit and rotting flesh. At the same time I was inspired by the courage of those caught up in war: the refugee families, the volunteers at hospitals that lacked sanitation, antibiotics, and sometimes even beds. The slender young Ugandan nun who smuggled Catholic believers out of a mad dictator's grasp. Less nobly, I was mesmerized by the adventure, by the adrenaline rush. I was thrilled, afterward, at my own escapes from peril. I saw myself as the heroic, calloused foreign correspondent. I drank. I had nightmares, outbursts of anger I could not explain. And I wanted more. To be clear: having once acted on my conviction that killing was morally abhorrent, and having been accorded the government-certified status of conscientious objector, I found war itself to be irresistible.

I left Africa after four years, returning to cover the Pentagon. I immersed myself in nuclear-war-fighting theory, defense budgeting, and weapons technology. With a small pool of reporters I traveled the world with the secretary of defense and even had my own desk in the Pentagon pressroom. But I got bored with Washington and was eager to learn what the military actually did. I discovered that they welcomed my interest, and I sailed on attack and strategic missile submarines and aircraft carriers, flew on bombers, and climbed down into a silo where an intercontinental ballistic missile, armed with multiple nuclear warheads, hummed on alert.

The most compelling work of the American military, I found, happens away from Washington, in its obsessive training in grueling combat exercises. I spent as much time as I could with troops in the field, out in the piney woods of Fort Bragg, Fort Drum, and Fort Polk and the swampy scrubland of Camp Lejeune, where the clatter of helicopters, the shrieking of tank turbine engines and rumble of treads, and the firing-range crackle of M4 carbines and thudding of .50-cal machine guns rise beyond the manicured lawns, neat split-level housing, child-care centers, and sports clubs of modern military life. At the vast training ranges at Twentynine Palms and Fort Irwin, in the Mojave Desert, I watched as marines and soldiers maneuvered by the thousands, with tanks, artillery, and air strikes by jets and helicopter gunships, replicating the tempo and confusion if not always the live ammunition of modern warfare. Every skirmish and battle would be followed by an after-action review: enlisted infantrymen and artillerymen, scouts and tank gunners, privates and sergeants and colonels gathered to review what went right and who did wrong, and I have seen commanders accepting responsibility for unclear commands or tactical errors pointed out by nineteen-year-olds. As the troops trained, I learned: when to duck and when (and where) to run. How to live out of a rucksack and stay relatively comfortable in rain, snow, heat. My Quaker mother was mildly offended but intrigued that I knew how to fire a mortar and treat a sucking chest wound and that I had worked for a few hours in the bowels of a Marine Corps M1A2 main battle tank as a loader, wrestling live fifty-four-pound high-explosive shells out of the rack, ramming them into the breech of a 120-millimeter gun, and then squeezing out of the way as the huge gun thundered and recoiled with flame, smoke, and bits of burning ash.

When there were wars, I went, wearing my own helmet and

body armor—a thirty-two-pound Kevlar vest with hardened ceramic plates front, side, and back—and living in the mud and rain and desert heat with soldiers and marines in their squads and platoons. Counterinsurgency missions with marines in Somalia, then the Persian Gulf tanker war, Saudi and Iraq for Desert Storm; Bosnia before and during the U.S. peacekeeping operations; then Afghanistan and Iraq again and again. I came to know guys like Nik Rudolph, Darren Doss, Stephen Canty, and others, men and women I like to think of as the blue-collar, working class of the military. They are the mostly young, mostly enlisted soldiers, airmen, sailors, and marines who are the infantry grunts, the trigger pullers, the wrench turners, the watch standers, the tank drivers, the helicopter crewmen, the medics. Those in higher ranks (referred to, usually not fondly, as "Higher") make strategy, write doctrine, and devise tactics. The working-class military is responsible for making it all work in the real world, even when they think Higher has it wrong. For all their youth, the twenty-three-year-old female turret gunner, the twenty-five-year-old jet fighter maintenance chief, the twenty-one-year-old infantry squad leader, carry immense responsibility. They handle it well and with passion. They get their hands dirty.

In Afghanistan I once met a young medic, Private First Class Randall Bone, a short, stocky guy with a boyish grin. On his first combat patrol, on a soft spring evening, the lead truck in his convoy was hit by a rocket-propelled grenade (RPG). It smashed into the cab, sliced across the face of the driver, and detonated in a blinding flash where a lieutenant was sitting beside him. The explosion drove glass shards into the driver's face and into the legs of the turret gunner. The lieutenant took the full force of the blast and shrapnel on his face and head.

Medic Bone ran up from a following vehicle and wrenched the door open and gently drew the lieutenant down from the wreckage. He was barely conscious, his skull covered in blood, his eyes swollen shut. As other soldiers took up security positions and began radioing for help, Bone tended to the lieutenant, gently wrapping his head in gauze and trying to keep him conscious through his pain, while patching up the gunner and the driver. The wounded officer needed brain surgery, Bone knew. In a story I wrote several weeks later, Bone explained: "It's extremely tough when all you can smell is blood and people are suffering and there's not a lot you can do for them. You can't miraculously heal somebody with an RPG wound. When you get somebody with head trauma as bad as the LT, there's not a lot you can do for him in the field." But Bone kept him alive. It took all night for the wounded to be medevaced and the damaged vehicle to be towed back to the U.S. base at Bagram. Bone helped clean the blood out of the truck, then went to check on the lieutenant at the base hospital. The officer had undergone emergency surgery and was doing well, Bone was told; he would be flown out shortly on an air force aeromedical plane. "As soon as I made sure I hadn't lost anybody, I asked if there was a sink I could use," Bone recalled. "The sleeves of my shirt were soaked with blood, there were patches of blood on my pants and face, and my hands were caked with blood." A nurse directed him to a sink. "I probably spent a long time at that sink," Bone said. The photo I took of Private First Class Bone shows him with a cocky smile and hard eyes. At the time, he was nineteen years old.

Living with people like Bone and others of the blue-collar military, I came to stand a little straighter, wear my hair a little shorter. From them I absorbed the creed of immediate and direct personal responsibility, taking care of your buddies always, no matter what; trusting they would do the same for you. Doing the right thing when no one's looking. I came to admire their grit, their sense of honor and commitment, their unfailing humor, their courage, their spontaneous generosity. I have watched them wrestle with difficult decisions and have sometimes winced at the directions they chose. I have known some of their families. I have watched tense leave-takings and joyful homecomings. In the chilly predawn hours beside a distant runway, I have stood motionless with hundreds of saluting soldiers as flag-draped coffins were carried gently up the ramp of a waiting cargo plane, and with grieving families I have attended burials at Arlington Cemetery. At war, I have seen Americans at their best. In a very personal way, I admire and honor their service.

Eventually, though, I could no longer ignore the nagging sense that something was wrong, that I was looking away from the dark side of war, which was causing real damage to the men and women I knew. Too many good people were returning home disquieted by their experiences. Some sought therapy, but most did not. Some were diagnosed with post-traumatic stress disorder. Most were not. But so many were ill at ease with something deep inside themselves, not entirely comfortable with the way they had changed. It's only now, as the flurry of combat deployments slows, that we can pause and take stock. Being at war, I've found, is rarely conducive to introspection; you're too anxious, too busy, or too stunned by heat and boredom or the sudden surge of adrenaline to find quiet. Stephen Canty explained it well. "None of us really knows what it's like until we go over there, and we go two, three, four times before we ever pause to think about what we're doing," he once told me, several years after his last combat tour, in Afghanistan. "Only now," he said, "do we start to look at the mental effects of killing other human beings.

"We keep going regardless of knowing the cost, regardless of knowing what it's gonna do," Canty said. "The question we have to ask the civilian population is, Is it worth it, knowing these mental issues we come home with? Is it worth it?"

In early 2008 I went to war with Stephen Canty's battalion, the First Battalion of the Sixth Marine Regiment—familiarly,

One-Six. Marines and soldiers—grunts—typically deploy as part of a brigade of three to four thousand people, divided into battalions of eight hundred to one thousand; the numbers vary by service and mission. Guys like Canty identify from the bottom up. First is their fire team of four. Three fire teams make up a squad, usually twelve or thirteen marines. Squads make up a platoon of forty to forty-five marines; four platoons make up a company of perhaps two hundred or two hundred fifty marines. Companies are identified by code words representing letters: Alpha, Bravo, Charlie. In combat, marines often fight in fire teams of four, perhaps led by a lance corporal who may not have reached legal drinking age.

Canty served with Second Platoon, Charlie Company, One-Six, along with others I would get to know, Nik Rudolph, Chuck Newton, Darren Doss, and Xavier Zell, and others who died before I could get to know them: Lance Corporal Zachary "Smitty" Smith, Sergeant Daniel M. Angus, and Lance Corporal Joseph Schiano. Two of the One-Six marines I did come to know would be killed in Afghanistan: Captain Brandon Barrett and Lieutenant Jason Mann. Gunnery Sergeant Rosendo DeLeon, who befriended me in Afghanistan, would die tragically at home after his combat tours were finished.

During weeks of training with One-Six before we left, I accompanied the marines as they practiced detecting IEDs and assaulting and clearing houses, rehearsed nighttime patrolling and hasty attacks, and slogged through swamps to ambush off-duty marines pretending to be insurgents. We lined up for shots and malaria pills and shopped at the PX for last-minute gear. I recall squirming on a folding chair in an overheated room for a droning lecture on Afghan culture, but I'm pretty sure there was no class on PTSD and definitely no mention of moral injury or how to prepare for any kind of psychological war trauma.

But the thousand marines of One-Six and its attached units

barreled into Afghanistan with impressive energy, enthusiasm, and confidence. And gear: They took their M4 carbines and anti-tank weapons, rockets and various explosives, and armored gun trucks—Humvees mounted with a .50-cal machine gun or a 40-millimeter grenade launcher. They took their attack and transport helos, seabags of personal gear, and wooden ammo crates of linked brass .50-cal machine-gun rounds, 5.56 ammo and grenades, boxes of MRE rations, computers, radios, spare parts, boots, mortar tubes and base plates, generators, Xboxes and video games, smokes and dip, trauma medical kits, and coils of razor wire, all logged on packing lists that ran to hundreds of pages and then packed into rugged steel shipping containers called conex boxes. The conexes went by ship to Karachi and then overland through Pakistan by truck. The marines and I flew out of the New River marine air base in North Carolina, stopped briefly at Manas Air Base in Kyrgyzstan, then loaded onto a C-17 cargo plane that flew us into Kandahar Airfield (KAF), the major U.S. air hub in southern Afghanistan. The conexes were waiting. Marines emptied them, and engineers stacked them two or three high in a stockade around their desert encampment adjacent to the runways.

I took a backpack with my laptop and a satellite phone and a duffel with my body armor and helmet (B-NEG, my blood type, embroidered on both). I also packed a stack of new notebooks and several dozen pens, a combat first-aid kit and tourniquets, and malaria pills. And a new softcover copy of Homer's *Odyssey,* a treasure at the end of a long day when I'd wrap myself up in my olive-drab poncho liner, an indestructible thin quilted blanket, click on my headlamp, and disappear into the aftermath of the Trojan War.

I was an embedded reporter, living as an observer inside the life of the battalion. I went where they did, carried what I needed on my back, slept where they did, and ate when and what they did. Marines couldn't get over the fact that I had volunteered to come—had fought to be with them. Having set up many embeds, I was familiar with the long process: convincing my editors to let me go, then running the gauntlet of required permissions from the Pentagon, and finally receiving officially stamped orders authorizing me to fly on military aircraft and excusing the Defense Department from responsibility if I was killed. It all moved quickly for us after that, in a blur of jumbled packs and gear, mounting excitement, and last-second hugs with anxious wives and crying children, until we departed Camp Lejeune in buses to the New River airfield.

In the weeks before their first combat mission in Afghanistan, One-Six learned to endure 120-degree heat and incessant wind-blown dust. We sweated through classes in detecting IEDs, struggled through close-order combat drills, jogged along the dusty airfield perimeter road with full packs, and idly speculated on the life span of the Afghan peasants hired to prod the soil of adjacent fields for land mines. At dusk, I'd thread my way through sweating marines sitting cross-legged, stripping and cleaning weapons, and between gun trucks swarming with marines doing maintenance. I'd prop up my laptop on an upended ammunition crate (empty). There, I'd peer at my notes with my head-lamp, trying to compose a story while sergeants bawled at their grunts, helicopters whined to life on an adjacent aircraft apron, generators rumbled, and, a short walk away, F-16 jets shrieked off KAF's main runway and thundered away over the distant mountains.

Story written, I'd unfold the foot-square wings of my satellite-phone antenna, rotate them toward the sky, and mutter a brief prayer. If I got a good signal from an Inmarsat satellite high over the Indian Ocean, I'd connect to the Internet and e-mail my story back home. It almost always worked.

★ ★ ★

I wrote a daily blog from Afghanistan, about marines and their lives; about the food (chow) and the weather; about the latrines (sparkling clean!), the grunts' wagers on whether they'd be home for Christmas as Higher kept promising; about the anxieties of young marines; and about the battalion's first two combat deaths, which left everyone shocked and sobered. One evening I opened my laptop and stood for a while. I'd gotten an e-mail from my wife that morning, a crisp, clear Sunday dawn in the Afghan desert. Call me, she wrote. I dialed the number on my satellite phone. Your mother died last night, she said. She died peacefully. Your sister Anne was with her. Is there somewhere you can go to be alone? I took a shaky breath and stared out through coiled razor wire at the bright, flat desert and the hazy horizon of barren mountains. Armored vehicles growled along a distant road. Two platoons of One-Six marines in battle gear trudged by, raising plumes of dust. On the runway behind me a C-17 cargo plane touched down and reversed its jet engines with a deafening roar. We will have a memorial service, I heard Beth say. I know you probably can't make it.

News of an event like this, a death in the family, is not uncommon here, I wrote, and when it comes, it penetrates painfully. A thousand marines are sent away to war knowing that among their many loved ones there will be triumph and tragedy. Babies will be birthed while they're gone, and grandparents lost. Romances will bloom and wither; a beaming child will excel, beyond expectations, on a math test. A championship game will be narrowly lost. Someone will be arrested, someone married. In this battalion alone, One-Six, fifty-eight marines would become fathers. Only faint and indirect echoes of this rich other life reach us from home, I realized, through a scratchy phone connection or a terse e-mail. *Can you call home?* Yet we clutch at these precious glimpses, preserving them like grainy snapshots folded lovingly into a wallet. It is perhaps the most we ask of those we send. Those rich moments occur far away and are lost forever. A child has a fourth birthday only once. The losses, like repeated body blows, accumulate in a deepening moral injury.

Men and women at war absorb the hard living with black humor, steel themselves against the risks of combat, temper their fatigue, homesickness, and apprehension by loving their buddies and being loved in return. They endure. Back home, we often count the cost of war in dollars, in the billions or trillions. We calculate strategic gain or loss. We honor with sorrow the dead and the wounded.

How do we measure the sacrifice of home?

It was here as well that I caught other glimpses of moral injury, how it differs from PTSD, and how people in combat deal with what the Marine Corps delicately calls combat and operational stress. One day in the spring of 2008, in the stifling tent that served as the mess hall for One-Six, Staff Sergeant Julian Lumm remembered the story of Molly and the leg. Lumm and Gunny [Gunnery Sergeant] DeLeon and a couple of others and I were dawdling over a table strewn with lunchtime remains of chili mac, tomato salad, and pineapple cake, the marines straddling the metal benches with their M4 carbines slung over their shoulders. The story had unfolded in Iraq the previous year, when One-Six had fought Sunni insurgents in Ramadi. One day a suicide bomber had come at the marines at a checkpoint, and when they got him stopped, he blew himself up. No marines had been hurt, but the bomber's body parts had landed all over the place. In the retelling, Lumm and DeLeon started to laugh. Both were handsome, tall and hefty with dark liquid eyes. DeLeon was forty at the time, on his second combat tour in two years.

On that deployment in Iraq, the marines had befriended a dog they named Molly, DeLeon explained to me, pushing aside his tray and hitching up his carbine. Already, he and Lumm and Gunny Carlos Orjuela, who had served with them in Iraq on that deployment, were starting to sputter and guffaw as they described that scene—Molly! Yeah! Here comes Molly, trotting back to where they'd taken cover, and she's got a piece of the guy's leg in her mouth, and the marines are going, "Molly! Bad dog! Put that thing down!" Lumm collapsed in helpless giggles, unable to continue telling the story.

Orjuela: "And Molly's going like *What'd I do?* She's lookin' so proud, ya know, like a cat bringing a mouse, and she keeps on comin' and we're goin' *No, Molly! Go away! Git that thing outta here!!*" We were all in stitches.

Lumm swiped a tear. Oh man, he managed. That was hilarious, wasn't it?

The marines of One-Six recently told me a similar story from their second deployment, in Afghanistan two years later, in 2010. This one had to do with what they called the Meat Wagon. They'd sometimes go out on patrol, get into a firefight, chase off the Taliban, then set up a primitive base, securing it with sandbags and razor wire. A day or two later, they'd be assigned to head out in a Humvee they designated as the Meat Wagon to pick up Taliban and civilian bodies, and after all that time in the sun, or in the shade of a tree, the corpses had started to putrefy and stink. Chuck Newton was often assigned to go get the bodies. Chuck is a tall, rangy guy from Brooklyn with a slow, deliberate manner. His dark hair, shaved down below stubble in Afghanistan, now is grown out almost shoulder length. He takes time to gather his thoughts before he speaks, as if his words are precious and not to be wasted or misunderstood; he lets them out a sentence or two at a time and checks your eyes to make sure you've got it. Often his stories start out dead serious and end in a burst of laughter. This story he'd told many times, but Canty, Xavier Zell, and other marine veterans from One-Six, sprawled across the beds in a New

Jersey hotel room on a Sunday afternoon drinking beer, were eager to hear it again.

The bodies, Chuck Newton said, "were, like, all blown up. Some of them you'd touch and they'd deflate. If it was in the sun, it had turned to jerky, or in the shade it would just melt and turn to goo, and you'd pick it up and the leg would stay there on the ground."

Zell interrupted. "The manicotti!" he prompted.

Newton: "Oh, yeah...The smell was like—you know those fake-cheese crackers? I couldn't get rid of it." On the drive back, "my foot was actually sticking to the gas pedal because I had like congealed blood on my boot, and my hands were sticking to the steering wheel.

"Anyway, we got back and I tried to clean up with, like, napkins. I was so hungry and I had a vegetable manicotti, this awful MRE, this tube with red goop on it, and I was eating it and my gunner on the truck goes, 'You got a little on your sleeve,' and I—Oh, God, that smell!—it was congealed blood from one of the...it was not manicotti! Well, at first everyone was like *uuuggghhh* [Newton making vomiting sounds], and for about five seconds I'm about to puke and cry at the same time, and then somebody starts laughing, and the floodgates open, and everybody is just like hilarious."

Zell: "And later I'm telling this guy, 'And then my buddy ate MAN-icotti!' Everything becomes a joke, man. Life's too fuckin' short!"

But that was still to come, when peril and death and gore had become commonplace. When I went with them on their first deployment, in 2008, they were new, unbloodied, excited, and anxious, jumpy. With days to go before their first op, an attack on the dusty market town of Garmsir in Afghanistan's Helmand Province, they lifted weights at dawn, shaved one another's heads, and relentlessly cleaned and oiled their carbines. They wound duct tape around their waists to keep their body armor from chafing. Sergeants came by to check gear and spread the word: *We're going into a Taliban hotbed so expect heavy resistance. Oh—and y'all carry three days' water.* That turned out to add forty or more pounds to everyone's rucksack, even after we'd discarded extra socks and underwear and the cardboard packaging inside our plastic-wrapped MREs. Wearing the pack and body armor and helmet, I found in combat drills that I could fling myself down to take cover all right. Getting back up to resume running was not so easy, and I managed it only with a strong yank from Gunny DeLeon. Even with all my gear, DeLeon could yank me upright; he was that strong. He was hefty, with noticeably plump cheeks, immensely respected by younger marines and by me. DeLeon had assumed my well-being as a personal mission, and everywhere I went he was right behind me, ready to yank me out of trouble.

As the Garmsir attack approached, nerves tightened. Outside the gates, a convoy hit an IED, and two marines were killed, First Sergeant Luke J. Mercardante and Corporal Kye Wilks, and the war suddenly got real. Sergeant Major Charlie Stanford, a balding, muscular man of forty-two, told me that the death of a marine in combat "is like losing a child." We were whispering inside a shelter during one of the frequent rocket attacks on Kandahar Airfield. Stanford, a martial-arts expert, had been in the marines more than two decades. A tough man, he was not given to expressing emotion. But he did now. Each death, he said, "drives you to your knees."

The choppers came for us after midnight, blacked-out twin-bladed CH-46s clattering down out of an immense starlit sky, lowering their rear ramps onto the moonscape of powdery dust where we'd been waiting. We ducked under the blades and awkwardly clambered aboard. During the roaring forty-minute flight, each of us mentally rehearsed: As the helo drops the ramp, the first fire team races out and goes left, the second goes right, both lay down suppressive fire as the third and fourth fire teams—and the correspondent—come off and go right and dig in. Self- and buddy aid for casualties until the corpsmen, the navy medics who accompany marines, get to you. We rechecked straps and snaps, adjusted the night-vision devices attached to our helmets, and squirmed in damp fatigues.

Suddenly our chopper flared nose-high, the skids bumped to the ground, and the ramp yawned open. At the last second, it occurred to me that if anyone was shooting at us, we'd never hear it over the roaring din of the helo. When our turn came, we sprinted out into a warm night and soft sand. I went right, cleared the spinning rotors, and dove for the sand. Gunny DeLeon flopped down protectively beside me.

Late that afternoon, huddled behind a wall with the battalion command group, I opened my laptop, and as I began writing an RPG whistled low overhead and exploded against a nearby tree. I scrunched down lower and kept going, wanting to get the story done before things got worse. Finished, I got a good sat-phone connection and with relief hit SEND. *Garmsir, Afghanistan, April 20—More than a thousand marines backed by artillery and helicopter gunships stormed into this Taliban stronghold before dawn yesterday . . .*

I didn't realize it at the time—too busy, too excited, my own brush with moral injury in the Ethiopian desert long forgotten. But the moral injury of One-Six was under way, as it was for many others who served before and after in Iraq and Afghanistan. The blue-collar military we sent to war was supposed to be strengthened against psychological injury by a rigid set of rules and values, hammered into them as new recruits. All of these rules would come under intense pressure in combat. Some would prove invaluable—*You are responsible for your buddy no matter what!* Most would not. And perversely, some would actually deepen the moral injury of those who went confidently into battle.

CHAPTER 3

The Rules: Made to Be Broken

I was doing what I was supposed to be doing, and bad things still happened.

— Clint Van Winkle, Combat Veteran, Iraq

It's near the end of their twelve weeks of Parris Island boot camp, and the marine recruits are struggling, wading through muddy South Carolina water with rifles held high, desperately heaving themselves over walls, squirming under barbed wire, and being blasted with the sound track of the opening minutes of *Saving Private Ryan:* the roar of battle, exploding shells, the snap and squeak of rifle rounds, bellowing sergeants, red-hot machine-gun slugs thudding into flesh, and the screams of gruesomely wounded men. Here, actual drill sergeants are yelling at the recruits: *Move it! Move it, move it, mooooove it! C'mon, recruit, git yer butt over the wall!* Up next: a grueling overnight march with forty-five-pound rucksacks. It's the culmination of their final exercise, two and a half days of hell when the drill sergeants keep them short of food and sleep, driving them day and night through exhausting obstacle courses. It will end as those recruits who've not fallen out struggle onto the parade ground at dawn, standing at weary attention to receive their coveted Eagle, Globe, and Anchor insignia and hear a senior officer declare them United States Marines. Then they'll summon their last reserves of strength and sprint for an all-you-can-eat breakfast of steak and eggs.

The next morning, here they are, all fresh and laundered, their burning resentment of the drill sergeants now coupled with beaming pride. They're coming at a trot down Parris Island's Boulevard de France, a blur of olive-drab PT shorts and tees shouting cadence from their precise ranks as they stream past the families gathered on the sidewalk. Before Stephen Canty got to Afghanistan, he and Darren Doss, Chuck Newton, Nik Rudolph, and the others who would fight together in Charlie One-Six endured the privations of boot camp and celebrated with this formation run for Family Day and the graduation ceremony on the following day. It happens like clockwork forty times a year here as young Americans are processed into the corps. For graduation, the visitors' parking lot is crammed with families emerging from vans and pickups with license plates from New Jersey and Indiana and Louisiana, the dads in pressed jeans and boots, Grandpa with his KOREAN WAR VETERAN ball cap, lots of MOM OF A MARINE T-shirts, and girlfriends decked out in frilly dressed-to-kill outfits. With shouts of "There he is!" the families strain to gawk at the miraculous transformation of the awkward teens they sent here three months ago into the tightly focused warriors now marching out in immaculate formations onto the parade field.

It's a proud and painful scene to watch, with the flags snapping in the breeze and the Sousa marches, blaring from loudspeakers, that bring the audience roaring to its feet. But there is an undertone. The toughness these new marines display is thin, fresh, and uncured. After all, it's been only eighty-four days since they arrived as nervous, self-conscious civilian recruits. Nik

Rudolph, like many others, rode a Marine Corps bus to get here early in 2008, a grim, sixteen-hour ordeal with one youngster already broken, weeping softly far in the backseat. But recruit training is only the first step of what is arguably the best combat training in the world. Young men and women go on from this and other marine and army recruit training bases to more advanced tactical fieldwork, mastering the techniques of warfighting and leadership far beyond what I've seen of other nations' military forces. They learn to kill, but nothing here or in their formal training prepares them for the acute moral dilemmas they will face in war.

Marine boot camp and army basic are famously rigorous, and by the end, the recruits, or "boots," have become lean and hard. They grow used to being shouted at. They learn to work in teams, to obey orders without hesitation or question, to shout back *"Aye, sir!"* in unison, to fire an assault rifle at human-silhouette targets. They march in close-order drill, demonstrate how to treat a sucking chest wound, and fight one another with pugil sticks and boxing gloves. They are constantly urged to emulate the heroes who have gone before them and reminded that they are preparing to fight and win no matter the cost. The weaker ones are bullied and grow protective calluses, or they may "recycle" and start over.

It's all part of building what the military calls resilience, its catchall word that encompasses the physical and mental toughening meant to stiffen recruits' outer shells, like body armor, against the physical and mental challenges of war.

Boot camp and army basic aren't just body and mind toughening; the long days are laced with lessons on morality and values. Drill instructors teach a rigid moral code of honor, courage, and commitment. The goal, according to the Marine Corps, is to produce young men and women "thoroughly indoctrinated in love of Corps and Country...the epitome of personal character, selflessness, and military virtue." The army's ethics codes are similar, demanding that soldiers "live the values of respect, duty, loyalty, selfless service, integrity and personal courage in everything you do" and always to do "what's right, legally and morally."

Loyalty, integrity, virtue: all these may sound like the ideals by which most of us hope to live. But the military's ethics codes have to be more exacting. They are issued to each recruit along with the means, the training, and eventually the authorization to kill. Success on the battlefield, accomplishing the mission, may call for the suspension of basic notions of civilian morality— such as the idea that it's wrong to kill a child. That is why the military backs up its list of values with a requirement for rigid and unquestioning discipline and obedience to orders. Every army recruit is required to memorize, and to recite on order, the Soldier's Creed:

> *I am an American Soldier.*
> *I am a warrior and a member of a team.*
> *I serve the people of the United States, and live the Army*
>   *Values.*
> *I will always place the mission first.*
> *I will never accept defeat.*
> *I will never quit.*
> *I will never leave a fallen comrade.*
> *I am disciplined, physically and mentally tough, trained and*
>   *proficient in my warrior tasks and drills.*
> *I always maintain my arms, my equipment, and myself.*
> *I am an expert and I am a professional.*
> *I stand ready to deploy, engage, and destroy the enemies of the*
>   *United States of America in close combat.*
> *I am a guardian of freedom and the American way of life.*
> *I am an American Soldier.*

Marine recruits bellow out the three marine values, sometimes while doing push-ups. The first is honor:

> This is the bedrock of our character. It is the quality that empowers Marines to exemplify the ultimate in ethical and moral behavior: to never lie, cheat, or steal; to abide by an uncompromising code of integrity; to respect human dignity; and to have respect and concern for each other.

But make no mistake: along with promising to respect human dignity, marine recruits are expected to be fighters, memorizing and internalizing the Rifleman's Creed. It is a bellicose call to arms, but notice it never uses the word "kill" to describe the act for which every marine is recruited, trained, and deployed:

> This is my rifle. There are many like it, but this one is mine. It is my life. I must master it as I must master my life. Without me my rifle is useless. Without my rifle, I am useless.
>
> I must fire my rifle true. I must shoot straighter than the enemy who is trying to kill me. I must shoot him before he shoots me. I will. My rifle and I know that what counts in war is not the rounds we fire, the noise of our burst, or the smoke we make. We know that it is the hits that count. We will hit.
>
> My rifle is human, even as I am human, because it is my life. Thus, I will learn it as a brother. I will learn its weaknesses, its strengths, its parts, its accessories, its sights and its barrel. I will keep my rifle clean and ready, even as I am clean and ready. We will become part of each other.

Before God I swear this creed. My rifle and I are the defenders of my country. We are the masters of our enemy. We are the saviors of my life.

So be it, until victory is America's and there is no enemy.

To civilians, all this may sound either appalling or ridiculous. In the confusion of battle, when terror and a desperate instinct for self-preservation can dominate, it is neither. If the military can be said to equip its warriors with a kind of emotional armor, this is it. I have heard them mutter the words in times of crisis, and I've watched them struggle to use these values in practice.

Curiously, though, none of this training prepares them to manage the moral challenges of warfare that everyone else knows are coming. It's an odd oversight. Recruits are taught to yank a tourniquet tight on the spurting stump of their own arm after an IED blast; they are not introduced to the idea that they may have to deal with their own moral injuries. Nothing in what the military teaches recruits about behavior in war instructs them to recognize, in the chaos and confusion, "what's right." They are required to master the complex process of assaulting and clearing a three-story house held by the enemy, and even the greenest privates memorize the nine-line radio message that will summon a helicopter to evacuate a casualty. They are taught to field-strip and reassemble an M60 machine gun while drill sergeants bellow at them and to use a topographic map and compass to find their way in the dark through miles of wooded hills. They are not taught how to think about the challenging moral terrain of war, much less how to navigate it safely. Marines who were taught at Parris Island to memorize "respect human dignity" as a bedrock marine value got to Afghanistan only to find themselves assigned to fight alongside and protect Afghan soldiers who were said to be using small boys as sex toys.

More challenging, after boot camp, they will find themselves killing without being helped to understand whether or not that violates the Old Testament commandment *Thou shalt not kill.* As army chaplain Paul D. Fritts explains, "The institution demands moral excellence of soldiers in order to maintain discipline but at the same time requires that combatants be prepared to perform the morally injurious act of killing human beings."

Like Nik Rudolph, Sendio Martz learned these same rules and values and recited the same creeds in marine boot camp. He never shot a child, though sometimes he wonders if he should have. His moral injury still pains him every day.

Sendio is a handsome, stocky man with a gentle demeanor and a quick laugh. We first talked around a picnic table outside the Wounded Warrior barracks at Camp Lejeune, a neat, three-story brick building with manicured lawns. He addressed me repeatedly as "sir." Born in Haiti, Sendio was adopted by an Illinois couple and homeschooled in an environment of loving support and high expectations. Before he enlisted, in 2006, he'd done two years of college, studying early childhood education, then worked with teenagers just out of prison. When he told his parents he'd decided to join the marines, they advised against it: the marines were too tough, they thought. Wrong answer! Tough was what he wanted, and shortly he was on his way to marine boot camp—this time to the West Coast version of Parris Island, at San Diego. It was tough, and he loved it. "A lot of the [Marine Corps] values matched up with what I already had," he told me. "Being responsible, disciplined, loyal. Training together to where you have trust in the other people to do what they're supposed to do." At San Diego he carried around what the marines refer to as the Book of Knowledge, a list of character-building guidelines on how you are supposed to conduct yourself.

"You get that training in the beginning, then you get to prove yourself and your worthiness for the next rank by how you took those basics and applied them," he said. "I thought it all made sense, because that's how my parents raised me."

In all the throngs of young men and women who have passed through marine boot camp, there have been perhaps few who absorbed the toughening and internalized the rules and values more seriously and thoroughly and eagerly than young Sendio Martz. He was the kind of brand-new marine about whom the drill sergeants would boast, Now *there's* a marine! I'd go to war with that guy!

Private First Class Martz was deployed right away to Falluja, Iraq, in 2006, a hard combat tour. The city was "blown to shreds" is how Sendio described it. He was assigned as the turret gunner on a gun truck, crouching in his body armor, helmet, scarf, and goggles and swiveling to target insurgents with his mounted .50-cal. machine gun. "You gotta stand up there, a lot of the attacks were on gunners, so our anxiety was very high," he said. His commander once told him his job was to "take one for the team." It was life on the edge: the next moment could hold boredom, the crack of a sniper rifle, or seeing your buddy's legs blown off. "You feel an invisible hand controlling stuff that you don't know nothing about," Sendio said. "But at the same time you got rules you gotta follow, because we are representing the U.S. nation. That falls under honor and courage." He did well, as the drill sergeants had expected. Promoted to corporal, he went again to Iraq in 2008, around the time I was in Afghanistan with One-Six. On his return Sendio reenlisted, made sergeant, got married, and had a child on the way before his third combat deployment in 2010. This time it was to Afghanistan, and he was assigned to lead eleven marines as a squad leader.

Parents and girlfriends and wives gathered at Camp Lejeune to see them off. "They were talking to me, saying like 'Make sure you bring my boy back!' and 'Keep my boy safe!'" Sendio fidgeted all the way on the long plane ride to Afghanistan. Bringing all his guys back safe was his responsibility, and it was a pretty high order, he thought, thinking back to the marines he'd seen die in combat, even guys you thought were invincible, guys who followed all the rules. He thought about all the near misses, the sniper shots and IED blasts that just missed his men, and he felt this good luck was accumulating day by day, mounting up on one side of a dangerously overbalanced ledger. And now they were headed to Kajaki Dam in southern Afghanistan's Helmand Province, an area whose arid rolling grassland was notorious for Taliban ambushes and the deadly pressure-detonated IED: a footstep would close its circuit and ignite the charge. Sendio vowed to put his faith in God and in the values and rules he'd learned at boot camp. Treat everyone with respect and dignity. Accomplish the mission. He could feel himself rigid with stress. Discipline, honor, courage.

Martz and his marines got to Kajaki around the same time that Chuck Newton, Darren Doss, Stephen Canty, and the rest of One-Six were arriving in Marjah, also in Afghanistan's Helmand Province but some ninety miles away. Kajaki was as bad as Martz had anticipated. Fighting was constant: close-in gun battles, IED blasts, long-range artillery barrages, mortar duels, and air strikes. It was exhilarating and terrifying. "I don't think I've ever been so stressed in my life," Sendio said. Patrols twice a day, with his riflemen plus attached specialists—engineers, intel guys, bomb-disposal experts, sometimes a forward air controller, the occasional reporter or visiting general, and some Afghan soldiers. Sendio was responsible for them all. "I had never been put in a position where I had so many souls in my charge," he said. "Wandering around on foot and you don't know where the next bomb is, you really have to watch the villagers, where one day there's a field with a bunch of people working, and the next day you do a patrol and there's no one there," a common indication of imminent trouble.

He sighed heavily. "And I have to be the one directing these guys where they had to go. And I don't know where anything is. I can't say to my guys, 'Don't go there, there's a bomb over there, stay away, and there's a guy over there, make sure you watch him and don't get shot.'" He paused and took a deep breath. As he recalled the scene to me, Sendio was getting agitated, his words tumbling out. "In the heat of it all you only have control over your guys and you are praying the decision you make is the right one, and if it's the wrong one, which a couple of my decisions *were* the wrong ones, you are paying the price and you're living with it."

He was thinking of the day when his squad was patrolling with another unit, and a buried sixty-pound IED was command-detonated beneath them, meaning that someone was watching and fired the device at the moment that would cause maximum casualties. The blast knocked Sendio and his guys unconscious and wounded, some severely. When he came to, he found that no one in his squad was dead, but some marines in the accompanying squad had been killed instantly, and others had lost legs and arms. Sendio ordered medevacs for the wounded, passing up medical help for himself. ("Just because you get banged up a bit doesn't mean you can take yourself out of the game," he explained. "I am not a quitter.") He quickly organized a defense perimeter and sent for reinforcements. "It was just very catastrophic, but as a leader you can't—I wasn't allowed and couldn't allow myself to crumble under the pressure or just give in to depression or...despair," he said. "As a leader you can't show a sign of weakness to your men."

In the following days they had to go out again and again. "I had issues, but I could hide them," he said. "I had some semblance of control. My fear was that they'd take me away from my men. Because as bad as it was, no one wanted to leave. It's the whole brotherhood thing, the courage and commitment it took to go back out there. Knowing it could be you next is really profound after someone gets hurt. I was scared out there, but I had to go back out. It's the honor among men, that we weren't gonna quit. It's what you learn in boot camp."

In the blast in Kajaki, Martz and his men suffered mild traumatic brain injuries and assorted other injuries. But the moral damage was worse than that. Earlier, they had befriended a young Afghan boy who would come around their forward operating base (FOB), trying out his English and bringing bread and other gifts; in return they gave him books and candy. The boy eventually would turn in villagers' weapons, and would point out places where IEDs had been planted. Then one day he disappeared—and a few days later came the IED blast. Soon they found out it had been the boy himself who set off the charge, and that discovery demolished their trust, soured their relations with the Afghans, and led some to question what the hell they were doing there anyway.

"To have the same kid turn around and blow you up...your trust has been ruined and broken," Sendio told me. "It shatters your reality of what's okay and what's not okay."

Sendio toughed it out. He followed the rules. He was that marine who made his drill sergeants proud. He came home with mild traumatic brain injury, PTSD, and other conditions, but he felt the moral injuries caused his sense of dislocation, bitterness. Bits and pieces of his old moral certainties and the newer realities of battle added up to a disjointed sense of himself, like a Picasso portrait. The rules and values had gotten him through combat, but when he got home, he said, "It's a different story.

"Even though you're home you don't feel at home. You don't feel safe—that was the case for me. And you become reserved. When you try to talk to someone, they don't understand, they start making their own assumptions about, like, 'Well, I don't think we should have been fighting that war in the first place.' Really?

"What you learn in boot camp, that you're not doing it for the money but because you want to serve and protect your country? It takes a long time to come back full circle and realize, Why do I care? The majority [of civilians] don't understand and don't care. We had brothers die in our arms, we've picked up the pieces of people . . . all the stuff you've seen and done, you went there with friends but came back without them—there's a guy [who was killed] back there who had a one-year-old son, and he's never going to see the light of day again, you know?"

Back home at Camp Lejeune, Sendio found himself replaying the IED blast detonated by the kid over and over in his mind, wondering what he should have done differently. "The only people you can trust," he decided, "are the guys you went and came back with."

As part of his treatment for traumatic brain injury he was assigned a therapist. Memories of the IED blast, his wounded soldiers, and the treachery of that young kid haunted him. "I constantly replay every decision I made while out there," he told her. "I'm just kind of stuck in a revolving, recurring thing, dreams and doubts."

Sendio's most acute moral injury was in the way he now felt about children. He and other marines sometimes experienced powerful impulses of murderous anger toward the Afghan kids who they believed were being used by the Taliban to spy on them, help plant and detonate IEDs, carry ammunition during running firefights, and even fire at them directly. "I'm still dealing with the effects of that set of moral issues," Sendio told me five years after the 2010 IED blast. "I hate being around children, because a child attacked me and my squad. I deal with the moral issue of whether or not I should engage [shoot] a child who is causing a very real threat or action toward us." Even today, medically retired from the military and at home in North Carolina, he said he has "a hard time seeing children in a different light. I know they are innocent but over there they are used as tools, spies. Do you want to attack a child even though a child is shooting at you? Is it right to end their existence? That was the kind of moral struggle that we dealt with on a regular basis."

Sendio Martz has three children of his own, all young girls. "That's where my moral conflict comes in," he said. "That's a struggle right there. I love them very much. I don't have any problem with my own children; it's with the other children the same age or older. I just don't trust the innocence of children." Birthday parties, family outings in the park, going to movies together, even attending his oldest daughter's dance recitals—he avoids them all. "It's sad that I can't give my kids what my parents gave me," he said.

Years of therapy have helped. One counselor tried to reassure him that he'd done the best he could, that he couldn't have foreseen the IED blast, that actually all his guys did come back. But Sendio was thinking, "All my guys got hurt and I let them down. And I'm angry because it's something I wasn't fully prepared for, and you start questioning, Why did I do this?

"It tests the foundations of your faith. What was this war all about? Guys got hurt for just doing their jobs and trying to save others. I question that. I had very angry talks with God, but at the same time, whenever we survived a close call, I thanked God for it."

But after five years, Sendio Martz is beginning to heal. He found therapists who were also Iraq War veterans to help with his TBI and PTSD. Inspired by them, he's gone back to school, studying psychology with the intention of becoming a mental health counselor for other combat veterans.

What's helped him the most is his community of other combat veterans. "You talk to your guys, and it's kind of reassuring to know that what you're going through, this guy is going through, so it's okay—I'm not losing my mind," he said. "You kind of reassure each other that we're not going insane."

★   ★   ★

While Martz was in Kajaki in 2010 struggling with the morality of children at war, the marines of Charlie One-Six in Marjah were engaged in a different kind of moral struggle, one in which the rules and values they'd memorized in boot camp seemed at best irrelevant to the reality of the war. Canty, who has a way of turning things over and over in his mind, trying to make sense of his experiences, once told me about manning a vehicle checkpoint. He and other marines were supposed to be working with an Afghan National Army (ANA) unit, training and mentoring Afghan soldiers and sharing living quarters with them. One day along came a middle-aged Afghan man on a moped with two little boys on the back, their faces and necks and arms blotched with darkening bruises. The kids had makeup on, and their mascara was running because they were crying. The marines knew they'd been raped.

"So you check 'em," Canty said of the man and boys, "and they have no weapons, and by our mission here, they're good to go—they're okay! And we're supposed to keep going on missions with these guys." Seeing that kind of stuff, he said, "your morals start to degrade. Your values do change real quickly."

War is morally corrosive not just for grunts like Sendio Martz and Stephen Canty. The generation of Americans who fought in Iraq and Afghanistan did so under a military high command that was trashing its own code of ethics in an astonishing and demoralizing display. Where, some grunts have wondered, was "the ultimate in ethical and moral behavior" when the George W. Bush administration based its decision to invade Iraq on fabricated evidence, widely debunked at the time, that Saddam was harboring nuclear weapons and building an unholy alliance with al-Qaeda? Where were the military values when the U.S. military authorities oversaw the atrocities at the notorious Abu Ghraib detention center and other detainee abuses?

In 2007, shortly after Canty had finished memorizing military creeds and rules at Parris Island and was able to recite them in a parade-ground yell, Army Lieutenant Colonel Stephen Jordan was dismissed from a military courtroom at Fort Meade, Maryland, and told to go home. Jordan, a heavyset, balding, fifty-year-old Army reservist, had been a commander at Abu Ghraib and was the only officer ever criminally charged with offenses relating to the abuse and torture of Iraqi men at the prison. After most of the charges against him were dropped on technicalities, Jordan had been convicted of disobeying an order not to discuss the case outside the courtroom. But even that minor wrist-slap eventually was dismissed.

From the highest levels of the Defense Department down to lowly enlisted soldiers, the treatment of Iraqi detainees at Abu Ghraib and the official response to public disclosures of the scandal amounted to a squalid evasion of moral responsibility. Under policies set and approved and supervised by the "chain of command" that ran from the senior U.S. commander in Iraq, Lieutenant General Ricardo Sanchez, to then defense secretary Donald Rumsfeld, U.S. Army prison guards and interrogators were "breaking chemical lights and pouring the phosphoric liquid on detainees; pouring cold water on naked detainees; beating detainees with a broom handle and a chair; threatening male detainees with rape; allowing a military police guard to stitch the wound of a detainee who was injured after being slammed against the wall in his cell; sodomizing a detainee with a chemical light and perhaps a broom stick, and using military working dogs to frighten and intimidate detainees with threats of attack, and in one instance actually biting a detainee." The investigation was ordered not by Rumsfeld or the Pentagon, but by Sanchez and the U.S. Central Command, the regional military headquarters. Sanchez appointed Major General Antonio Taguba to head the investigation but dictated that the investigation be confined to alleged wrongdoing by junior soldiers; senior officers and policy makers were not to be investigated.

The Defense Department sought to suppress news of the atrocities at Abu Ghraib, but once it leaked out, Pentagon officials professed to be stunned by the revelations. "It breaks our hearts that in fact someone didn't say, 'Wait, look, this is terrible. We need to do something,'" Rumsfeld told a congressional committee after he saw the Taguba report. "I wish we had known more, sooner, and been able to tell you more sooner, but we didn't." After that guileless remark, Taguba told journalist Seymour Hersh of *The New Yorker* that "a lot of people are lying to protect themselves...From what I knew, troops don't just take it upon themselves to initiate what they did without any form of knowledge of the higher-ups." But, he added, "I was legally prevented from further investigation into higher authority."

Ninety-two low-ranking enlisted soldiers were convicted of abuses. The most senior soldier convicted was a staff sergeant, precisely halfway up the enlisted rank ladder from private. Sanchez, nominally in charge of the prison, was allowed to quietly retire, as were other senior commanders. No one in Washington was officially accused of wrongdoing. While Canty and tens of thousands of other young Americans were headed into the war to do their best with duty, honor, courage—doing "what's right"—the war's entire chain of command evaded responsibility for the most damaging atrocities of the war.

But more moral rot was becoming evident. A rising army star, Brigadier General Jeffrey Sinclair, admitted to military charges of adultery, improper relationships with female subordinates, and other violations; he tearfully pleaded for leniency from a military court and was allowed to retire at a slightly lower rank, keeping his military pension and benefits. William "Kip" Ward, a four-star army general, was forced to retire after investigators found a pattern of lavish and improper spending. While marines and I were sleeping in the rain and eating cauliflower-and-potato hash for dinner in western Iraq, Ward was billing the government for personal travel and lavish hotel suites and having his staff take his wife shopping and to a spa, among other acts of misconduct detailed by the Pentagon's inspector general. Ward was ordered to repay $82,000, but he was allowed to retire as a three-star, collecting an annual pension of $208,802. In 2010, while Stephen Canty and his buddies were fighting in Marjah, Gary Alexander, a senior employee of the navy's Space and Naval Warfare Systems Command, was sentenced to seventy-five months in prison after admitting that he accepted $400,000 in cash bribes in a contract-award scheme. Air force missile-launch officers were found cheating on exams, as were navy sailors training on nuclear-reactor operations. Three navy admirals were censured and allowed to retire after investigations found they had accepted gifts and sexual favors from a ship provisions contractor known as Fat Leonard. In the ongoing investigation, another naval officer admitted having accepted cash bribes, luxury-hotel vacations, and the services of a prostitute.

A top military ethicist, Don M. Snider of the army's Strategic Studies Institute and professor emeritus at West Point, observed that the moral standards of the U.S. military profession had been "deeply corroded" by a decade of war. "How else," he thundered in a November 2012 essay for the institute, to account for the "as-yet uncontrolled escalation in suicides among the military, the unprofessional levels of sexual harassment and assault within the ranks, the spiked divorce rate in military families…the high rates of toxic leadership in command and resulting reliefs for cause?" The eruption of high-profile corruption and misconduct cases forced General Martin Dempsey, then chairman of the Joint Chiefs of Staff, to order in late December 2012 that all officers undergo new training to "reinforce" the military's values.

But the problem went much deeper than a few sensational

cases. The pressure of war had warped the moral code of the army's officer ranks, and lying had become not just common but essential, according to a study by the U.S. Army War College published in 2015. War College professors Leonard Wong and Stephen J. Gerras confirmed what warfighters like Sendio Martz and Nik Rudolph knew from experience: that while they were struggling to apply their moral codes to the chaos of combat, those above them were blatantly violating the military's own moral code of values, both to accomplish their mission and for their own career advancement. Certifying, for instance, that under-strength battalions were fully manned, that vehicles all had passed required maintenance checks, or that soldiers had been adequately trained when in fact there was insufficient time before deployment. After fourteen years of high-stress war, the War College study found, army officers "have become ethically numb...Sadly, much of the deception that occurs in the profession of arms is encouraged and sanctioned by the military institution. As a result, untruthfulness is surprisingly common in the U.S. military even though members of the profession are loath to admit it." It was a damning indictment of an institution that claimed to be built on high moral values.

Yet pinning blame on officers who set aside the code of ethics is letting the institution off too easy, a trio of army officers wrote in *Military Review,* the army's professional journal on the art and science of land warfare. The military's values themselves are the source of trouble, wrote Lieutenant Colonel Peter Fromm, a retired officer who taught ethics at West Point; Lieutenant Colonel Douglas Pryer, an intelligence officer serving at the Pentagon; and Lieutenant Colonel Kevin Cutright, a graduate of the army's elite School of Advanced Military Studies who also taught ethics at West Point.

By requiring strict adherence to its values, the three officers argued, the army "contributes to self-deception by convincing people that they are good, an ethical member of a values-based organization, even though [the army] does very little to actually encourage the right action."

For example, they wrote, until the Detainee Treatment Act of 2005 made "enhanced interrogation" illegal, "one could employ army values to endorse harsh treatment of detainees. Those who used torture could argue they displayed 'loyalty' to their nation and fellow troops by helping extract intelligence that might save lives. They could display adherence to 'duty, country and selfless service' by their hard, dirty work for good ends."

In fact, they wrote, it's hard to think of any tough ethical problem that army values could help a soldier actually resolve. By sloganeering its values, the military has in effect provided moral cover for almost any act: lying, for instance, to protect one's fellow soldiers and to accomplish the mission. Army values, they wrote, "can actually set the stage for unethical action by inspiring moral complacency and allowing us to justify nearly any action that appears legal."

"During my combat deployments," Pryer wrote elsewhere, "I never once witnessed a staff debate about the perceived justice of an act. Unless a lawyer says a tactic is illegal, the typical U.S. military leader believes he or she has the moral 'green light' to do it."

Put another way, the military's own values thrust its troops into conditions of intolerable moral dissonance. Alyssa Peterson, a Mormon with a degree in psychology, was a young Arabic-speaking intelligence specialist with the 101st Airborne Division, assigned to interrogate Iraqi prisoners inside the detainee cage at the U.S. base in Tal Afar in northern Iraq. According to reporting by Kevin Elston of public radio station KNAU in Flagstaff, Arizona, Peterson's hometown, she refused to participate further after only two nights of interrogations. Elston reported that an army investigation found that Peterson had been reprimanded for showing "empathy" for the prisoners. Echoing the dislocation many warriors experience as they straddle the separate moral worlds of war and home, she told army investigators that "she did not know how to be two people; she . . . could not be one person in the cage and another outside the wire." She was reassigned to guard duty and sent to suicide-prevention training. But on the night of September 15, 2003, she killed herself with her service rifle. She was twenty-seven.

As the wars deepened, the military continued to demand that its recruits memorize high moral standards and rules, and the American public continued to believe that the military acted on a higher moral plane than they did. Few spoke of the reality. "The whole 'moral code' thing is bullshit, a fake," Stephen Canty said to me one day recently, looking back on his two tours in Afghanistan. "Things are more complicated."

CHAPTER 4

A Friend Was Liquefied

Cry havoc, and let slip the dogs of war.
—William Shakespeare, *Julius Caesar*

Darren Doss had just come back from a morning patrol on the outskirts of Marjah, Afghanistan, when his best friend, Kruger, got shot. It was a blazing-hot day, June 1, 2010, and Americans and Taliban fighters were locked in a desperate fight along Marjah's narrow, shadowed streets and back alleys and across its outlying poppy fields and irrigation canals. The White House and the Pentagon had vowed to wrest Marjah from Taliban control and create a prosperous, safe, democratically run city as a model for the new Afghanistan. Doss and Marine Corporal Zachary Kruger and the marines of One-Six, along with thousands of other American troops, had been struggling since January to make this happen. The Taliban were dug in and determined to stay. The fighting was continuous and deadly.

Darren Doss is a slender man with dense black hair, a prominent nose, and soulful brown eyes that often reflect unvoiced pain and sorrow. Like the combat marines I know, Doss is outwardly tough; he's endured extremes of discomfort, deprivation, and grueling physical and emotional stress that most of us will never know. During his two combat tours as an infantryman in Afghanistan he was an aggressive fighter, not one to hang back. And yet Doss seems the most sensitive among the marines of One-Six, more vulnerable to emotional bruising. To this group of men hardened by the violence of war, it felt as if Doss was the youngest, everyone's little brother. In Marjah, he was about to turn twenty-two.

That morning, Doss was the last man in a line of marines heading back to their outpost after a routine patrol. Climbing a low wall, he heard AK-47 rounds impacting around him and realized that someone was trying to shoot him in the back. He scrambled quickly over the wall, cursing loudly, and made it back okay, but he barely had time to catch his breath before guys came running, yelling "Marine down! Marine down!" and grabbing their body armor and helmets and weapons. Doss raced out with them, and as they sprinted across an open field he could hear on another marine's radio that there was a firefight under way, it was bad, and the casualty was Kruger.

"I was tight with Kruger," Doss said. "My heart just sank." With reason: death was a constant in their lives. Two marines had been killed within days of their arrival in January. Others followed, including Corporal Jonathan Porto, who drowned when his armored vehicle tipped over into an irrigation canal and he was trapped inside. That May, the marines of One-Six had been shaken by the death of a popular leader, First Lieutenant Brandon Barrett, who was shot by a sniper. In the following three weeks, Joshua DesForges, Nicolas Parada-Rodriguez, and Philip Clark were killed. On Monday, May 31, Anthony Dilisio was killed. Now, on Tuesday, Kruger was down.

The marines leaped into the gully where Kruger's squad was

hunkered down in a firefight so intense that the barrel of one marine's SAW was glowing red. Doss fell to his knees beside Kruger, who had been shot in the thigh and was bleeding heavily. They got a tourniquet on; a medevac helicopter had been called. Doss grabbed Kruger's hand and squeezed, making jokes, trying to keep Kruger conscious. An army chopper landed a distance away, and a crewman came sprinting through gunfire across an open field and flung himself down. He hadn't brought a stretcher. As the marines returned fire to cover him, the medic ran back to the chopper and returned with a stretcher. Doss and another marine grabbed Kruger's arms and dragged him up and out of the gully and got him on the stretcher. Then they ran. The field they had to cross had recently been plowed, leaving foot-high ridges, making it difficult to run without turning an ankle. The larger danger was the Taliban gunfire raking the field. All hell was breaking loose, Doss thought. He could hear rounds impacting the dirt. By chance a *New York Times* photographer was riding on the chopper; one of his images shows Doss, his right hand gripping the stretcher handle, helping to shove Kruger into the chopper. Doss waited as it lifted off in a blizzard of pebbles and grit and tilted away. Then he ran back through sporadic gunfire. Within a few minutes the firefight died away, leaving an enormous emptiness, and the marines trudged home. Kruger survived. The army medic received a medal for bravery. No medals were awarded to the marines, who resumed their work without pause.

The shock and grief of seeing his best buddy grievously wounded, in pain, and at risk of dying clearly were an emotional blow to Darren Doss. But in the continuing maelstrom of Marjah, there was no opportunity to quietly absorb what would be a shattering experience for any human being. Here, it became just another emotional injury to a young man already wounded by loss.

"Over there, you don't really talk about it," Doss once told me. "You don't have time to sit there and cry about shit. You got shit to do, go on patrol. You don't dwell on it."

Darren Doss told me the story about Kruger over lunch recently at the Blue Ribbon Diner in Schenectady, New York. I had picked him up that morning at the VA medical center in nearby Albany, where Doss was an outpatient in the mental health clinic. He is diagnosed with PTSD, but his moral injuries have cut more broadly and deeper. He carries wounds of the soul that are eating away at him. Five years after Marjah, Doss was able to name six separate prescription drugs he is currently taking for anxiety, depression, pain, and insomnia. All for his experiences at war. At lunch his head drooped, his eyelids sagged, and occasionally he appeared to doze off. When we were done, he stepped outside to smoke a Newport. He stood alone in the parking lot, gazing out into the distance.

The politicians and policy makers and generals who rushed the United States into war in 2001 and again two years later never thought to prepare for the length and intensity of those conflicts and the psychological wounds the troops would bring home. Thousands of military professionals and intelligence analysts work briskly in offices along the Pentagon's seventeen miles of fluorescent-lit corridors, but when the United States went to war in Afghanistan in the autumn of 2001, few of them foresaw that cleaning out the ragtag bands of Taliban would last much beyond the spring of 2002. Attention had quickly turned to Iraq, which the Pentagon and the White House gave assurances would be a short campaign. After all, the most recent war in the experience of many officers, Operation Desert Storm in 1991, took only three weeks of air strikes and a four-day ground war to achieve victory over Iraq's military, and psychological injuries seemed to be minimal. By the time American troops poured over the border into Iraq in March 2003, the invincibility of the U.S. war machine was a bedrock conviction within military and political circles. On May 1, six weeks after U.S. troops invaded in the spring of 2003, President George W. Bush declared that "major combat operations have ended." That was something of a surprise to the grunts of the Second Armored Cavalry Regiment with whom I was embedded as they conducted patrols and weapons searches that summer in East Baghdad. The small-scale skirmishes and bombings then breaking out were modest compared with what was coming. But Washington held to its belief that the war in Iraq was winding down. By October, despite the battle losses of 225 Americans dead, the Pentagon was making plans to recall 30,000 troops from Iraq as not needed.

GIs were assumed to be bedrock strong as well. A report prepared for VA clinicians in 2004 acknowledged "insufficient" understanding of the impact of severe war-zone stress. But judging from how quickly people seemed to recover from car crashes, the report said, "it is safe to assume that although acute stress reactions are very common after exposure to severe trauma in war, the majority of soldiers who initially display distress will naturally adapt and recover normal functioning during the coming months."

There had been early signs that Afghanistan and Iraq would be different, more challenging for the troops, and at a higher human cost. In July 2003, the army surgeon general, Lieutenant General James B. Peake, sent a team of mental health specialists to Iraq. It was an act of courage and foresight not appreciated within Washington's ruling circles at the time. But Peake knew combat stress and its effects on troops. As a young enlisted soldier, he'd been selected for West Point, was commissioned an officer, and won a Silver Star for combat valor in Vietnam before becoming a physician. He was aware of the lingering physical and mental health problems that followed the troops' return from previous wars. When the invasion of Iraq was launched, he told me recently, "we recognized that the quicker we got on this, the quicker we would understand what the realities were of the current war, the better prepared we'd be to deal with it."

Peake's team found what he suspected. That December the army's Mental Health Advisory Team (MHAT) reported that 15 percent of the troops then serving in Iraq, or roughly 20,000 soldiers, screened positive for "traumatic stress." A larger group was tagged with depression, anxiety, or traumatic stress. But fewer than one in four of them had gotten any help, because they were afraid of the stigma of seeking help or because no help was available. The military's overriding culture, by necessity, was one of stoic acceptance of pain and discomfort. Not complaining. But the cost was becoming evident: the surgeon general's report noted the rising suicide rate among troops in Iraq—15.6 suicides per 100,000—was already dramatically higher than the army's peacetime average rate of 11.6. The numbers might be an aberration, the mental health team concluded, adding somewhat hopefully that the data "did not signify an escalating rate of suicide." But the flood of military mental health injuries was under way. In 2005, the VA began frantically hiring some seventy-five hundred additional mental health professionals to care for the rising tide of returning troops in need of psychological care. It wouldn't be enough.

By 2006, the year Stephen Canty was itching to join the marines, fighting in Iraq had increased in intensity and savagery. Eight hundred twenty-three Americans were killed in combat there that year; 6,412 were wounded. Fifteen hundred miles away, the war in Afghanistan was bogging down in its fourth year of bloody slogging; American combat deaths had doubled since 2002. And back home, a majority of Americans for the first time agreed that the war in Iraq was a mistake and that President Bush had no plan to end it. John Murtha, a retired marine and a conservative senior congressman, declared that the war was "flawed policy wrapped in illusion." Regardless, voters kept returning to office politicians who were determined to press ahead with the wars.

The army surgeon general's Mental Health Advisory Team returned to Iraq that summer of 2006, where it again conducted surveys and focus groups among soldiers and marines and found significant psychological trauma. Two-thirds of marines then serving in Iraq had seen the severe wounding or death of a buddy. In individual interviews, one soldier told the army researchers he had witnessed "my sergeant's leg getting blown off." Another had seen "friends burned to death." Others reported, "I had to police up my friends off the ground because they got blown up," "A friend was liquified [*sic*] in the driver's position on a tank, and I saw everything," and "A huge fucking bomb blew my friend's head off like 50m from me."

Like Darren Doss, most of the Americans we sent to war seemed capable of toughing their way through even this level of emotional stress, at least temporarily. But the survey team documented high levels of anxiety and depression: 20 percent of soldiers, just over twenty-eight thousand, screened positive for depression or anxiety, and some were diagnosed with PTSD. More significant, the detailed surveys also turned up strong evidence of damaging moral injury: the personal and military moral codes that young Americans took with them to war were being corroded by their experiences in battle. Despite what they'd been taught about honor and dignity, for instance, almost two-thirds of the marines surveyed told the MHAT researchers they would not report a buddy for injuring or killing an innocent noncombatant. Fewer than half of soldiers and marines believed that Iraqi civilians should be treated with dignity and respect, the MHAT found.

Equally distressing, the military suicide rate kept rising, by the end of 2006 reaching 16.1 per 100,000. Over the next six years the rate for active-duty soldiers would double, rising to a shocking 29.6 suicides per 100,000. The survey team, reporting back to Washington, strongly urged that the Defense Department develop "battlefield ethics training so soldiers and marines know exactly what is expected of them."

In other words, train soldiers to recognize the key to preventing moral injury: helping them see and act on "what is right." But it was already too late.

For the physically wounded, astonishing advances in military trauma medicine meant that almost everyone in these new wars who fell wounded in battle was being saved. In World War II, seven of ten wounded GIs survived; the others died of their wounds. In Afghanistan, nine of ten wounded troops were being saved, a rate of 93.3 percent. The surviving wounded were carried home grateful to be alive but often weighed down with the trauma of losing limbs or genitals, guilt for having survived buddies who died, angry at themselves for getting hurt, shame at having to leave buddies behind. The battle wounded were beginning to attract attention as they recuperated. At Walter Reed Army Medical Center in Washington, D.C., I watched cheerleaders, politicians, rock stars, and baseball players arrive to visit, and occasionally the president would quietly slip inside. The wounded were feted at regular off-campus steak dinners held in their honor and at annual July 4 extravaganzas on the Mall in Washington.

But larger numbers of patients were quietly evacuated from the war zones with invisible mental health injuries, a testament both to the ferocity of the wars and to the psychological damage they were causing. By 2011, the army's medical community had acknowledged an "epidemic" of psychological trauma, with a half-million troops diagnosed with symptoms common to PTSD and moral injury. Some of the damage was severe. Across the military forces, the rate at which troops were hospitalized for mental illness had risen 87 percent since 2000. Roughly a quarter-million army soldiers were receiving outpatient mental health therapy a year; ten thousand a year were hospitalized for mental health treatment. At least seventy-six thousand army soldiers had been prescribed opiate drugs; other pills, for anxiety and insomnia, were handed out informally to troops in combat. A study by the Institute of Medicine (IOM), the health arm of the independent, nonprofit, and nongovernmental National Academy of Sciences, concluded that the rapid rate of multiple deployments was having a cumulative effect. Thirty-three thousand soldiers who had deployed three or four times had received a diagnosis of depression, anxiety, or acute stress, according to the IOM report. Many were being returned to battle nonetheless, but by 2010, the army was holding back thirteen thousand active-duty army soldiers, physically and mentally battered, who had been declared unfit to deploy.

The repercussions of these psychological injuries didn't just impact individuals; they resulted in a deterioration of the military itself, a faint echo of the demoralized, crime-ridden post-Vietnam army of the 1970s. An alarmed army report published in 2012 found that violent crime in the ranks shot up 31 percent between 2006 and 2011; that year the army recorded 122 homicides among its soldiers. On active duty at the time were 42,698 convicted criminal offenders and 11,257 convicted drug and alcohol offenders. The roster of criminal offenders included 4,877 soldiers convicted of multiple felonies; 438 active-duty soldiers had been convicted of multiple violent sex crimes. Some families were breaking under the stress: domestic violence cases across the army rose 50 percent between 2008 and 2011, while incidents of child abuse climbed 62 percent. By 2010 almost 4,000 military personnel from all services were hospitalized for attempting or threatening suicide. That year, 280 active-duty, reserve, and Army National Guard soldiers died by suicide, along with 15 military family members. Suicides among women veterans rose 40 percent between 2000 and 2010; suicides among comparable nonveteran women rose only 13 percent during that period. By 2010, suicides per 100,000 had risen to 35.9 for veterans, nearly three times the civilian suicide rate of 12.4.

But it wasn't until June 2013 that the full extent of the psychological damage became evident, in a detailed analysis by the Armed Forces Health Surveillance Center. It found that the most frequent diagnosis for patients medically evacuated from Afghanistan for treatment between 2001 and 2012 was not traumatic amputation or blast injury but "adjustment reaction," a medical diagnostic code that includes anxiety, depression, and acute stress. Also high on the medevac list: patients with episodic mood disorders and dissociative, somatoform disorders.

In short, the military was experiencing moral injury on a scale that was both massive and unrecognized outside a small circle of researchers.

America had been to war before. Why was this psychological wounding of troops so widespread? It was the new kind of warfare U.S. troops were facing, forms of conflict that began to surface when I was with marines in Somalia in 1993. It was evident in Chechnya in 1994 and Liberia in the late 1990s: chaotic, extremely violent conflicts fought by ruthless, often-suicidal extremists who violated every Western concept of warfare. Three-fourths of U.S. battle casualties in Iraq and Afghanistan were caused not by direct action—gunshots in a firefight—but indirectly, by blast injuries from the tens of thousands of land mines left over from decades of war in Afghanistan, then from booby traps or IEDs. These "improvised" devices were made from bombs and artillery shells looted from Saddam Hussein's arsenals in the lawlessness unleashed by the U.S. invasion. Later on in Afghanistan, IEDs were constructed of simple fertilizer and fuel oil packed in a bucket with stones or nails and scrap metal and a detonator and buried with a simple trigger made of two sticks, a discarded double-A battery, and a piece of wire. Such devices exploded anonymously, leaving the survivors no one to fight back against. And because they exploded almost anywhere and without warning, the troops learned that each footstep in Afghanistan could ignite a fireball and shatter limbs. I attended an early mine-awareness class in Afghanistan in January 2002, given by an army explosives expert. He had just finished clearing mines from a dirt path that led from the runway at Bagram, which would become a major U.S. base. Days later he walked the same path, and a land mine that had worked its way up through the mud detonated and severed his leg.

Danger in these wars was like that, random and often deadly, leaving troops constantly in dread of, or resigned to, the sudden blast that would shear off arms and legs, rip through soft bodies, crush organs and bone, and drive dirt, rocks, and filth deep into torn flesh, often leaving the genitals shredded or missing. Several soldiers and marines told me they'd rather be dead than live without their genitals and sex. Often it was the first question the wounded would ask as they awoke from surgery: Do I still have my nuts? But by 2012 several hundred soldiers and marines were listed with these "genitourinary" wounds.

These new wars also threw young troops into legal and moral swamps that GIs of past wars could hardly imagine. Certainly men have caused atrocities in every war: World War II saw war crimes of unimaginable horror; atrocities in Vietnam were rare, but they happened and for the most part were prosecuted. Generally speaking, though, soldiers on all sides of twentieth-century conflicts fought under common understandings that prisoners were not shot, for instance, and civilians were not considered targets. But in the alien world of combat in Iraq and Afghanistan, the enemy used the tactics of atrocity at will. The last-century signposts of behavior, the Geneva Conventions and the laws of war, seemed to disappear in the fiery blasts of IEDs and suicide vests worn by women and teens that killed and maimed indiscriminately in places like civilian markets and mosques. At ground level in these wars, the insistence of Higher headquarters that American troops play by those old rules seemed quaint and irrelevant, even dangerous. A young infantryman, for instance, might watch an idle Afghan villager scope a crowd with binoculars, then dial his cell phone seconds before an IED exploded in a crowded market. But the infantryman might hesitate to take a shot as the spotter fled: appearances to the contrary, he could be an innocent civilian noncombatant, protected under international law. Or he could be part of an IED gang and kill again.

Complicating these choices were the increasingly strict rules of engagement (ROE). Issued on plastic-laminated cards to every military service member in Iraq and Afghanistan by U.S. Central Command, the regional military headquarters, the rules governed the circumstances in which deadly force could be used. The ROE, backed up by the threat of court-martial if they were violated, demanded that every armed serviceman and -woman make a tangled legal calculation—while trying to stay alive and kill the enemy. That calculation generally required a PID, positive identification of a potentially threatening person as an actual and legal enemy. That meant making a determination that someone "is engaging in a hostile act or demonstrating hostile intent," according to the ROE. In Iraq, families were allowed by U.S. occupation authorities to keep an AK-47 at home. (The rule was changed during the summer of 2003 to allow three weapons.) That sometimes put soldiers in the dangerous position of trying to determine if some guy down the alley at dusk was holding a weapon in a threatening manner or just carrying it home, whether his intent was "hostile," whether he was about to open fire. For an American soldier, guessing wrong could mean court-martial. Or death.

In Afghanistan, the ROE were tightened further under the counterinsurgency strategy of Generals David Petraeus and Stanley McChrystal, to provide greater protection for civilians. The practical effect was to transfer some portion of risk from Afghan civilians onto guys like Darren Doss and Stephen Canty. Marines told me that when Taliban fighters realized that the Americans couldn't shoot back unless they were holding a weapon (demonstrating "hostile intent"), the Taliban sometimes would shoot and then throw down the weapon, knowing the marines probably wouldn't fire back.

And if a military police soldier serving as a turret gunner in a gun truck felt her position was under attack by a car speeding toward her, for instance, she was supposed to employ a process of "escalation of force." That required shouting, waving a flag, or blowing a whistle and, if that didn't work, then brandishing a weapon, then firing a warning shot, then shooting for the tires, and only then shooting to kill. All that was supposed to happen in seconds. The enemy, of course, had no such rules, giving rise to the burning conviction of many grunts that they were fighting with a huge disadvantage imposed by Higher sitting in far-off, immaculate air-conditioned offices. Justified or not, the ROE caused frustration and bitterness among the working-class military. It's understandable that the surgeon general's 2006 report found that 10 percent of soldiers and marines acknowledged to military researchers that they "modified" their ROE in order "to accomplish the mission."

But even attempting to follow the rules could lead to sickening self-recrimination. Lieutenant Colonel Rob Campbell, a tall officer with sandy hair and freckles, commanded a cavalry squadron in eastern Afghanistan when we talked during a foot patrol outside the city of Gardez in 2009. We were picking our way through ankle-high weeds, keeping one eye on the horizon for snipers while also scanning the ground for telltale detonation wires or the fresh dirt of a newly buried IED. One night, Campbell said, overhead surveillance that was beamed into his command center showed what looked like a team of insurgents planting IEDs beside a road. He and his staff watched until they were certain that the ROE and international law had been satisfied and then called in a strike. The dead men turned out to be local farmers engaged in midnight planting. "It was horrible, something I'll have to live with," Campbell said with anguish on his angular face.

In Garmsir, Afghanistan, on the sweltering afternoon in 2008 when a rocket-propelled grenade (RPG) suddenly whooshed overhead and detonated, none of the marines of One-Six was hurt. But they boiled up like angry wasps, taking positions behind a wall and peering at a distant ridgeline where two Afghan teens were riding a motorbike back and forth, watching us. The marines were certain the two either had shot at us or were signaling to a hidden shooter. But unless the marines could see a weapon, they had to hold fire. Staring intently through their rifle scopes, they could see no weapon. "We got PID?" someone demanded. "C'mon, c'mon pick it up," another marine kept urging, convinced the RPG launcher lay just out of sight at the youths' feet. Eventually the two moved off on the motorbike, and the disgruntled marines returned to pick at their MREs.

The rules seemed most difficult to interpret and follow at vehicle checkpoints, where often the most-junior soldier or marine was given the job of turret gunner, responsible for spotting and halting suspected suicide bombers. That's the situation Jake Sexton found himself in during his first combat deployment to Iraq in 2007. Jake had grown up in the crossroads hamlet of Farmland, in the corn-and-soybean belt of eastern Indiana. Now he was a twenty-year-old soldier with the Indiana National Guard, sitting atop a Humvee gun truck behind a .50-cal machine gun.

Jake's dad, Jeff Sexton, told me the rest of the story, as he came to understand it. Jeff is an army veteran and a short-haul truck driver; he runs air-conditioner parts every day from Muncie down to the Honda plant outside Columbus. Late one April afternoon after work, he sat on his back porch in Farmland and talked. His son Jake had spent eight months in Iraq. "When he came home, I knew he was different, but it wasn't really that much different. But then as things went on, he started opening up about Iraq a little more," he said in his slow, quiet voice. "He, ah, told me about this situation where he was manning the turret where they had this roadblock, and a car came up and didn't stop, and so he had to open fire on the car, and when they went to investigate, it ended up being a family of four. No weapons. Just a miscommunication. And that really tore into him. He was the only one who fired, so there was no doubt he was the one that caused... you know, caused it. I said, 'What did they do?' And he said, Well, they had the investigation and said it was a clear-cut case of he had no choice. He said he didn't want to be back in the turret after that, and they took him off it. He was home almost a year and a half before I knew that happened."

Had Jake Sexton served in World War II, he would have had time to decompress with his buddies on the long trip home by troopship. Soldiers coming home from Iraq and Afghanistan returned in a disorienting two or three days (as did Vietnam veterans). I have convoyed out of a combat forward operating base in Iraq, caught a ride to the Baghdad airport, flown to Kuwait and on into the peaceful summer twilight of Washington, D.C.—all in the same day. Active-duty troops returned to Fort Hood, Texas, or Camp Lejeune with their buddies and stayed with their unit more or less intact. But National Guard soldiers like Jake Sexton returned abruptly to civilian life, civilian friends, and civilian jobs, often with no one around who understood what they'd just gone through. And that added to Jake's problems.

Come to find out, Jeff said, his son was having trouble sleeping and was drinking heavily and never was offered or sought the help of mental health experts. But he volunteered for another deployment, serving this time in Afghanistan on a quick-reaction force, racing out every time someone hit an IED to secure the site and brace for the inevitable second attack. Mostly, Jeff understood, it was Afghan civilians getting blown up. "He had all kinds of pictures on his computer of the devastation and all that; it really bothered him," Jeff told me. "He loved kids. And seeing all these kids getting blown up . . ."

Jake came home on leave, and one afternoon he and his dad talked some in the garage. With the little bit Jeff could get out of him, he could sense his son's anguish and frustration. As Jeff remembered it later, what was eating away at Jake was "the senseless killing of innocent people and then not knowing who you are fighting when it did happen." Like most soldiers, Jeff said, "he'd get a little alcohol in him, and he'd open up a little bit, but any other time he kind of kept it all inside."

A few days later, Jake and his brothers and other friends went to the movies at the Muncie Mall to see the horror-comedy film *Zombieland* and settled in. After twenty minutes or so, Jake took a handgun and shot himself in the temple and died instantly. He was twenty-one years old.

Shattered, Jeff Sexton went to see the master sergeant in his son's unit and found out the sergeant knew Jake had PTSD. "And I'm sittin' there going, 'Well, why didn't somebody say something?' And it was, 'Well, we can't interfere unless they step up,'" Jeff told me. And of course the military code of honor is you don't admit to weakness and you don't ask for help. And Jake didn't. That wasn't okay, Jeff thought. So even before the funeral, he went back to Jake's National Guard unit and spoke to the assembled soldiers, urging them to see a mental health specialist if they felt they needed to, not to put it off. "I went and told them flat out, 'If you've got a problem, to hell with *Suck it up, soldier.*' I said,

'Jake's buddies in Afghanistan had to do that because they still had a mission to do, but you guys are home now, and if you got a problem it's time to take care of it, so step up.'" A couple of days later Jeff got a call from the first sergeant. "He thanked me for coming by, and he said he already had three guys step up and say they're having problems. And I told him, 'Well, that's three less we gotta worry about.'"

It wasn't as if the military brass and the Pentagon's vast civilian workforce in Washington didn't care about the psychological health of the men and women they were sending to war. True, they were primarily concerned with warfighting and with the daily drudgery of defense budgets, acquisition programs, and congressional appropriations and the ceaseless politicking that went along with all of that. What made it difficult to find a way to tackle the issue of war trauma was the deep disagreements inside the mental health community about the very nature of trauma: what exactly was it?

Most people thought any kind of war trauma was simply post-traumatic stress disorder. By the time of the terrorist attacks on 9/11, it had been two decades since PTSD had been officially recognized. The American Psychiatric Association, after studying psychologically damaged Vietnam veterans for over a decade, finally in 1980 certified post-traumatic stress as an official disorder in its *Diagnostic and Statistical Manual of Mental Disorders,* used by physicians, insurance companies, and the government as the final word on illness. A diagnosis of PTSD, it said in the third edition of the *DSM* published that year, must be based on the patient's experience of "intense fear, terror and/or helplessness," must be reexperienced in "recurrent, intrusive" dreams, flashbacks, or memories that provoke intense distress, and must cause the patient to react with emotional numbness or avoidance—staying away from fireworks, for instance, or isolating yourself from your family. You could get help from military and VA therapists if you met those criteria. If not, good luck.

While the public accepted PTSD as the explanation for all war trauma, inside the mental health profession the view was far from unanimous. "The views of what PTSD was were very confusing. At least fifty blind men and an elephant," said Dr. Harold Kudler, a psychiatrist and chief mental health consultant at the VA. Nobody, for instance, agreed on exactly what constituted "intense fear," since its intensity depended on the ability of the patient to articulate precisely how fearful he or she had been. And some rejected entirely the idea that war trauma had to be fear based. "A lot of my friends who are major authorities got excited about fear, but I don't believe there is a great scientific basis to say that trauma is a fear phenomenon," Kudler said. "When you boil PTSD down to fear, you're saying, 'Oh, you were afraid, that's your problem,' and I don't think that's the case." Under fire, the APA retreated. In its fifth edition of the *DSM,* published in 2013, it added that you could have PTSD if you were exposed to possible death directly or indirectly (through the death of a relative, for instance). "It turned out," Kudler told me, "that even though fear and a feeling of helplessness made sense, it did not predict who would develop PTSD. And that put us back at square one." In a stunning acknowledgment, coming as it did after more than a decade of continual war, Kudler concluded: "We do not know what trauma is."

Very gradually, it has become clear that the disturbing psychological effects that troops were experiencing in Iraq and Afghanistan were broader than any of the specific diagnostic specifications for PTSD laid down by the APA. As early as 1994, psychiatrist Jonathan Shay published his groundbreaking book *Achilles in Vietnam,* which described the modern U.S. military as a moral construct: not because its actions are always moral, but because it is "defined by shared expectations and values," Shay wrote.

Even then, Shay could see that the moral codes that grunts really lived by did not rely solely on the military's own values and ethics that it demanded be memorized by recruits. Instead, he wrote, they combined some formal regulations, some shared traditions, and some generally accepted truths among warfighters about what is okay and what is not. All together, Shay wrote, "these form a moral world that most of the participants most of the time regard as legitimate, 'natural,' and personally binding." Moral injury, as Shay saw it in his decades of work with Vietnam veterans, was a violation of this collective and deeply personal sense of "what's right." Not fear-based trauma. "I do not believe the official PTSD criteria capture the devastation of mental life after severe combat trauma," he wrote. In Shay's subsequent book, *Odysseus in America* (2002), about veterans' homecoming, he writes of "the moral dimension of trauma" and complains with evident irritation that the APA's diagnostic manual "has saddled us with the jargon 'Post-Traumatic Stress *Disorder*' (PTSD)—which sounds like an ailment—even though it is evident from the definition that what we are dealing with is an *injury*."

For instance, the moral injury of the soldier who saw his buddy "liquified."

The accumulating evidence of war trauma made it more and more difficult to cling to the notion that most veterans experiencing psychological problems simply had PTSD. Researchers studying psychological autopsy data following military suicides, for instance, found that the majority of completed suicides did not meet criteria for a *DSM-IV* disorder, or PTSD, at the time of suicide. Shira Maguen, the research and clinical psychologist at the VA in San Francisco, had published much peer-reviewed clinical research on the effects of combat, especially of killing. In her work she found PTSD to be an important but minor part of war trauma. "While the predominant view is that the majority of war zone traumas involve a fear-based reaction to life-threatening situations, there is accumulating evidence that trauma types are far more diverse, involving a much wider range of emotions at the time of the trauma, and varying post-trauma reactions in the aftermath," she wrote in 2013. The powerful emotions Darren Doss was feeling, for instance, when Kruger was shot.

While the mental health community was struggling to simply define "war trauma," the Pentagon and the VA were scrambling to find practical ways to respond to the psychological problems evident among the thousands of troops rotating home from war. In 2005 the Defense Department instituted mandatory physical and mental health screenings for soldiers back from deployment. The mental health portion of the four-page checklist had items to check if you'd had a frightening experience, were having trouble sleeping, or were easily startled. The Defense Department hired health-care contractors to ask additional questions, including "Have you ever felt you'd be better off dead?" This Post-Deployment Health Reassessment was a start. But there was no system to track whether individuals who were flagged with serious mental health concerns ever got help. Many did not. There was a serious short-age of mental health specialists in the military services and at the overwhelmed VA, where the suicide hotline was drawing 170,000 calls *a month*. When the military could hire outside contractors to help, they often had no familiarity with the military and no insight into soldiers' lives.

The experience of Mike McMichael, a North Carolina National Guard officer, was typical of those whom the military mental health system had failed. Mike is a stocky, well-muscled man whose commanding presence, friendly backwoods demeanor, and liquid Carolina diction camouflage a world of hurt and struggle. He came home damaged, with an undiagnosed traumatic brain injury from an IED blast. And suffering nightmares, shame, and guilt over his experiences. In an incident in 2004, a convoy he was commanding was trapped and ambushed north of Baghdad, and one of his fuel tankers was shot up and leaked fuel, which caught fire, engulfing Iraqi civilian bystanders. In his nightmares: the frantic bellowing of his soldiers, his own desperate struggle to get the convoy moving. And as he pushes his trucks through the wreckage, the screams of the Iraqi civilians, shaking their fists at him as they burn.

On his return home, a military nurse gave Mike the checklist of PTSD symptoms. He filled it out and handed a copy back. He never heard from the army. Years later he looked at the copy he'd kept and realized he'd checked every indicator of severe traumatic stress on the sheet: Were you ever in fear of your life? Check. Felt hopeless? Check. Ever see bodies, check; ever see civilian injuries, check. Anxious and sleepless? Oh yeah, check. And so on. But Mike was never examined for his psychological wounds and never got effective treatment. Over the ensuing years, he fought his memory lapses, tremors, fits of rage, blackouts, and anxiety attacks that left him gasping on the floor. Occasional screaming nightmares. He lost his job at the local power company and had to resign his commission as a National Guard officer. The unwritten warrior's code kept him from admitting his problems. "I had guys that lost legs; what's wrong with me that I can't handle this, there isn't anything really wrong with me. I didn't want to show weakness," he told me. He narrowly resisted the lure of suicide and eventually found a sympathetic psychologist at the VA; intensive therapy helped. Now Mike runs a program to train and certify veterans to become peer counselors for the VA. But life is a continuing struggle, and his marriage has fallen apart.

Such realities belied the feel-good rhetoric that had been coming from defense officials and generals. During a congressional hearing in the summer of 2006, I heard Jack Keane, a gruff retired army four-star general, angrily reject the idea that the military was breaking under the stress of repeated combat deployments. "This is a war, and we should expect stress and strain on our soldiers and marines," he said dismissively. Despite that, he said, "They are performing magnificently." True enough, perhaps, but that was a testament to their grit and determination, not to the troops' mental health. Amber Robinson, a sergeant with the Tenth Mountain Division, told me later that summer about a friend who was killed in combat in Afghanistan. She had collected her friend's bloody clothes and personal gear and carried them all back to base. "A lot of soldiers are depressed, angry, having drinking problems," she said. "But you get desensitized. I don't cry anymore." After a few moments she added in a soft voice, "Sometimes I wake up and cry for no reason."

As the wars ground on, the accumulating evidence of their psychological costs was causing concern among politicians on Capitol Hill, who began hearing demands for help from constituents with sons and daughters returning from Iraq and Afghanistan. Defense Secretary Donald Rumsfeld and other Pentagon officials were regularly lambasted in congressional hearing rooms for having rushed to war without providing proper armor protection against IEDs and for fumbling the response to the increasing mental health demands of troops at war. ("You go to war with the army you have...not the army you might want" was Rumsfeld's shrugging response.) That October 2006, Congress passed legislation requiring the Pentagon to expand the testing of troops before and after their deployment to the war zones and to tighten its tracking procedures to ensure that troops flagged with mental health conditions, like Mike McMichael, be seen by mental health practitioners. The conclusions of a Defense Department task force on mental health, published a year later in June 2007, confirmed what many soldiers, marines, and their families already knew: that the Pentagon's mental health services were "woefully inadequate" to meet the demand. Unprepared—six years after we went to war.

"Our involvement in the Global War on Terrorism has created unforeseen demands not only on individual military service members and their families, but also on the Department of Defense itself, which must expand its capabilities to support the psychological health of its service members and their families," the task force reported. "New demands have exposed shortfalls in a health care system that in previous decades had been oriented away from a wartime focus. Staffing levels were poorly matched to the high operational tempo even prior to the current conflict, and the system has become even more strained by the increased deployment of active duty providers with mental health expertise... the system of care for psychological health that has evolved over recent decades is insufficient to meet the needs of today's forces and their beneficiaries, and will not be sufficient to meet their needs in the future."

Things weren't much better over at the sprawling VA, where its 280,000 employees were struggling unsuccessfully to keep up with the unanticipated demand by Iraq and Afghanistan War veterans for mental health services despite its $140 billion budget. Senior VA officials assured me things were fine, but in 2009, a coalition of veterans groups sued the VA, and the U.S. Court of Appeals for the Ninth Circuit agreed that the VA, because of inadequate mental health care and other medical lapses, had violated veterans' constitutional rights. It found the "influx of injured troops returning from deployment in Iraq and Afghanistan has placed an unprecedented strain on the VA and has overwhelmed the system." As a consequence, the court determined, veterans were forced to endure lengthy delays for treatment, especially for mental health care. Some, it found, had committed suicide. "The VA's unchecked incompetence has gone on long enough," the court declared. "No more veterans should be compelled to agonize or perish while the government fails to perform its obligations."

Few veterans disputed the court's findings, but its decision eventually was overturned on constitutional grounds. The VA continued to sink. Its employees worked fast, but new benefits claims came in even faster: between 2009 and 2013, the VA's clerks processed 4.1 million claims for benefits; but during that period 4.6 million new claims came in the door. Eventually, VA officials were discovered lying to cover up their inability to handle the workload, and in 2014, Secretary of Veterans Affairs Eric Shinseki, a decorated combat veteran himself, was forced to resign to make way for a promised bureaucratic housecleaning.

The army, meantime, decided it better get serious about preventing battlefield trauma, even if the experts couldn't agree on what exactly trauma was. In 2008 General George Casey, the army's chief of staff, began working with the Positive Psychology Center at the University of Pennsylvania, whose director, psychologist Martin Seligman, had written such popular self-help books as *Authentic Happiness: Using the New Positive Psychology to Realize Your Potential for Lasting Fulfillment*. Together, Seligman and the army came up with a program they called Comprehensive Soldier Fitness, later expanded to Comprehensive Soldier and Family Fitness, or, as the army refers to it, CSF2. The army hired Seligman and his center, on a no-bid $125 million contract, to develop a way to build "resilience" in soldiers. The goal was to increase their psychological strength and positive performance and "reduce the incidence of maladaptive responses of the entire U.S. Army," according to Rhonda Cornum, the retired army brigadier general who oversaw CSF2. Cornum, a biochemist and board-certified surgeon, had been a POW during Desert Storm, when she was sexually assaulted by Iraqi soldiers.

CSF2 requires every soldier to complete an annual self-assessment test and, based on that score, to master one or more online training programs to strengthen their resilience. Master "resilience trainers" are scattered throughout army units to provide further encouragement and training. The idea is to enable soldiers to "bounce back from adversity and to grow and thrive," Sergeant First Class Eric Tobin, a master resilience trainer, told me in 2014. "Not to eliminate adversity, we all know bad stuff happens, but to work through those situations...change your thoughts to be more productive in the moment."

Say a buddy is killed in combat, Tobin said. "My thoughts in that moment could be, Shit, that guy's dead, which is gonna make me feel terrible. I may freeze. Or my thought may be that we're all gonna die, and that leads to freezing. If my thoughts are, That guy's dead, but I have to save the rest of us, that's gonna drive a different reaction. Lean on my [CSF2] training, do that battle drill, and keep everyone else alive. In that moment," Tobin said, "I can still function."

Sharyn Saunders, the director of army resilience programs, told me the training modules "don't really talk about how to emotionally handle" morally tough issues that might arise on the battlefield, such as seeing a buddy killed or killing a civilian. Although the mental resiliency program is six years old, she said, "We have not yet addressed the mental perspective or the psychological perspective or the emotional perspective of that particular moment." What is addressed, she said, is "how do I support my own optimism at that moment." As the army builds more programming, she said, "It will be interesting to see how that connects to future PTSD." How could it not? I asked, and she shot back, "That's my thinking! We are really pushing forward in this particular area to robust that," she said. "The good stuff is yet to come."

The army's CSF2 and similar programs by the other military services were studied in 2014 by the IOM's sober graybeards, who cast a bleak eye on all of them, observing the lack of evidence that any of them actually work. "A majority of DOD [Department of Defense] resilience, prevention and reintegration programs are not consistently based on evidence," the IOM said. "There has been no systematic use of national performance measures to assess current DOD screening programs." In short, these outside experts said, the army had no way of telling whether its resiliency programs were effective or a total waste of time and money.

Veterans and families frustrated by all this have found some leverage in Congress, which has been hounding the Pentagon and VA for failing to care for the troops. Congress has forced the VA to adopt such reforms as adding new mental health caregivers and increasing research into war trauma.

Some individuals have taken direct action. In the years after his son's suicide, Jeff Sexton worked tirelessly to try to find ways to improve the military's mental health services. He wrote letters. Heard nothing back from the Indiana National Guard, received polite form letters from army and Defense Department officials — We're sorry for your loss, we're working on the problem. "But as far as anyone doing anything," Jeff said. "Nobody. Ever." Then one day he heard his new senator, Indiana Democrat Joe Donnelly, talking about the need to do something about military suicides. Jeff sat down and wrote an e-mail.

Dear Senator Donnelly,

Me and my wife know all too well the pain of military suicide. Our son Jacob took his life Oct 12, 2009. I'm glad to see you talking about the suicide rate among our service members. For too long I felt like the military has tried to hide the facts from everyone and not let the true cost of 10 years of war be told.

I'm willing to help you in any way I can. All you need do is ask and I will be there by your side to tell anyone who is willing to hear how a young man takes his own life and leaves the ones he loved behind. And how his PTSD did not go to the grave with him but passed on to his father.

The next day in Farmland, Jeff's phone rang. The number indicated the call originated from a Senate office in Washington. This is Joe, a deep voice said. I want you to come to Washington.

In late 2014, the Jacob Sexton Military Suicide Prevention Act, sponsored by Senator Joe Donnelly and Senator Roger Wicker, Republican of Mississippi, passed Congress and was signed into law by President Obama. It required the military to give annual mental health assessments to all service members, strengthened privacy provisions for those seeking psychological help, and directed the Pentagon to experiment with giving training and responsibility to sergeants to monitor the mental health of their troops. All were measures that might have kept Jake Sexton alive and helped veterans like Darren Doss manage their own demons.

As I dug into stories of people like Darren Doss and Jake and Jeff Sexton, I began to realize the breadth and depth of the moral blows that American troops were absorbing. I felt angry that we were sending them to war without any emotional protection, spiritual armor. Apart from the threadbare homilies about punishing the terrorists of 9/11, or fighting them over there so we didn't have to fight them here at home, there seemed to be no grand purpose that might justify the damage being done to them. Years ago I had written some about the doctrine of just war. I never heard any grunts mention it, but I thought it might apply to the two wars. I went back and reread, and what I found was surprising.

CHAPTER 5

Just War

War is a morally dubious and difficult activity.
  —Michael Walzer, "The Triumph of Just War Theory
                    (and the Dangers of Success)"

In early January of 2010, a squad from Charlie Company One-Six got pinned down in a gully under fire from Taliban fighters holed up in an adobe farm compound in southern Afghanistan. The marines had just arrived in the country, part of a "surge" of thirty thousand troops President Obama had ordered to strengthen prosecution of the war. The president had used his Nobel Peace Prize acceptance speech a few weeks earlier to justify his decision to expand the U.S. effort. After eight years of fighting, the physical, mental, and moral casualties were mounting. Jacob Sexton had shot himself that fall in a movie theater near Farmland, Indiana. Obama had visited the wounded at the Walter Reed Army Medical Center in Washington and had come out shaken. "I don't want to be going to Walter Reed for another eight years," he said. Now in his Nobel speech in Stockholm, he explained:

I face the world as it is, and cannot stand idle in the face of threats to the American people. For make no mistake: Evil does exist in the world. A non-violent movement could not have halted Hitler's armies. Negotiations cannot convince al Qaeda's leaders to lay down their arms. To say that force may sometimes be necessary is not a call to cynicism—it is a recognition of history; the imperfections of man and the limits of reason.

"We must begin by acknowledging the hard truth," Obama said. "We will not eradicate violent conflict in our lifetimes. There will be times when nations—acting individually or in concert—will find the use of force not only necessary but morally justified."

It's unlikely anyone in Charlie One-Six had heard the president's endorsement of war as a necessary, lesser evil. Had any of them recalled and repeated aloud the eloquent phrases about "morally justifiable" war in the desperation of their shallow, stony gully on that awful day in early 2010, he might have been greeted with hoots of derisive laughter. At the moment, unable to move forward or back without exposing themselves to the Taliban's deadly gunfire, the handful of marines of Charlie One-Six were too busy trying to survive.

It was a bad situation in Afghanistan's Helmand Province in early 2010. Marjah, the town U.S. troops were charged with liberating from the Taliban, was spread out across a labyrinth of cross-hatching irrigation canals, adobe-walled compounds separated by dirt paths, and acres of alternating bare stony ground and steamy poppy fields. The marines of Charlie One-Six faced, at some distance, a compound typical of that part of southern Afghanistan: a modest farmhouse of three or four dirt-floored rooms, with perhaps a lean-to shelter for cooking and crude pens for goats and chickens, all of them enclosed by adobe walls that rose,

in places, to five or six feet. Families living this hardscrabble existence would scatter when American troops moved into the area,
fearing the gun battles that would ensue. And sure enough, this
marine patrol came under fire from gunmen hidden somewhere
within the compound, and the marines dove down into the gully's modest cover to figure out what to do next.

Two of them, Joey Schiano and Chuck Newton, took turns
cautiously raising their heads to see if they could pinpoint where
the shots were coming from. Despite their age—Joey was
twenty-two, Chuck twenty-five—they were seasoned combat
infantrymen on their second deployment. They ducked at a
whooshing sound, and a rocket-propelled grenade exploded in
the tree over their heads, and branches and twigs clattered down
on them. Finally Joey spotted a muzzle flash and slid down excit-
edly. Newton inched up to take a cautious look.

"I don't see 'em—which window? Where?" Newton was
trained and assigned as a SMAW gunner. The shoulder-fired mul-
tipurpose assault weapon was the squad's most powerful weapon.
But he couldn't see the shooters.

"Lemme do it," Joey yelled, and Newton shouted, "I'll cover
for you!" and handed over the SMAW. Joey lifted the fifty-four-
inch tube to his shoulder, rose into a crouch, squinted into the
viewfinder, and focused on a section of blank wall. Then he fired.

The SMAW is a descendant of the World War II bazooka,
designed to disable tanks and blow apart concrete bunkers. Against
adobe, it is devastating. The blast demolished one end of the
building. As the rubble and dust settled, the marines could hear
shouting and wailing. "They want to bring out the wounded,"
the marines' interpreter reported. The Taliban gunners fled, and
the survivors dragged out the torn and bleeding bodies, some
draped over wheelbarrows. It became clear that the Taliban had
intended to use women and children as human shields, herding
them behind the wall that the SMAW had struck. The marines

were stunned. "I mean, all of us would have stopped for a kid. We would rather have the entire squad mowed down than to put a family in jeopardy," Newton said later. "Joey's thing was, we're taking fire from that building and there are Taliban there. Who would ever think they'd put a family in there? That's how they won the day," Newton told me, still furious five years later at what he saw as the Taliban's moral deceit. "That's the only way they can get over on us, by tricking us. They didn't outgun us or kill any of our guys, but they won the day by baiting us into killing civilians."

Joey Schiano was shattered at the carnage he'd caused. "He just broke down sobbing," said Stephen Canty, Schiano's squadmate. "The thing is, you couldn't have known." It wasn't within the marines' mind-set at that time that the enemy would deliberately put women and children at risk for tactical advantage. Charlie One-Six was not yet hardened to the butchery that would characterize this combat tour in Marjah. But they were learning fast. And as Canty often reminded himself, once you know the truth of war, you can't unknow it. Ever.

The doctrine of just war holds, as Obama noted, that war should be a moral response to a grave wrong, a self-defense response to aggression, or an effort to rescue or protect the victims of injustice. The value of just war lies in its being not only a salve to the conscience of the king or president who orders troops into battle, but as a reassurance to the troops themselves that the killing they do is morally righteous. Otherwise, it is murder.

Rationales for war have been around a long time. Political theorist Michael Walzer, professor emeritus at Princeton's Institute for Advanced Study, notes that ancient Greeks argued about the conditions under which war could be justified, and so did early Islamic scholars. There are references to such debates in the Bible. In Plato's *Republic*, written some twenty-four centuries ago, the Greek philosopher justified war as a natural instinct for survival of a just state—that is, Athens—against the threat of surrounding unjust states. War making, the Greeks believed, was a legitimate and justified right of the people.

The early Christian church swerved sharply away from that idea, unambiguously rejecting participation in the military and in war in any form. Over time, that position proved untenable as the church sought to defend its holdings against the rising Germanic tribes, including the Visigoths, who sacked Rome in 410. Christians needed to make war and kill, and in the fifth century the theologian Saint Augustine, an African bishop, came to the rescue. Killing was okay, Augustine declared in *City of God* (published in A.D. 426), if God or political leaders said so:

> They who have waged war in obedience to the divine command, or in conformity with His laws, have represented in their persons the public justice or the wisdom of government, and in this capacity have put to death wicked men; such persons have by no means violated the commandment, "Thou shalt not kill."

In essence, Augustine's new doctrine relieved individual soldiers of responsibility for killing and put this immense power, to declare killing just or not, in the hands of higher authority. That was the church. By Augustine's writ, Christian pacifists became Christian warriors.

Of course it was easy, demonstrably too easy, to claim "divine command" as your *jus ad bellum*. It was the concept of "just war" that enabled thirteenth-century Christians, directed by Pope Urban II, to crusade against—slaughter—Muslims. But the elaborate rhetorical and philosophical gymnastics that religious and secular leaders performed as they battled over religion and conquest largely faded away with the rise of sovereign nation-states, whose leaders felt their military excursions needed no justification. Save for some outspoken moralists, few raised just war objections to the Civil War, the Franco-Prussian War, the opium wars, or the Spanish-American War. The United States swept into the final year of slaughter in World War I on a wave of indignant moral determination to "end all wars," as President Wilson put it. That idea culminated in the 1928 Kellogg-Briand Pact outlawing war altogether. It was solemnly signed by all the major nations that plunged into a global conflict just a few years later.

Not until the Vietnam War in the 1960s did just war doctrine come back into vogue, seized upon by the antiwar left as a legitimate basis for opposing what was seen as an unjust war. But critically, it was the military's own embrace of just war that revived the doctrine as a useful tool of modern statecraft. The United States fought in Vietnam under a counterinsurgency doctrine, which required winning the hearts and minds of the local populations. That meant the American cause, its warfighting methods, and especially its treatment of civilians had to be seen as just. In practice, of course, carpet-bombing, Agent Orange defoliants, napalm, assassinations, and forced relocations made our hearts-and-minds counterinsurgency campaign a cruel hoax. But the idea was implanted, and some military strategists began speaking of the U.S. defeat in Vietnam as a failure to pursue a just war. That idea became thoroughly embedded in the strategies that framed the wars in Iraq and Afghanistan.

As Princeton's Michael Walzer wrote in 2002, "There are now reasons of state for fighting justly. One might almost say that Justice has become a military necessity." That meant, he wrote, "that we should not fight wars about whose justice we are doubtful, and that once we are engaged we have to fight justly so as not to antagonize the civilian population whose political support is necessary to a military victory."

Much of the way the United States fights today stems from

just war doctrine: the military's rigorous effort, if imperfectly realized, to avoid causing civilian casualties; its practice of paying cash to the families of each civilian killed by U.S. forces; its placement of lawyers into tactical operations centers to ensure compliance with just war concepts; and issuing rules of engagement to guide the behavior of individual troops.

The modern adaptation of just war doctrine neatly resolves the problem of determining whether a killing is justified or murder. Fifteen centuries after Augustine, we have returned to the idea that if you are fighting evil, you are excused from the biblical commandment *Thou shalt not kill.* Your cause has to be just a bit less evil than the enemy's. The Catholic Church put it this way in its 1992 catechism: "The use of arms must not produce evils and disorders greater than the evil to be eliminated." Lesser evils, okay.

In its most recent incarnation, though, the application of just war has been too easy, too convenient. After the terrorist attacks of 9/11, as confusion and fear hardened into a demand for revenge, President George W. Bush and many others invoked just war doctrine as the basis for the morally righteous killing of the alleged perpetrators in Afghanistan. But Bush, rather than simply acknowledging the emotionally satisfying and morally justifiable decision to strike back, invoked the concepts of good and evil, vowing to use the military to "rid the world of evildoers." With U.S. troops pouring into Afghanistan to pursue evildoers, in February 2002, Bush declared: "Our cause is just... our war against terror is only beginning." Within a few weeks, the terrorists responsible for the 9/11 attacks were gone from Afghanistan, fled into neighboring Pakistan. Washington accelerated the war inside Afghanistan anyway, with more troops, more and bigger American bases, more casualties, more destruction. When I arrived there with a company of Tenth Mountain Division troops in January 2002, we slept in leaky tents, shaved outdoors in icy buckets, and used a splintery plywood two-seat latrine (waste was burned off each day with diesel fuel). We dreamed of showers. A decade later, a half-dozen three-story brick apartment buildings had risen to house the military, with paved streets and parking lots, giant fitness facilities, and dining halls, and Pizza Hut and Burger King offering free delivery.

When the invasion of Iraq was ordered, it was against broad public misgivings: even if the president's dubious claims about weapons of mass destruction were true, there was no basis in international law or precedent for his proclaimed right to pursue a "preemptive" war to prevent Saddam Hussein from ever attacking the United States. It was difficult to see how self-defense under just war doctrine could be applied to aggression that hadn't yet happened. But Bush went ahead anyway. "If we wait for threats to materialize," the president explained at West Point in 2002, "we will have waited too long."

Of course, the bearded riflemen and suicide bombers who thronged back into Afghanistan to confront the Americans and, two years later, rose against the American presence in Iraq were armed with their own just war doctrine: "Do not kill the soul sanctified by God," the Koran dictates, "except for just cause."

In both Iraq and Afghanistan, the U.S. military applied just war ideas to its tactical operations, with results that will be debated for years. It's already clear, however, that just war provided little comfort to the troops on the ground. The men and women we agreed to send into our longest wars fought under clouds of doubt. If just war comforted the politicians and think-tank savants who supported the wars, those who did the fighting were left on their own to decide whether their actions in combat were justified killing or murder. The result was an epidemic of moral injury and personal tragedy.

★ ★ ★

When nineteen-year-old Joseph Schiano had come home to tell his mother, Debbie, that he was joining the marines, she reacted in a way most mothers would understand. She grabbed him around the throat with both hands, pushed him against the wall, and yelled, *"You can't do this! I have given you life and I am the only one who can take life from you!"* Then she sighed and wrapped him in a bear hug. "I saw this was what he wanted to do," Debbie told me.

Despite her deepest fears, Joseph came home after that second combat tour in Marjah physically unharmed. But the demons of his moral injuries, the nightmares of those torn bodies, the guilt over what he had done, followed close behind and eventually closed in on him, finally spilling over onto Debbie herself. It turned out, she realized too late, that war's aftermath was more dangerous for Joseph than being in war.

Debbie and Joseph and her two other children, Tyler and Nicole, were close, intimate in the way families can get when times are hard. Debbie was a single mom, and they were scraping by. Their small two-story town house in a moderate-income housing development in Greenwich, Connecticut, was cramped and sparse. They did without. At one point they slept on the floor. They were proud and defiant. They fought and yelled at one another, but they always ended up laughing. They stood together. And her kids were smart. Joseph, her eldest, had a sharp memory, the kind of student who could neglect his homework and then ace his tests. By fifth grade at the redbrick Hamilton Avenue School, he'd published three poems in the school newspaper. One, written after a class lecture about drinking and driving, described the thoughts of a driver as he was dying in a car crash.

At elementary school, Joseph was bullied. Debbie complained to the school. When a teacher suggested her son might be "instigating" attacks on himself, Debbie marched into the classroom and told her: "You are instigating me to bounce a ball on your head!" Riding home in the car one day, Joseph pointed out the kid who'd bullied him. Debbie made him get out of the car and go punch him. "He didn't want to hurt anybody," she said, remembering his reluctance. Once, she punished Joseph for misbehavior, and he objected. "I can't believe you did that—you're supposed to be my friend," he complained. She shot back: "I am your mother first. Then we can be friends." And they were.

When Joseph grew into his teens, he kept his two most distinctively boyish features: his rosy cheeks and his short stature, around five-six. He compensated: earring, lip ring, eyebrow ring. He tried to harden himself by working out, but he was never what Debbie called "a washboard kid." He went through what she remembers as his "black phase," when he painted his fingernails black. Once he dyed his hair, yellow on one side, red on the other. Debbie and Nicole called him Half Head. All that dropped away when he went to Parris Island in 2007. When the other marines found out he hated the name Joey, they fondly called him Joey and taunted him for his rosy cheeks. "We made fun of the people we liked," Chuck Newton once explained. "People we didn't like, we never talked to."

Joseph and Debbie stayed close, even after he and Charlie One-Six went away for seven months in Afghanistan in 2008, fighting in the southern town of Garmsir. "One thing Joseph and I have—had," she corrected herself, "is communication." She knew he had worried about the children in Afghanistan; he'd heard they could be aggressive, sometimes dangerous. Joseph had asked her once, What should I do if a kid threatens me with a gun? Shoot him, she'd replied. You're okay defending yourself. She worried while he was gone. She knew his company was sometimes called Suicide Charlie because they felt they were always being dangled out as bait for the Taliban. Like moms across the country, Debbie stifled her fear with action: she sent them box after box of goodies, snacks, toiletries, boxers, cigarettes, socks, and ziplock bags. Cartloads of stuff from Costco. At home, she fretted, feeling alone in a sea of upscale suburban-Connecticut families whose kids were not fighting in Afghanistan. "You just go around like everything's fine," she said. "But I was losing my mind." She wondered, Is it normal to be planning your child's funeral? She was grateful when she found a website for marine parents that answered that question: Yes, normal. Something many military parents did.

Charlie One-Six was home at Camp Lejeune for fourteen months before they were sent back to Afghanistan, in December 2009. This time they were assigned to help clear insurgents from Marjah. The fighting was fierce and prolonged, and Charlie One-Six was in the thick of it. They started taking casualties even before the battle officially began. There was a lot of killing. "I know he was having anxiety issues over there," Debbie said. "They lost close friends. They blamed themselves."

It wasn't until much later that she learned the details of that day when Joey fired the SMAW at a building where women and children were cowering behind Taliban gunmen shooting from windows and doorways. For Joey Schiano, it was a classic moral injury. Using a SMAW to try to stop the gunfire pinning the marines down was tactically correct and allowed under every international law and U.S. military doctrine. It was a military necessity. In the words of President Obama, Joey's commander in chief back in Washington, it was "morally justified." But the moral burden, the image of those bloody innocents, the guilt, the shame—the inescapable truth of what he had done—that's what Joey evidently took away from Afghanistan. The way Debbie described it, the moral pain he felt was acute. "He loved people. He would do anything for anyone," Debbie said. One image in particular haunted him, she said: he was convinced that the rocket he had fired had gone through the head of one of the children.

Even before One-Six got back to Camp Lejeune from Marjah in July 2010, navy psychologists had diagnosed Joey with PTSD. He was having trouble sleeping, so they dosed him with Xanax, an antianxiety drug, but when he did drift off, he'd jerk awake, sweating and trembling from nightmares of maimed children. In a panic he'd call home. To make Joey laugh and break the tension, Debbie would try to quickly think up something silly his brother, Tyler, had done. One by one his platoon buddies were getting out of the marines. Finally Joey did, too, and came home to Connecticut on January 12, 2011. He left behind Frankie, his beloved pit-bull mix; there was no place for him in Debbie's crowded town house.

A day or two after he got home, Joseph called the VA to get help with his PTSD. He was told to send an e-mail request. As Debbie remembers it, he received a form letter from the VA two weeks later saying they'd get back to him in eight or ten weeks. That was a blow. After four years of hard-driven, mission-oriented life in the marines, Joseph was adrift back home in the civilian world. The sudden disappearance of his closest buddies stirred feelings of loss and grief. As much as he had chafed against the institutional confines of military service, he missed its structure, its predictability, its ideal of service. Like other veterans, he thought he could regain some of that by getting involved in law enforcement or emergency medicine. He got the books and studied, but none of it stuck. "Mom, I just can't remember anything," he said.

"It's okay," Debbie told him. "Take your time."

One night, he came home from drinking with friends and stormed upstairs. Nicole yelled to Debbie, "Mom, you better come up here, there's something wrong with Joe." Debbie raced up the stairs. He was shouting at himself in the mirror: "I'm a marine! I don't need anyone! I can do this by myself!" When Debbie tried to intervene, Joseph exploded, shouting that they were being shot at and needed to shoot back. Tyler tried to grab him, and Joseph turned with a look of hatred and screamed, "I'm gonna come fuck you up!" That's when Debbie put her hand firmly on Joseph's shoulder, and he slid down to the floor, his back against the wall. Debbie slid down with him, and as he burst into tears, she held him and rocked him.

"It broke my heart, he just cried so hard," Debbie told me, through her own tears. "He just couldn't understand why he had to lose so many friends, why he was the way he was. He kept saying it should have been him out there [who got killed]. And he just saw the image of those kids all the time. He lived with that image every time he went to sleep."

But then he seemed to pull himself together.

He stopped drinking. Tried to quit smoking. Made plans to fix up a room for himself in his grandmother's house and bring his dog, Frankie, up from North Carolina. He found a new girlfriend and would drive his Volkswagen Jetta the forty minutes up to Somers, New York, to see her. He'd go Friday night, come back Sunday, and along the way he'd put on Zac Brown. The music, with its haunting lines, often made him cry.

Just after noon on Sunday, March 20, 2011, Debbie felt sick and canceled plans to get a manicure. She was lying down when the police came to the door. Joey's Jetta had run off Route 139, a narrow winding road in Somers, and struck a utility pole. At twenty-three years old, he was dead.

Joey Schiano had gone to war with the other marines of Charlie One-Six and hundreds of thousands of others, trusting—along with their families—that the United States held the moral high ground, that they fought under the banner of just war. Translated to an actual battlefield, that assurance meant that the killing Charlie One-Six would do was virtuous and morally sanctioned. Otherwise it would be murder, a profound violation of the moral dictates of the world's great religions. It meant that even though the accidental killing of Afghan women and children was tragic, it was not murder.

But if U.S. military interventions in Iraq and Afghanistan were believed to be morally just—not only by politicians far distant from any battlefield, but on a personal level by the working-class military, the trigger pullers—then why did the conduct of those wars produce so much moral pain among those who fought in them?

How did Joseph Schiano, who followed the rules and values he'd learned from Debbie and been taught at Parris Island, who fired his weapon against an enemy in a morally justified war, come to be haunted by that act? So haunted that he told his mother he wished he'd died on the battlefield? And why is it that we who sent Joey and the others to war have not also felt their moral pain?

The machinery of war continued to grind forward, the cycle of growing threat and growing response powering both wars well beyond their shaky moral origins. Instead of just war, these conflicts became war justified by war. And we let it happen. Not only was there no serious antiwar movement, there was precious little questioning of the moral justifications of the wars at all. Three days after the terrorist attacks in 2001 Congress had enacted the Authorization for the Use of Military Force (AUMF), which sanctified American killing of alleged terrorists anywhere on the globe. The war in Iraq was begun, fought, and ended, and new U.S. military interventions began in Iraq and Syria without any significant public pressure to rewrite the AUMF or even to discuss it. In 2014 and 2015 a few members of Congress wondered whether or how to renew the AUMF, but as of this writing, despite a raucous presidential campaign and an angry debate over how to fight the Islamic State, nobody could be bothered.

Thus the high moral purpose that fired our united response to

9/11 was allowed to wither, and the soldiers and marines I lived with at war after 2002 fought without the certainty that their cause was just, that every action, every decision, came under the umbrella of just war, that the killing in which they were engaged was not murder. In that sense, we all let them down. Because war is morally complex and constantly changing, Michael Walzer wrote, "decisions about when and how to fight require constant scrutiny, exactly as they always have...the ongoing critique of war-making is a centrally important democratic activity."

News of Joseph's death knocked the breath out of Debbie. For hours she could hardly move. Finally she levered herself up from the sofa, tottered into the kitchen, and smashed glasses, plates, and dishes. Then the tears came, the regret and anger and aching sorrow. At Joseph's funeral, the marines of Charlie One-Six served as pallbearers and stood at attention as his casket was lowered into a grave under towering beeches and cedars at Putnam Cemetery, just off Parsonage Road in Greenwich. A glass display holding a folded flag and Joseph's medals graces a wall in Debbie's living room; on another wall, a large color photograph of Joseph, bare chested at the beach, embracing his dog, Frankie, and grinning at the camera. The VA never had gotten back to Joey. But after his funeral, they offered counseling for Debbie and Tyler and Nicole. Debbie and Nicole declined. Tyler went a few times, then gave up and enlisted in the marines. Debbie's own grief runs deep, her loss beyond words. She can manage to say, "I miss Joey. But I think he's in a better place."

There are inevitable questions about whether he took his own life. "I know for a fact he didn't commit suicide," said Debbie. "He had problems. He felt like he didn't belong. But he was making plans." Like other veterans, Joey said he missed the adrenaline rush of combat. Maybe that's why he drove so fast, Debbie thought. Tempting death.

It is a tragic measure of his moral injury that Joey may have felt the only way to surmount his pain was with reckless speed. Certainly he needed professional help, steady, insightful, and caring. The VA has acknowledged its shortage of mental health therapists and has hired additional therapists in recent years. But long waiting lists still are common. And while there are promising experimental therapies for moral injury under way, the therapy provided by the VA has had disappointing results. The mental health community, both military and civilian, is a long way from being able to reach veterans like Joey Schiano with consistent healing help. After all, the origins of his moral injury lay not in him but in the inability or unwillingness of our political leaders to pursue war under a clear, convincing, publicly articulated moral justification. Joey went to war without any moral structure to support him, and in that sense his wound may have been untreatable. Talking with an understanding therapist might have helped, but Joey was on a wait list when he died.

"It wasn't Afghanistan where he died," Debbie once reminded me. "It was right here." Betrayal is at the center of her moral injury: the failure of her country to support her son at war, and its unwillingness to care for him when he came home. Betrayal, grief, anger. "Joey was dead inside of twelve weeks! How many guys are dead that were waiting those twelve weeks? Hire some more people!" Debbie said. "You've got a lot of kids coming home — this is a time of war. Cut back *after* the war!"

Toward the end of a long conversation, Debbie paused, exhausted. "I don't know what the answer is," she admitted. Except the obvious: "There need to be more people who can listen," she said. "I don't care how much the story makes you sick to your stomach, just listen. Don't turn your back."

CHAPTER 6

Trotting Heart, Shell Shock, Moral Injury

The moral dimension of psychological injury remains largely
unexplored, at least within mainstream mental health.
— George Loeffler, Lieutenant Commander, U.S. Navy,
and Psychiatrist, Naval Medical Center San Diego

That fresh Saturday morning at the end of October promised
some relief from the ferocious heat of an Iraqi autumn. But not
from the war. It was 2004; Joey Schiano was a junior in high
school, dreaming of joining the marines even as the war was
accelerating. In Iraq that October, sixty-four Americans were
killed in battle. On this day, bombings were leaving broken glass
and body parts in the streets of Baghdad and other cities, a Japanese hostage was found decapitated, an American convoy was
attacked south of Baghdad, and fourteen civilians were killed in
the resulting firefights. Outside Falluja, a city wrecked by
house-to-house fighting and now held by insurgents, marines
were responding to a mortar-and-rocket attack with a barrage of
artillery shells they sent whistling into the city.

A convoy of marines in heavy trucks and Humvee gun trucks, meantime, was moving warily down the main road on the outskirts of the city. An officer later recalled glancing at a black Chevy Suburban creeping along the shoulder, thinking it was odd that the Iraqi driver was sitting with his head down. Moments later, the explosives-packed SUV erupted. A hurricane of fire and jagged red-hot steel shrapnel struck directly at dozens of marines standing unprotected in the bed of a seven-ton truck. Eight were killed immediately, three under the age of twenty-one; another eight fell wounded. Then insurgents struck with small arms and RPG fire. Under constant attack for ten more hours, the surviving marines set up a security perimeter and returned fire as the bodies burned in the wreckage. When the flames died down and the insurgents withdrew, the marines gathered the charred corpses of their buddies from the wreckage to zip into body bags.

Bill Nash rushed to help. As a navy psychiatrist, he had deployed to Iraq with these marines as one of the military's top experts on psychological trauma. But this was no place for the niceties of research or office-call therapy. His job now was to swallow his own horror and help the shocked marines absorb what had happened and enable them to move on. This was a war, after all, and the marines were assigned to take part in a major assault into the deadly back alleys of Falluja within a few days. As he leaped from his Humvee at the gruesome scene of the attack, Nash recoiled for a moment, feeling a weight of inadequacy before the awful trauma etched on the faces of these young marines.

"I know what it's like," Nash wrote home later, "to watch their wracking sobs and feel their anger and fear and grief and see their eyes looking at me like I am supposed to respond with some magical words that will somehow make it better...

"I hate this shit, more than almost anything in my business."

★   ★   ★

Nash is a bear of a man whose broad face, booming laugh, and intense manner make him seem larger than his six-foot frame and instantly likable. At home now in a suburban split-level outside Washington, D.C., he wears comfortable sweatpants, running shoes and a loose black shirt, military-short brown hair, a close-cropped beard, and wire-rim glasses. Passion runs close to the Nash surface. He likes to laugh and laughs often, a gleeful, shoulder-shaking *heh-heh-heh*. Unable to sit still for long, he'd often jump up from his dining room table where we talked and pace to let the words tumble out. Until I learned to rest my tape recorder on a folded napkin, it would register loud detonations whenever he slapped the table for emphasis. His living room is bachelor-neat, slightly crowded with a high-end bicycle trainer wedged between easy chairs, a reminder of his intention, at age sixty-three, to work his way back to the bike-racing trim of his youth. On the fireplace mantel, a reproduction of Vermeer's *Girl with a Pearl Earring,* tastefully lit from below.

It's easy to imagine Bill Nash in body armor and helmet among boisterous marines a decade ago in Falluja, so it's surprising to find that he's been painfully shy much of his life. That he grew up one of six kids in a dysfunctional blue-collar family on Chicago's South Side; that he felt "pretty much motherless" as a kid ("There's my mother," he once told me, pointing to the Vermeer); and that his fantasies of a loving family were nurtured by TV sitcoms like *Leave It to Beaver.* That he was bullied by neighborhood kids until the day in fourth grade he picked up Tommy Gannon and dumped him sprawling on the ground. And that his bedrock belief in cleansing and redemption and forgiveness came from the Catholic Church, where he served as an altar boy. On Saturdays, rather than goofing off, he'd walk the thirteen minutes from home, heading west on Eighty-Seventh Street to the red-brick edifice of Saint Kilian's for confession, so that on Sundays he could receive communion with a pure heart. "I remember," he told me with a shy smile, "the feeling of walking home — clean, you know? Renewed. So spirituality and all that was an important part of my coping."

The marines were still pinned down in firefights around the burning truck near Falluja when Nash arrived, and he threw himself into the initial first aid to the psychologically wounded while absorbing their outpouring of shock and anger and grief. In the following hours and days he met with marines individually and listened to their stories and held more formal debriefing sessions in which he encouraged marines to talk about the experience and to articulate their emotions. He organized and led memorial services for the dead. It was the emotional equivalent of the tourniquets and blood plasma of combat trauma medicine. Whatever succor the marines found, however they managed their emotional and moral wounds, there was little time for healing. Days later, they joined the assault into Falluja in a major two-month battle that would kill 95 American troops and wound 560. Nash went with them, and when their combat tour was complete and they all rotated home to Camp Pendleton, near San Diego, Nash plunged back into clinical work. He carried with him critical new insights into psychological war trauma and a fresh determination to break free of the prevailing doctrine for treating war trauma, a creaky and harmful century-old model used during World War I. That was all he'd had to help the marines of Falluja and it wasn't enough.

Eventually, Nash would recognize the psychological damage suffered by those marines and so many others in war as moral injury, the term first used by VA psychiatrist Jonathan Shay. Nash's groundbreaking work, along with that of a handful of others, would begin to form an entirely new basis for helping Iraq and Afghanistan veterans cope with their war experiences.

★   ★   ★

Until recently, the most common model for treating traumatized combat troops, the one Nash had been taught, was formalized in 1916 during a gathering of German psychiatrists and neuroscientists in Munich. Their concern was not so much the staggering slaughter then under way on the battlefields of Europe. It was the tens of thousands of soldiers returning from the trenches so traumatized that they had been declared unfit to fight and sent home, flooding the hospitals and city streets of the German Empire, supported by generous pensions. The streams of "shell-shocked" troops vividly demonstrated the effects of industrial warfare on human beings, and the hemorrhaging of manpower and treasure was draining the kaiser's coffers. It couldn't continue. Something, the graybeards were told, had to be done.

What they devised was a new doctrine stating that if you were traumatized by war, it was because you came to war with a preexisting weakness, what today is termed a personality disorder. This fit nicely with the prevailing understanding that once you grew out of childhood, your personality was fixed; subsequent experiences were fleeting, and whatever pain they caused was temporary. As Freud once wrote, "the primitive mind is, in the fullest meaning of the word, imperishable." It was a neat solution. War didn't make you sick, they decided. If the bloody terrors of trench warfare or charging into the machine guns at Ypres or the Marne drove you into an emotional breakdown, it was because you were already sick and war made it worse. But only temporarily.

To the doctors at least, this was heartening. It meant traumatized soldiers no longer had to be sent home (and no longer needed to be paid pensions). They could be treated briefly, near the front—"within the sound of the guns" was a common prescription—and sent back into the trenches. As Freud understood it, at least in the opening months of the First World War, "When the fierce struggle of this war will have reached a decision every victorious warrior will joyfully and without delay return home to his wife and children, undisturbed by thoughts of the enemy he has killed either at close quarters or with weapons operating at a distance."

The model agreed upon at Munich swept away a century or more of confusion, experimentation, and hand-wringing within the mental health profession about how to deal with wartime trauma. During the Civil War, soldiers suffering psychological damage were ignored and simply deserted or were accused of malingering and sometimes shot. Those who survived long enough to reach medical attention were told they suffered a cardiac condition, "soldier's heart" or "trotting heart," although there were discomfiting signs that the trauma went deeper. Peter Reed, a Union infantryman, was confined to the Indiana Hospital for the Insane in Indianapolis in 1862; his doctors noted with some puzzlement that Reed insisted that "he was guilty of great crimes... he thinks he is lost for all eternity." It became evident, at least to some, that war trauma was not temporary and could continue to do damage if untreated: in 1888, Civil War veteran David Wiltsee was confined at the same Indiana hospital; his chart noted that "his delusion seems to be that he has done something terrible," a description that today would be recognized as the shame and guilt of moral injury.

Prior to World War I, British surgeons asserted that soldiers suffering from shortness of breath, anxiety, chest pain, palpitations, or other manifestations of trauma were merely suffering from knapsack straps that were drawn too tight; they recommended that soldiers loosen the straps and avoid "stooping." That proved an insufficient medical remedy as well as bad tactical advice for troops facing murderous German guns after the war broke out. Soldiers found wandering aimlessly in the mud and shell craters of the battlefield were sometimes hauled back, court-martialed, and executed on the spot. German doctors had used electric shock to try to bring traumatized soldiers to their senses, often ordering them first to strip naked, the better to stun them with the current. Ironically, the British military medical establishment seems to have stumbled on what is now known as traumatic brain injury; they called it shell shock and applied the diagnosis to anyone suffering not just the physical effects of brain damage but the emotional ones as well, including nightmares, fatigue, tremors, and confusion. All that was caused, according to Frederick Mott, Britain's leading neuropathologist at the time, by the blast of exploding artillery shells, which damaged "the delicate colloidal structures of the living tissues of the brain and spinal cord." British theory also had it that exploding ammunition released carbon monoxide fumes into the air, which caused damage to the central nervous system.

Such debilitating conditions couldn't be treated casually, the British authorities decided. Rather than risking "lunatics at the loose," as one Allied psychiatrist put it, shell-shock victims were hurriedly evacuated back to twenty newly built mental hospitals in Britain, a humane response that soon became unsustainable: in the first four months of 1916, 24,000 men were sent home. During that summer's Battle of the Somme, 40 percent of the casualties, or some 140,000 men, were declared shell-shock patients. Like the Germans, the British began to search for a way out, and in 1917 a British physician and psychologist, who had worked with troops on the front lines and had coined the term "shell shock," came to the same conclusion the Germans had in Munich the previous year. Given the small international community working on trauma at the time, that was not surprising. Charles Samuel Myers, a handsome English intellectual who had studied experimental psychology, determined that shell shock had emotional as well as physical causes and that emotional trauma could be treated with rest and a respite from battle, close to the front. Implicit in his work was the idea that psychological trauma was an understandable and "normal" response. The promise of a quick return to battle appealed to generals desperate for manpower, and Myers's approach was quickly adopted. During the fourteen-week Battle of Passchendaele, in 1917, psychological casualties were temporarily withdrawn from the trenches and provided a safe bed, warm food, and a ration of rum. Then they were sent back.

Skip forward a generation to find that this treatment, devised under wartime pressure, survived into World War II and beyond—as Bill Nash experienced at Falluja in 2004. Nearly ninety years after the Munich meeting, Nash was treating troops just as the kaiser's doctors had treated psychological casualties of the trenches. One custom, though, has been discontinued: punishing traumatized soldiers. Shocked and horrified troops have often deserted; during World War II some twenty-one thousand American GIs were charged with desertion, but only one, Eddie Slovik, was executed for it. General George S. Patton was famously (and temporarily) fired by Eisenhower after he slapped and threatened to shoot two soldiers hospitalized with exhaustion. One of them was Private Paul G. Bennett, an artilleryman who witnessed the severe wounding of a buddy and was carried from the front with fever and dehydration, even though he had pleaded to be allowed to stay with his unit. When Patton came through the hospital ward, Bennett struggled to sit up, explaining that "it's my nerves." Patton exploded. "Your nerves, hell—you are just a goddamned coward. Shut up that goddamned crying," Patton bellowed. He drew his pistol and slapped the man before aides restrained him. Patton later complained that shell shock was "an invention of the Jews." But for the most part, soldiers were treated with food and rest, a remedy American troops popularized as "three hots and a cot."

In hindsight, it seems ludicrous to have treated mental health casualties of war under the conviction that war trauma is merely a temporary aggravation of childhood psychological injury, a condition that can be relieved by rest and conversation. As Nash wrote in a letter home from Falluja in 2004, when a person experiences trauma and moral injury, "part of one's sense of competence and worth as a human being is torn away, sometimes never to return." Yet the notions that were endorsed in Munich in 1916 are still the basis of much of today's battlefield treatment of war trauma. In modern U.S. military terms, the technique is codified as PIES, which specifies the principles of treatment: *proximity,* that treatment should take place close to the battlefield; *immediacy,* without waiting for lengthy medical evacuation; *expectancy,* the assumption that the patient will quickly return to normal; and *simplicity,* without any prolonged or complex psychological treatment. Often the acronym is modified to BICEPS, indicating that intervention should be *brief, immediate,* performed by a *central* authority—that is, someone in the patient's chain of command—and should meet the requirements of *expectancy, proximity,* and *simplicity.* PIES and BICEPS are the basis for the most commonly used trauma intervention in the United States, the critical incident stress debriefing. Widely practiced by police, firefighters, and emergency medical technicians, CISD is a group discussion facilitated by a trusted leader immediately after a traumatic event to share perceptions and emotions and to support one another's coping skills. The technique assumes the participants will return to normal quickly without prolonged treatment.

One reason that critical incident stress debriefing has only limited success, in the view of practitioners like Bill Nash, is it doesn't allow you time after a traumatic incident to think about what happened and to reach for some perspective. "Time does indeed heal at least some wounds," University of Virginia psychologist Timothy D. Wilson writes in his book on trauma and memory, *Redirect: Changing the Stories We Live By.* "Once we are done throwing furniture or sobbing into our pillows, we can take a step back and put as good a spin as we can on what happened."

Corralling people into a group discussion immediately after a traumatic event "can even solidify memories of it, which makes it harder for people to reinterpret the event as time goes by." But the principle of CISD still underlies the U.S. military's approach to the treatment of trauma: that trauma is a normal reaction, and if you weren't psychologically damaged in childhood, you should be able to get over it fairly quickly (three hots and a cot) with a quick stress debriefing. If that doesn't work, you are just... weak.

"What a massively destructive thing to do to somebody!" Nash snorted. I was thinking of Nik Rudolph, who was neither damaged in childhood nor weak, but he shot a child and came home from Afghanistan with a bruise on his soul. Nash and I were talking across his dining room table one winter morning. He'd made us coffee in a Keurig single-serving pod machine. My tape recorder rested protectively on a folded cup towel.

"If you read the military combat-stress-control doctrines and manuals going back to at least World War One," Nash was saying, "they all say the same thing, that a combat-stress reaction is entirely normal and it is not to be confused with real mental pathology. No matter how extreme or persistent or protracted, it's normal!" Wham! Nash's hand slapped the table. "So somebody could have a full-blown psychotic break on the battlefield, and just because it happened in the stress of something traumatic in combat, we are defining it as 'normal'?" Nash said with a chuckle. "When I know full well that if that same kid had the same symptoms in any other setting, any other stress that tipped him over the edge, he would get a psychiatric diagnosis, be treated with medication, get a medical board—who knows? But we sure wouldn't say, Oh, that's normal. You're hearing voices and you think the devil's trying to recruit you for his band? That's totally normal, that happens to everybody who goes to war, don't worry about it!"

Nash pushed back his chair, heaved himself to his feet, and began pacing, gesturing as he spoke.

"And it's all based on PIES and BICEPS, where the key is expectancy. It is, no shit, the power of suggestion! Telling these kids, There's nothing wrong with you, you will get over this, and you will go back to your job and we'll hear no more about it." Here, Nash's broad shoulders shook with laughter. "Heh-heh-heh...right?" he said, in case I hadn't appreciated the full absurdity of PIES and BICEPS. "I'm not sure we even totally believe that this *is* normal, but we need to believe that it is in order to avoid epidemics, which to the leadership was the number one concern. Not what to do with the fifteen or twenty percent who are damaged by the experience."

But Nash used the PIES and CISD concepts, too, early in his career, because there was no other approved way to treat trauma. As a young navy psychiatrist in 1989, long before he was deployed in Falluja, he was summoned to the scene of a crash on the deck of the USS *Lexington,* an old aircraft carrier used for practice landings near the naval aviation training station at Pensacola, Florida. One trainee miscalculated and crashed, his jet cartwheeling in flames down the flight deck, killing the pilot and four others and injuring seventeen. Nash gathered small groups of the survivors and had them talk about the event, describing the details of it and sharing their emotional reactions. "Clearing that stuff out of the way," as Nash described it. "A very attractive procedure for the organization [the navy] because it gave them the impression that we were really preventing mental illness. That if somebody went through this hour and a half debriefing group, they were good to go," he said. "But there was not the slightest attempt to follow up to see if, for any of them, this was not enough. And we knew that, when you have these command-directed debriefings after an event, not everyone's gonna go, and the people who don't even show up are probably the people who are the most badly damaged, and that's why they don't want to go, because they know they can't handle it, they'll just be retraumatized and be even more ashamed because they'll break down, they won't be able to communicate, they'll dissociate, zone out, it'll be worse than use-less." He took a deep breath. "Right?" He grinned. "And most of the people who do show up would do fine no matter what you did!"

For the others, he said, rising on tiptoes and spreading his arms, "Might's well *buy 'em a hot dog!* Heh-heh-heh. But, yeah... But people didn't challenge this idea to say, 'Wait a minute, is that the best sense we can make out of this?'" Deep down, Nash knew PIES and BICEPS weren't right, that CISD wasn't enough. "All you gotta do to see how absolutely absurd it is—is talk to a marine and be there with him." Nevertheless, it was all he had as he was summoned to heal the marines at Falluja. "We were supposed to coerce them into going back to the fight," he said, adding softly: "No matter what we believed."

Nash began his military medical career as a naval flight surgeon. The navy paid for undergrad and medical school and he did his residency in orthopedics. But during his first job, providing pri-mary health care to the navy community, he realized his best moments were spent working with mental health cases. He switched and did a three-year residency in psychiatry at the Naval Medical Center San Diego and in 2001 was swiftly hired for the mental health program at the nearby Marine Corps Base Camp Pendleton.

That's where Nash developed his full-blown panic attacks. One day he was scheduled to give a noontime lecture on depres-sion to family practice residents. They sat with their lunches while he stood at the podium sweating and gasping and unable to speak, and the worst part of it was the shocked look on their faces. Relat-ing the story, Nash took a huge shaky breath. "The part of me that believes in God says, you know, these are experiences I needed to have so that, when the time came for me to go with the marines to Iraq in 2004, I would be prepared."

Soon after 9/11, marines recently back from Afghanistan began coming to him for help, and it was here that he started to realize that what they had was not PTSD, that it was not terror that had cut deep into their nervous system, that it was something different. Something Nash and his staff had never seen before. Acute war trauma, they called it. They'd had plenty of cases of PTSD, mostly Vietnam veterans. "I knew this was not the same animal," Nash explained to me. "The prevailing view—an untested belief since World War I—was that if you had war trauma it was because you had a preexisting weakness, a personality disorder. And there were studies correlating personality disorders with PTSD, and so it just allowed us all to sort of write them off." But with the marines coming back from Afghanistan, Nash said, "I could see what every spouse or mother who knows their kid or husband sees," that those who return from war "are not the same person anymore. They come back and they're different. I had a marine wife who brought her husband in. She had no reason to exaggerate, didn't know about the disability system, but she was saying, 'This is the way he was before, and this is the way he is now. Help!' And I was changed by my experiences working with these patients at Pendleton hospital between 2001 and 2003 and feeling like, number one, realizing how wrong I had it, personally in my own understanding, and then making me rethink a whole lot of other things I believed. Like, what is the optimal prevention strategy?"

That question kept Nash up at night. If being traumatized in combat is a "normal" reaction to horror, what is there to prevent? The marines coming to see him at Camp Pendleton were experiencing deep trauma; clearly they needed something beyond PIES and BICEPS. It seemed suddenly obvious to Nash that the kind of war trauma he was seeing was not normal—not a result of childhood psychosis—but a wound. An actual wound. That term, Nash saw, wasn't just semantics. It suggested that the condition could be treated and healed.

Just before he left for Iraq in 2004, Nash tried out his new ideas at a Marine Corps conference on combat and operational stress control, an umbrella term the corps uses to refer to the identification and treatment of any form of mental difficulty. As the name implies, its central concept is that any adverse psychological reactions to war are normal, temporary, and can be—must be—controlled. The idea that one could be psychologically wounded, as surely as any other combat injury, had never arisen inside military circles. A wound or an injury can be healed, perhaps, but not controlled.

Nash, despite his senior rank as a navy captain, was an outlier in the sessions. The idea of standing up and proclaiming to hardened warfighters that they should see emotional trauma as an actual wound made him worry that he'd get one of his old panic attacks. But his excitement drove him forward. "I was sharing with them some of the stuff I'd learned about trauma being a literal wound, right? A wound! And if you think about it that way, then the wound is the intermediate stage between 'good to go' and 'fucked up for life.' And most wounds, people get over them. But your chances of getting over it are far better if you acknowledge that you've been wounded" and are given appropriate treatment.

Stress injury, Nash called it. The term hung in the air at this Marine Corps conference, then dissipated. Days later, Nash gathered his combat gear and left for Iraq, packing his manuals on PIES and BICEPS because there wasn't any other approved treatment doctrine. But he came home burning with frustration at what he felt was his inability to heal the shaken, weeping marines of Falluja. He burrowed deeper into the idea of trauma as an injury or a wound. Within two years he had published a book,

Combat Stress Injury, with trauma psychologist Charles R. Figley and an introduction by Jonathan Shay, the Boston VA psychiatrist who has written widely on combat trauma.

Nash hit the road to lecture on his ideas, arguing and fighting with his colleagues and seniors. Soon, he'd created such a stir among marine commanders and senior mental health experts that he was summoned to marine headquarters in Washington to explain himself. The tempo of battle was rising in Iraq and Afghanistan, casualties were mounting, and the corps was struggling to meet its manpower commitments. The last thing the generals wanted was another category of injury—especially given the bedrock military tradition of "suck it up," treating psychological casualties as weenies. What the corps wanted was a way to prevent combat stress from overwhelming its marines, not another injury requiring treatment. Determined to head off this threat, three senior marine combat commanders, those who held the corps's most revered positions as warfighters and keepers of the corps's warrior ethos, had written an open letter to the Marine Corps commandant. They didn't believe in Nash's "stress injury," they said. They wanted the term removed from official documents, and they never wanted to hear it mentioned again. Ever.

As Nash packed for Washington, his colleagues in military mental health were ducking for cover. "People thought I was in so much hot water that they were auctioning off my office furniture. They knew I was not coming back," Nash told me gleefully. At Marine Corps headquarters, a series of stormy meetings ensued that included the three senior commanders and other warfighters, medical and mental health authorities, and a handful of chaplains. It was a curious echo of the 1916 Munich conference but with a dramatically different outcome. They agreed to define psychological health with a simple color-coded "stress continuum" chart. The chart acknowledged that some marines would emerge unscathed from combat, able to rely on their own internal coping skills. On Nash's scale they occupied the green zone on the far left. Others would experience a temporary stress reaction (yellow). Those with more severe and prolonged symptoms were "injured" (orange), and, on the far right, a red zone for those with major depression, anxiety, or diagnosable PTSD.

The agreement was a significant advance in the acknowledgment and treatment of war trauma. It was the first time the United States Marine Corps recognized that the young men and women it sends into combat could become not just temporarily stunned by combat but actually injured with a psychological wound. Just as significant, it enabled front-line leaders—young sergeants, lieutenants, and captains—to sort out after a combat engagement which of their marines were okay, who needed three hots and a cot, and whose injuries put them at risk of future problems, such as drug and alcohol abuse, risky motorcycle racing, or even suicide, and thus needed psychiatric intervention. "The three generals started this conference to kill the stress injury idea," Nash said. "And they ended by saying, in effect, that we have solved the problem—stress injury is a terrible idea, it doesn't fit with our culture, we don't like it, it's not true, so instead we want all of our training to be based on the stress continuum model," Nash said. "It was a way to have their cake and eat it, too."

Emboldened and a little giddy by this victory, Nash publicly confronted his most severe critic, Lieutenant General Keith J. Stalder, the gruff commander of the Second Marine Expeditionary Force, an air-ground task force of some sixty-two thousand marines and sailors who fought in both Iraq and Afghanistan. At a briefing for hundreds of marines on the new stress continuum, Stalder strode the auditorium stage, imposing in his battle dress uniform, taking questions. Finally he recognized Nash, who was sitting nearby. Nash stood under Stalder's glare. "I said, 'General

Stalder, sir, do you believe stress injuries are real?' And he was walking back and forth in front of me, and his eyes were locked on mine. And finally he said, 'Yes, I do.' "

"Thank you, sir," said Nash, and sat down with a smile.

It was not long after he returned from Iraq that Nash, working at Marine Corps headquarters in Washington, dialed a phone number at Camp Pendleton, the massive home of some forty-two thousand marines, where he had worked for years. He asked for a therapist named Michael Castellana. A friend had lent him a copy of a treatment model for war trauma that Castellana had written. It incorporated many of the new ideas that had been circulating in Nash's head. It was a way of helping marines, far beyond the tired notions of PIES and BICEPS. Castellana was unknown to Nash; he wasn't even a psychologist, Nash noted. But the model he'd written was brilliant. When Nash read it, he was exhilarated. The traumas marines were bringing home were intensifying, and he felt a growing urgency to respond.

"I read your therapy model," Nash said when Castellana came on the line. In what he intended as a friendly, bantering tone, he said: "Who the hell *are* you?"

CHAPTER 7

Grief Is a Combat Injury

The fallen, the fallen!
The buddies, the sharers of foxholes
the tellers of stories, the dreamers
without words, the singers without music
Our fallen, our fallen!
We clasp them — once and for good —
mightily, tearfully, each to our breast.
                    —Dan Levin, Marine Staff Sergeant,
                              Iwo Jima, March 1945

On a routine combat patrol outside Marjah in January 2010, a squad of marines from Second Platoon, Charlie One-Six, crept cautiously toward an adobe compound in a farm village, hunting a Taliban gang who were making and planting IEDs, the deadly bombs responsible for the majority of American dead and wounded. The marines had just arrived in Afghanistan, and three squads — about thirty men in all — were assigned to a remote base called Outpost Husker. It would be a few weeks before Joey Schiano would raise his rocket launcher against the adobe wall of a farm-er's compound not far away.

Now, stepping warily at point, at the head of the patrol was Lance Corporal Zachary "Smitty" Smith. He was nineteen years old, taller than his dad—a New York state trooper—but with his dad's engaging grin. Growing up in small-town Hornell, New York, he'd been deeply affected by the terror attacks on 9/11. When he was in the sixth grade, he'd glued an image of Osama bin Laden on a cardboard box and took potshots at it with his grandfather's .22 rifle. Before he left Camp Lejeune with One-Six that November, Smitty had gone home and married his high-school sweetheart, Anne. Now he was barely a month into his first com-bat experience.

As he stepped carefully, an IED suddenly erupted beneath him, tearing off his legs and scything down other marines with shrapnel and blast wounds. Corporal Zachary Auclair rushed to save him, kneeling and frantically pulling out tourniquets and bandages, and Auclair was soon bathed in Smitty's blood.

"Watch for the second one! Watch for the second one!" The Taliban often laid IED traps in pairs of bombs, and the senior leader on the patrol, twenty-eight-year-old platoon sergeant Dan-iel M. Angus, was frantically warning his marines, and then he himself stepped on the second IED. The blast blew him apart, killing him instantly and spraying Auclair with blood and viscera. In the chaos, Staff Sergeant Warren Repsher, wounded in the face by shrapnel, was on the radio calling for a medevac bird, and Smitty lay dying in Auclair's arms.

It is difficult to comprehend the emotional shock and grief that slammed into the marines of Charlie One-Six. Of course they realized that they were at war, and they knew, as they often said, that bad shit happens. Most of them had already done one deployment in Afghanistan, but that was a relatively benign tour in Garmsir, the trading-post river town down south where I had deployed with the marines. This was different: the Taliban would fight viciously to keep the Americans out of Marjah, and Charlie One-Six knew that, even though they'd been here barely a week. So the emotional shock didn't come from surprise as much as from the catastrophic loss of deeply loved comrades, obliterated in an instant of horror seared forever into the souls of the survivors.

What lingers after the shock wears off is the deep moral injury of grief, perhaps the most common psychological wound of the generation that fought in Iraq and Afghanistan. While Charlie One-Six was attempting to absorb the loss of Smitty and Angus, the army surgeon general's Mental Health Advisory Team was arriving for its seventh survey of the emotional health of the troops, finding that just under 80 percent of combat soldiers and marines had experienced a death in their unit.

The pain that these men and women carry is not only the most common emotion but perhaps the most difficult to share with outsiders. The survivors often feel guilt for having not spotted the IED that killed their buddy or for surviving when a buddy goes home in a body bag. Many veterans find it impossible to convey the depth of emotion that binds members of a small unit like Second Platoon and why each combat death thus cuts so deep. Coming together as they do, these emotions of grief, sorrow, shame, guilt, and loss endure as a powerful moral injury.

Relationships that develop and deepen at war are different from those most civilians experience. By some mysterious process the moral obligation hammered into green recruits—*You are responsible for your battle buddy, no matter what!*—grows into a loving and steely devotion that leads military people and especially those engaged in ground combat to value the lives and well-being of their comrades more deeply than their own. Friendships are shorn of pretense and affectation by shared hardship and the forced intimacies of communal living under stress. It's difficult to act aloof and superior when everyone in your squad is bathed in the sweat and filth of weeks without a shower and has been defecating in holes in the ground or in bags of kitty litter. There are no secrets out there; the strengths and weaknesses of every man and woman are magnified and exposed. It is life lived vividly.

The narcotic of this web of relationships is why wounded grunts, medevaced to distant surgical wards and swathed in bandages and tubes, will struggle to get back to their guys. It is why returning combat troops may find old relationships with spouses and friends to be flat and dull. It is why, when their tour of duty is complete and they're back in civilian life, the separation from their buddies produces the empty ache of loss. The shared intimacies and shared risks are experiences that separate them forever from those who weren't there.

But camaraderie in war is dangerous. As in any loving relationship, death can be devastating to the survivor. Soldiers and marines at war are used to seeing dead bodies, even those of other Americans. But you can't distance yourself from the mangled face of a dead loved one. Psychologist Ilona Pivar once studied the prevalence of grief among Vietnam War combat veterans. What she found was stunning: many of them had lost beloved buddies in combat; their grief, more than thirty years later, was deeper and more painful than their sorrow at the recent loss of their spouse.

In the bloody chaos of that awful day in Afghanistan, Angus was dead, and Smitty was dying, and his best friend, Xavier Zell, knew he should go over and grip Smitty's hand to give some comfort in his last moments. But Smitty was a bloody mess, and Zell, twenty-two, told himself he had to pull security, taking his place in the outward-facing defense perimeter the marines had set up, anticipating an attack and waiting frantically for the medevac chopper to come in. Zell was torn, knowing he should go to his friend, but he was afraid. It was too much. He couldn't even look.

The helicopter came, and Smitty and Angus were zipped into body bags and put on stretchers and carried out to the landing zone and loaded on board, and away they went. Darren Doss watched them go. Afterward, he thought, We just got here and this already happened? How the fuck are we going to make it out of here?

In some ways, Doss seemed the most fragile of Charlie One-Six. He depended heavily on his buddies for support, yet he could appear untethered, so that events would lift him to giddy heights or drop him into black despair. He laughed the loudest and sorrowed more deeply than the others. That Christmas of 2009, he told me, "I woke up early and [Lance Corporal Justin] Shreve was on fire watch, and he was like 'Hey man,' and he puts his arm around my shoulder, and he's like 'Merry Christmas, Doss,' and I'm like 'Merry Christmas, Shreve,' and he just, like, slips me two little shooter bottles of vodka." Remembering, Doss blinked away tears. "It was just…yeah."

Doss told me this story years later, when he and Nik Rudolph and Stephen Canty and I met to talk one long afternoon in a Philadelphia hotel room. They'd gone out for smokes and more beer and then settled back in and took up the story.

The day that Smitty and Angus were killed was bad. Doss had just come back from a patrol with his squad. From a distance, he'd heard the blast and seen the column of smoke, and he knew. In telling the story now, Doss spoke mechanically, his words dead.

"I saw the gunny and first sergeant zip them up in the body bags. Angus, both his legs were gone, and one arm was gone, and the other was kind of fused in an awkward position. They put the bags on stretchers and went out to the helo single file, and the helo took 'em away. And I went back to my tent, and Auclair was sitting there, and there were, like, guts hanging off his helmet and blood all over his stuff. He was crying, and he had baby wipes, but the baby wipes were all dried up, covered with blood. He was trying to clean under his fingernails, and I sat down and I wanted to talk with him, maybe try to cheer him up. But I didn't know what to say. I like gave him a pack of baby wipes I'd gotten in the mail, and I went outside and just…that was about it."

The next day the three marine squads occupying the combat outpost held a memorial for Smitty and Angus. Auclair had taken off his stained cloth helmet cover and never wore it again. He and the others stood respectfully. "The chaplain came and pulled us together and, like, gave us this speech," Doss remembered. "And it was basically, he said, like, this shit, you know, happens, and… he didn't really help much, everyone was kind of like 'Yeah, he meant well,' but everybody was walking around with tears in their eyes the whole day. We had to go out the next day. We had the memorial, and [later] that day we went out on patrol, and we got ambushed.

"We were in open desert," Doss said, "and you could hear rounds bouncing off the rocks, and no one could take cover because we are like just flat open." Finally they were able to fire back with rockets and grenade launchers. "We hit this [Taliban] dude and fucked him up, and another guy was dragging him, dragging him behind a wall, and he was fuckin' throwing up after he dragged the dude, and then we leveled the place, we went insane, and the gunny was yelling 'That's enough! That's enough!'"

The room was silent for a moment. "What happened next?" I asked.

Doss: "We walked back in and I had an MRE!" The room exploded with laughter.

Laughter, in fact, is the mental health therapy that combat marines and soldiers use to survive. The explosive release of laughter can keep grief at bay, at least for a while. "If we really get down and think about what we did," Canty said once, "it's a slippery slope. Avoidance is a great strategy."

As the story of Smitty and Angus was still reverberating, someone started telling the one about the tent stakes. Adjacent to the marines' outpost was an encampment of Afghan National Army soldiers who lived in a U.S. military tent that was pegged to the desert floor with huge wooden stakes. Across the way, the marines would build a fire at night, and since wood was scarce, they began eyeing those tent stakes.

Doss: "Every night we'd go over to the ANA tent and sneak off with a couple of their stakes and use 'em for the fire, but we were careful to take only one or two at a time."

One night a transport helo came in with water resupply, landing in a hurricane blast of dirt and pebbles, and the marines took cover. "When we went out to get the water," Doss said, "we look across the dirt and, like, the Afghan army tent is one hundred percent gone! All their cots are sitting in a row, but the tent itself is gone because we had burned every one of the stakes." We're all helpless with laughter at this. "They had no idea what happened," Doss said, recovering and wiping tears from his eyes. "They were standing around, like, baffled!"

Then there was the Christmas-tree caper. At their base in Marjah, the marines had stacked their empty conex boxes three high, and that December, the battalion chaplain had a couple of marines erect a decorated Christmas tree on the top. One day, one of the platoon sergeants said to the Charlie One-Six marines, "Hey, I got a mission for you guys. See that Christmas tree? After chow I want that Christmas tree in our tent. Get the Christmas spirit!"

So that night, said Doss, "we dress in all black. Fuckin' climb up there and cut the rope securing it, and we make it down to like the first conex box, and all of a sudden 'Hey! What are you doing?'" No matter how many times the marines have told and retold this story, they are laughing and shouting over one another trying to tell it again.

Nik Rudolph takes over. "We get caught, and we're up there and some of the guys book it out of there, and we're, like, fucked. And the chaplain comes, and he's like 'I want your fuckin' name and rank and who you're with.' And I'm like 'I'm Second Platoon,' and he goes 'What's your name?' and I'm like 'Rudolph, sir.'" And the chaplain is beet red with rage, bellowing up at Rudolph. "And he's like 'You're trying to tell me your name is Rudolph and you're stealing my Christmas tree? On Christmas? I don't fuckin' believe it.'" They put the tree back up but hopped down off the other side of the conex boxes and escaped punishment. "But...oh, man," Rudolph said, chuckling and shaking his head.

Around that time there was an Afghan kid who used to come around the marines' outpost, basking in their attention. One day he kept trying to get them to go outside, wanting to show them something. Doss and Canty and some others finally went with him into an adjacent field toward a tree line and discovered a desiccated corpse, a man the marines had shot a while back. Canty remembered the shooting. The man had been acting suspiciously and wouldn't respond to the warning shots the marines had fired in accordance with the ROE, and so he was shot and killed. Now his body had been ravaged by dogs.

It turned out that the corpse was the boy's father, who was deaf and mute and couldn't hear or respond to warning shots, the boy explained, and that's why he appeared to ignore the marines and why he was shot and killed and was now lying dead in a field.

"I'm not sure how that feels," Canty said, when I asked him how he'd reacted to that awful news. "Here we are trying to do our American ideals all over the place, and we're being arrogant cowboys." In the accumulation of such events, he said, "the morality did wear down."

But Doss took it harder. That killing, and the realization of how it had taken place, created a grief that seemed to penetrate deep into his soul. Few knew it at the time, but his own father was in poor health, in and out of hospitals with an autoimmune condition among other problems, and he'd had surgery and a pacemaker implanted in his chest. He'd been sick since Doss was in the sixth grade. He would joke to Darren and his two sisters that his pacemaker sometimes would "shock the shit out of me," and the kids would laugh. But they realized that meant his heart was stopping. Michael Doss died in 2012, two years after Darren came home from Afghanistan.

After his father's funeral and burial at the Niskayuna Reformed Church just outside Schenectady, New York, Darren began to have nightmares, exploding awake in horror. He spoke about it in the videotaped interviews that Stephen Canty has done with members of Charlie One-Six, and we watched the interview with Doss one afternoon as a dozen marines and I were sprawled across hotel-room beds. Doss had gone home earlier.

In the video, Doss is saying that in his nightmares he is back in Afghanistan, going out into that field with Canty and the Afghan boy, and they find the corpse, but instead of the Afghan man who'd been dead for days, it's his father, and his father's face is partially eaten away... And on the videotape Doss is breaking down in gulping sobs of anguish. But he manages to finish "eaten away... by dogs," and he ducks down out of the camera's view, and the sound of sobbing fades slowly.

In our hotel room there is dead silence for long moments. Then someone says, "I love you, Doss."

CHAPTER 8

It's Really About Killing

War makes us killers. We must confront this horror directly
if we're to be honest about the true cost of war...I'm no
longer the "good" person I once thought I was.
— Timothy Kudo, U.S. Marine Corps, Iraq 2009,
Afghanistan 2010–2011

Like many other American kids, Chuck Newton went to war to
kill. It was after 9/11, and he was burning for revenge. I want to
go fight, he told his parents when he was seventeen. Understandably, they said no. But after he was old enough to enlist without
their permission, off he went to marine boot camp at Parris Island
and then to two combat tours in Afghanistan with Charlie One-Six.
By the time he got home, he had killed many times, with different weapons and in many different circumstances, and in my conversations with him he seemed awash in conflicting emotions of
pride, remorse, bitterness, and defiance. In combat there are
things you know you shouldn't do, but everybody does them, he
said one day. It's a dichotomy.

"I wanted to kill people — badly. In the same way you wanted the people responsible for the [9/11] massacres to get killed. And I went and did it, and thinking back on it, you know...that's too heavy for one person to take on. I don't know that there's anybody who's not psychopathic who isn't hurt by it."

Killing seems like such a natural part of war, so central to the existence of the Defense Department and so implicit in the duties of everyone in military service, that it's easy to assume that if the act of killing carries any moral consequences, they are marginal. That soldiers and marines can kill without being disturbed by it later on; that the crews of bombers and strike fighters and the pilots of armed drones, those who launch rockets and mortars and who fire high-explosive artillery rounds, all emerge with their consciences unmarked by what they have done.

They do not. Even the most hardened of our military killers, as I found out, are haunted in the end by the taking of life, justifiable though it may be. Our newest generation of veterans may have experienced grief and loss, remorse and regret, even anger at having felt betrayed. But it is killing that lies at the heart of their moral injury.

I once walked the gentle green hills of Fort Benning, Georgia, with a retired Army Ranger who early in his career had served several combat tours in Vietnam. He couldn't help pointing out good fields of fire, ideal spots for machine-gun emplacements and channelized kill zones. As we walked, he enthused about the properties of various weapons without mentioning their effect; in all, he seemed a tough, hard man, inured to close-up killing. Yet his demeanor changed when he described a trip he'd recently made back to old battlefields in Vietnam. At one point, he said, he had climbed over a ridgeline to find a vast cemetery spread out before him with hundreds of white crosses marking the graves of Vietnamese soldiers and civilians. "All those people," he said as tears wet his eyes. "We shouldn't have killed all those people. We should not have killed all those people."

It's a profound and unpleasant truth, and each one of us knows it, deep down. Under any circumstance, killing another human exacts a moral cost. We send men and women into war knowing that they will collide with a moral choice no one can resolve: in order to be good soldiers they must kill; and killing violates one of our oldest taboos.

But rather than confronting the morality of killing, we've just surrounded it with a conspiracy of silence. We smother the truth of killing with video games and television dramas in which the act is done casually, usually without evident pain, gore, or consequence. Except in escapist fantasy or frenzied political posturing, the word "kill" itself is impolite. The father of a new military enlistee doesn't say with pride "My daughter has signed up to kill." Military recruiters avoid the word. Many of the young recruits I've talked with say they never really thought about killing. The Rifleman's Creed memorized by every young marine demands not that the rifleman kill but only that he must fire his weapon "true" and adds, "We will hit." Asking a combat veteran if he ever killed someone is considered rude and, for the veteran, cause for excruciating discomfort: most likely, the answer lies tightly wrapped in layers of pride and guilt and confusion, an experience that's been hard-earned and not lightly shared. In his blog, *Thoughts of a Soldier-Ethicist,* Army Lieutenant Colonel Pete Kilner, who teaches philosophy and military science at West Point, acknowledged some moral squeamishness when he wrote: "We don't tell our family members and civilian friends that we killed in war. If they ask, we answer matter of factly and move on. When acquaintances and strangers ask if we killed anyone in war, we lie or ignore them; they have no right to know. Those who haven't experienced combat couldn't possibly understand what it means to kill another human being, and we want to be looked at for the purpose we achieved (protecting them) not for the means we used (killing others)."

That justification for silence—outsiders have no right to know about the moral cost of killing—rises to the institutional level as well. Killing is rarely discussed or even mentioned in the public statements and documents and training manuals of the Department of Defense (which was the Department of War until 1947, when the name began to seem too belligerent). There was a major fuss, for instance, when then major general James Mattis told his First Marine Division on the eve of the invasion of Iraq, and within earshot of journalists, "Be polite, be professional, but have a plan to kill everybody you meet." The Defense Department publicly distanced itself from that advice, as if killing were not the central purpose of the war.

Theologians and philosophers and religious and secular leaders have wrestled with the morality of killing in war for centuries, but rather than looking away in silence they have acknowledged the moral damage of killing and searched for ways to sanitize warriors after battle. The understanding that killing contaminates the killer has persisted stubbornly down through the ages. It's a constant theme in Greek tragedies. Samurai warriors used Zen meditation to assuage their fear and guilt over killing. Ancient Hebrew texts and modern-day moralists have sought to distinguish between killing in combat and murder, disagreeing sharply about whether the sixth commandment dictates that one should not kill or that one should not murder. The fourth-century bishop of Alexandria, Athanasius, put his finger on the moral dichotomy Nik Rudolph experienced when he killed an Afghan boy in a firefight: "It is not right to kill," Athanasius wrote sometime before A.D. 354, "yet in war it is lawful and praiseworthy to destroy the enemy . . . so that the same act is at one time and under some circumstances unlawful, while under others, and at the right time, it is lawful and permissible."

That's a lovely philosophical point for theoreticians to ponder. But religious and secular authorities in centuries past also recognized that killing even under legally and morally justifiable conditions demanded that the killers afterward cleanse themselves by making amends. So medieval foot soldiers and archers and battle-ax wielders and mounted lancers found themselves thrown into battle and, if they survived, were sentenced to acts of penance, some of them severe. In the seventh century, warriors who killed in battle underwent a period of forty days of penance and banishment from the church by the order of the archbishop of Canterbury, Theodore of Tarsus, whose revulsion at killing came from his childhood during a period of devastating wars.

By the tenth century the church had gone so far as to sanction even those who fought in self-defense: it required three years' penance "for anyone who kills an enemy while trying to repulse an invasion of his own country." The fine print added that if the war was waged by a king, only one year of penance was required. Penance was heavy-duty stuff: it might include abstinence from sleep and from sex; public confessions; wearing sackcloth and ashes; and kneeling before the congregation and groaning and crying out for their intercession with God. How many soldiers actually performed these acts of penance is not recorded.

After the Battle of Hastings in 1066, a gathering of bishops ruled that "anyone who knows he killed a man in the great battle must do penance for one year for each man he killed." Those who couldn't recall how many they'd killed were required to do one day of penance each week for the rest of their lives. Or they could get off by financing a new church.

All that seems rather quaint and even backward. But I'm struck by the sharp difference with our own treatment of returning warriors. On the battlefield, in the heat of life-and-death struggle, an individual simply cannot make fine distinctions between killing and murder that wise men have argued over for centuries; the warrior must trust that if he acts in accordance with his conscience, whatever his decision he will be forgiven, cleansed, welcomed home. A thousand years ago, societies acknowledged that killing in wartime imposed a moral cost on warriors, and however odd their methods might seem, they did recognize and honor that moral pain and offered healing. Today we send the young into war, and when they return we call them heroes and ignore whatever moral struggles they bring home. Any moral or spiritual cleaning up we leave to the individual or, if the wounds of killing are disabling enough, we label them as mental illness and send the injured off to the VA to be cured with therapy and drugs. Unlike societies of old, we have decided: not our job. That's a tragic loss for veterans, and for us.

Yet in the aftermath of our wars in Iraq and Afghanistan, there is an awakening recognition that killing does wound the killer, specifically with moral injury. "Taking a human life, in the point of view of most Americans, is immoral," the Reverend Robert G. Certain told me. Certain was a B-52 navigator who was shot down during a bombing run over Hanoi in late 1972 and held as a POW; on his release he became an Episcopal priest and air force chaplain. Now retired, Certain is not a pacifist by any means. But he sees wartime killing clearly as "a violation of the commandment not to do murder."

The moral injury of killing, of participating in the death and destruction of our longest wars, seems evident as combat veterans pour back into civilian life, often seeming angry or depressed, unwilling to talk about the war. Wanting to go off by themselves or hang out at the bar with other veterans. New research is providing glimmers of understanding of these effects of wartime killing. Brett Litz, the Boston trauma researcher, conducted a series of focus groups in 2014 with combat veterans from Vietnam, Iraq, and Afghanistan. He found deep trauma:

> For example, group members articulated that they distanced themselves from loved ones because of their

experiences with killing, due to fear of what others might think if they knew the truth about their actions. Many members felt that they did not deserve to have intimates due to killing, and identified several self-handicapping behaviors that they engaged in due to killing in war (e.g., abusing alcohol prior to an exam or job interview due to the belief that happiness and advancement is undeserved). Another significant theme that arose during the focus groups was the topic of spirituality. Group members expressed loss of spirituality as well as beliefs that they could not be forgiven due to killing actions in war; struggles with self-forgiveness were central, as were the ways in which this impacted sense of self. We have also examined the relationship between killing in war and a number of mental health and functional outcomes, including PTSD symptoms, depression symptoms, alcohol problems, dissociation, relationship problems, anger, violent behaviors, and functional impairment. After controlling for a number of demographic variables and combat exposure, killing was a significant predictor of multiple mental health and functional outcomes.

For several days in the summer of 2014, Jim Gant sat at my dining room table and talked about killing. Of all the men and women I have met in war and all the veterans I have known or interviewed even briefly, Gant is the apotheosis of the ancient and modern warrior, the pure killer. Listening to him over many hours, it occurred to me that if you decide to go to war and want to win, if your goal is to kill as many of the enemy as necessary, then Gant is your guy.

He grew up in southern New Mexico and enlisted in the army out of high school. Bright and ambitious, he served in the army's elite Special Forces, then went to college and returned to Special

Forces as an officer and a commander. He served a fourteen-month tour in Iraq and three tours in Afghanistan, including twenty-two months of continuous combat there from 2010 to 2011. He has been awarded, among other commendations, a Silver Star for combat valor for his actions after an extended firefight in which he deliberately drove over three IEDs, detonating two against his vehicle, to protect his troops following him. Beyond the killing, he was an extraordinarily effective soldier. In Afghanistan he developed a way to organize local tribes to defend themselves against the Taliban. He lived a spartan life with the tribes, shunning the cumbersome U.S. military machinery. General David Petraeus called him "the perfect counterinsurgent." Osama bin Laden demanded his head.

It felt easy having Gant in my home. He is a likable companion, softening his high-strung temperament with a courtly, self-deprecating manner. He tells good stories. He is above all an intensely proud man for whom honor is the highest moral value. He is lean and wiry and wore a navy baseball cap even indoors, a thin beard, and a plain T-shirt. His face was weathered by stress and sun. On his sinewy arms: elaborate tattoos of Achilles, the Greek hero of the Trojan War, and Hecate, a goddess associated with victory and glory in war. When we talked, he kneaded his fingers together, as if squeezing out difficult or painful ideas. He was forty-seven, and his career had ended abruptly with an official reprimand, the revocation of his Special Forces status, and a denial of promotion, an ugly and humiliating debacle detailed in the book *American Spartan* by the journalist Ann Scott Tyson, his wife. As Petraeus told me, Gant's downfall was his "willingness to push the envelope" of the military's rigid bureaucracy.

Gant saw war as the most challenging and honorable endeavor of life. "War is a gift from God," he declared one day. "The opportunity to prove yourself on the battlefield. In Iraq we were killing people every day. There's a lot of satisfaction in the hunt, getting a target, going after a specific person, which I did many, many times, and, like I said, I enjoyed it a lot." There are some people, Gant said, who will not fire their weapon. Most people in combat will fire when they feel threatened. "It takes a completely different person to hunt another human being down and shoot him in the face. For me, it was a lot of enjoyment and satisfaction." In Iraq, he said, "we'd go through a village, three or four IEDs'd go off, they [the insurgents] would open up, and we'd take a casualty. Now, most units would evacuate. That's not what we would do. We would right there hunt those motherfuckers down, chase 'em through the village, hunt them down and fucking kill them."

In Iraq, Gant commanded an Iraqi police commando unit that conducted hunter-killer missions and acted as a quick-reaction force that would respond when American or Iraqi troops were in trouble. Once, he told me, "an American patrol hit a couple of IEDs and got hung up there real bad, and by the time we got there, there was an up-armored Humvee on its side, pretty much blown in half. And as we got there the Americans were pulling out with their casualties, trying to get the hell out of there, and there were still gunshots and about twenty-five Iraqis with guns were jumping around and the [U.S.] vehicles were on fire and they [the insurgents] were doing, you know, their killing dance."

I was dying to know what happened next, figuring Gant waded in and killed all the bad guys. But Gant would not be hurried. By the second or third year into the war, he explained by way of background, the rules of engagement were getting more and more restrictive, in an effort to reduce unintended civilian casualties. Whenever an American fired a shot, it had to be reported and investigated. Gant snorted. "There was a time in Iraq when, if you fired even a warning shot, you had to report it, you know? Fuck that! Warning shot hell! There's no such thing as a warning shot! I'm just saying that over time it became more and more dangerous for the individual soldier to fire his weapon system, not because of the combat but because of what he would have to answer for. Fuck that!"

Now, with jihadis dancing in jubilation atop burning American vehicles, Gant never hesitated. "We opened fire on those fuckers. That's hostile fucking intent—you are dancing on a fucking vehicle that fifteen minutes before there was a couple of guys killed on it? I opened fire on that and reported it and there was a fifteen-six [military investigation] or whatever the fuck, and I said, 'Hey! Hostile intent! Couldn't *be* more hostile intent!'" The investigation was dropped.

Gant thought killing was just and honorable and also effective. "Once you get a taste for it and once you, you know, get good at that, there is absolutely nothing like it and you seek out engagements and you seek out those moments in time when your life and the lives of your men are right there. I do not believe killing another human being, for most people, is a natural thing to do. I and others like me did really, really enjoy it."

After his years in Afghanistan and then Iraq, Gant rotated home to work at Fort Bragg, North Carolina. There he had time to think, and what he wondered was, What is all this killing actually accomplishing? Because a lot of killing was going on in Iraq and Afghanistan, and things were not getting better. "See, if all you're doing is killing, and you're not gaining security with that, something is wrong, okay? And there are a lot of times in a lot of places tactically and otherwise where you gotta do a whole bunch of killing in order to even give security a chance. But at some point, when you're killing hundreds and hundreds and hundreds and thousands and thousands of these fuckin' guys and there is no increase in security—well, you have to relook at what it is that you're doing."

With all that killing, Gant said to me, "did it do what we

needed it to do? Clearly the answer is no. Clearly. I mean clearly, clearly. At some point, you gotta do something different."

Gant's epiphany led him to develop a strikingly new counter-insurgency doctrine based on helping local tribes develop their own security. Rather than trying to kill all the Taliban, enable the locals to stand up to them so that some kind of deal, even rec-onciliation, can take place. The key was working locally. The idea caught the attention of senior commanders and worked well, until Gant ran afoul of Big Army, the institutional military, and he was ordered home in disgrace.

When I asked Gant if there was a moral cost, a personal cost, for all that killing, he didn't hesitate. To get me to understand it, he described his own moral principles as being a series of walls that demarcate right from wrong. An internal honor code that dictates, for instance, that killing an innocent civilian is wrong; helping an injured noncombatant is right. The innermost wall, as he described it, is the moral prohibition against killing, one he ignored repeatedly for much of his career.

"Over the course of time, what happened to me is that pretty much all the moral walls I had, in regards to anything and every-thing, were pretty much obliterated. That's not just in combat; it was my personal life. It was everything. I was gonna die tomor-row so I didn't give a fuck. So those moral walls broke down. And this last little one that you have around yourself, the one you're asking about, has to do with killing—what you've done to other people, and what they've tried to do to you. It's the last thing you have, and you keep it right here"—he thumped his chest hard—"because you know you're gonna go again. And our lives cen-tered around combat and so we kept this last place, the killing and the dying part, what we did to others and what they did to us, we kept it..."

Gant bowed his head. After a long silence, he was able to go on. When he was forced out of the army, when he no longer had to gird himself for combat, "then that last little wall [against kill-ing] was taken away. And now I am having to deal with...what I did to others. At the very basic level, was all of that worth it?"

On another day I asked Gant to help me understand the emo-tional storms that have swept through his life, the effect of repeated moral injuries. "I have a lot of very violent dreams, sometimes extremely violent. Disturbing. I struggle with these things every day. It's been absolutely...horrible. I almost com-mitted suicide a couple of times. Pretty much tried to drink myself to death. See, because I already decided I would die. When I get on that fuckin' plane [to deploy] I'm already dead. I said that for ten years, say good-bye to my family, I am dead. I don't have any intention of coming home. I have made that decision a thousand fuckin' times. When the time and place comes, that decision is already made, and I've proved it dozens and dozens of times. Well, that does something to you."

Several years after this conversation Gant wrote me a long let-ter to explain the perspective he felt he'd gained since he left Afghanistan and the army. He seemed, on the surface, better. He is happily married, engaged in outdoor sports, and deeply reli-gious. "I am getting a second chance as a father and a parent," he wrote. "It is a wonderful life and I am a blessed, fortunate, and lucky man."

But Gant also wrote that the war and the killing have not left him alone. "Just about six months ago my commander from Iraq killed himself. What the fuck? He called three days before he killed himself and I didn't answer the phone. I don't remember what I was doing but it wasn't important. Here was a guy I trusted unequivocally in battle and had become a true friend." Gant spoke at his memorial and placed his own Silver Star Medal at the foot of his casket at Arlington National Cemetery.

"There are dark, very dark, echoes and shadows in my head," Gant wrote to me. "I hate laying my head on my pillow at night.

It is at night that the demons gather. Tonight when I close my eyes I will dream of killing or dying, whichever is necessary."

Gant and the men who fought alongside him are outliers, it seemed to me. Forever separated from the rest of society by the killing they've seen and done. He reminded me of an army sergeant I'd met on a warm, moonless night in northern Afghanistan. He was on lone sentry duty. I'd been unable to sleep and wandered out to talk. For an hour we spoke softly. I never saw his face. But I did jot down in my notebook one thing he said after talking about his combat experiences and how he felt killing forever separated him from civilian America. "We can't ever really go home," he said. "We're the ones society no longer needs."

Now Gant was voicing a similar conclusion. "My closest friends are not okay," he once told me. "It's never going to be okay for us."

Shira Maguen, the clinical and research psychologist at the San Francisco VA Medical Center, has done landmark work on the impact of killing. In 2010 she published the results of a study of 2,797 soldiers returning from Iraq, of whom 40 percent reported killing or being responsible for killing during the deployment. "Even after controlling for combat exposure," she found, "killing was a significant predictor of posttraumatic disorder (PTSD) symptoms, alcohol abuse, anger, and relationship problems. Military personnel returning from modern deployments are at risk of adverse mental health conditions and related psychosocial functioning related to killing in war." A year later, Maguen reported that veterans with higher killing experiences had thoughts of suicide at a rate twice that of veterans with fewer or no combat killing experiences.

In her clinical work, Maguen asks combat veterans to fill out a measure called the Killing Cognitions Scale, capturing the ways in which killing has impacted the person. "We look for guilt and shame, contamination, feeling like you are functionally impaired in certain ways," she explained to me. "We found a lot of people who felt that because of the killing they've done, they can't go back to their spiritual community, some who felt that because they killed, they don't deserve to be happy, to have a family, to have kids, a successful relationship."

Chuck Newton is not functionally impaired, although he has done his share of killing in two combat deployments with Charlie One-Six in Afghanistan. A faint Brooklyn accent betrays his origins in New York, where he's working as a welder in his new post-Afghanistan, civilian life. He's a gifted guitar player, like his father. He's read the Bible from cover to cover. He has thought deeply about issues of morality and holds firm positions on his own moral culpabilities.

In boot camp, he said, killing is only mentioned after they shut the barracks doors and not as a part of the formal training. "Middle of the night they woke everybody up, closed all the doors, had us stand on line with our weapon. We said the Rifleman's Creed. The drill instructor looked like a human GI Joe, giant arms and a kung-fu grip, he's walking around with his M16 and telling us, 'This is a weapon of death, this is a weapon of destruction, you are now a weapon of death, you will be killing.' He's telling guys who will be cooks and accountants that they are here to kill. And I was extremely high on that for days, and then I find out this guy is a refrigerator repairman! This guy hadn't killed. But they make a point of telling you you're going to kill people. And they get people who are either crying about it or, like me, excited about it."

I said, "But this is not part of the official indoctrination or training."

"It can't be!" Chuck said.

"But it should be," I argued.

"You're right! Yes—but it's part of the underground brotherhood."

In 1999, then Major Kilner, an enlisted soldier who had risen to command in the Eighty-Second Airborne Division, published an essay in the army's influential journal *Military Review*. Kilner, who wrote the *Thoughts of a Soldier-Ethicist* blog, intended to cut through much of the official obfuscation about the subject of military killing. He had come to see that killing was a problem for the army—not because it was immoral, he thought, but because soldiers were not being trained how to think about the morality of killing. After the killing was done, he knew, many soldiers felt they had committed an immoral act. And no one, he wrote—not military chaplains or lawyers, not the army, not the Defense Department, or academia, "not even my own religion—provided a satisfactory justification for looking down my sights and placing two rounds into the head of an insurgent." Consequently, he wrote, "many of the soldiers entrusted to our care suffer needless guilt after killing in war." He dismissed the idea of just war as valid only for nations engaged in international conflict but of little use in explaining to individual troops why killing in war can be "a morally right choice." Killing, Kilner wrote, "is central to our profession, and it is a huge moral issue. We already train our soldiers to kill effectively. Let's train them to live effectively after they kill."

Kilner's urgent plea, that the army begin talking about killing and morality, came at a time when the military was getting much better at the business of killing. At least since the Civil War, it had been known that in combat some soldiers would not fire their weapons at the enemy, even at the risk of being overrun. But the army was astonished to be told definitively, at the close of World War II, that most of its soldiers would not fire or would not fire persistently even in close-quarter fighting. This was the conclusion of a disheveled former sportswriter turned military historian, one of dozens of analysts hired by the army to get out on the battlefield and document how well existing tactics and operations were working and to recommend changes. S. L. A. Marshall, inevitably known as Slam, showed up just before Thanksgiving 1943 at a South Pacific atoll called Makin Island, and after witnessing three days of heavy fighting against a Japanese force "crazed with sake," Marshall reported that the island was captured. He spent the next few days interviewing individual soldiers about their roles in the fighting, a technique he would continue in both the Pacific and European campaigns of World War II. He later reported to astonished War Department brass that "on average not more than 15 percent of the men had actually fired at the enemy positions or personnel with rifles, carbines, grenades, bazookas, BARs [Browning automatic rifles] or machine guns during the course of an entire engagement." He later wrote, in his classic 1947 account, *Men Against Fire,* that, overall, 75 percent of American troops would not fire or persist in firing at the enemy. "These men may face the danger," he wrote, "but they will not fight."

Although he never backed up his conclusions with actual data, Marshall had a profound effect on American combat training and infantry weapons. "The teaching and the ideals of that civilization [from which American soldiers come] are against killing," he explained. "The fear of killing, rather than the fear of being killed, was the most common cause of battle failure in the individual." His solution: "We need to free the rifleman's mind with respect to the nature of targets." Soon the army had its eye on a new rapid-fire weapon that could be sprayed at the enemy rather than requiring a soldier to wait for a target and take careful aim before firing—a pause believed to encourage second thoughts about killing. The M16 rifle, introduced in 1963, could be fired on semiautomatic or full automatic. And new combat training emphasized quick-reaction drills. I've watched soldiers and marines training to deploy to Iraq and Afghanistan in these react-to-fire drills: as they walk along a road with their weapons at the ready, targets pop up, and the infantryman swivels and shoots. No time to consider; reaction becomes automatic. The theory is—no time to think about it.

Until afterward.

When the killing is done, as Kilner recognized, soldiers and marines often begin to question what they've done. Kilner believed that killing in war could be justified as a moral right, akin to amputating a diseased limb: painful, requiring courage, but the morally right choice among bad alternatives. To help them think through the morality of killing, Kilner came up with what he refers to as the "bubble theory." He described it to me in its most simple form. Think of every human being, he told me, walking around inside a protective bubble, which represents the right to life, the right not to be killed. Puncturing that bubble to hurt the person inside is immoral, a violation of one's right to live. But an aggressor can forfeit that right to live—for example, by attacking an innocent person. A soldier is then morally permitted to kill the aggressor because he has forfeited his bubble of protection. It's an almost-cartoonish idea, but one that sparks animated discussions among the West Point cadets in his ethics class. Since Kilner introduced the idea in 2006, he's briefed it to groups at the army's Command and General Staff College and to the entire West Point class of 2015. But overall, he said, "the army is very uncomfortable with it. People can talk about killing, about their feelings about killing, but when you actually want to say, 'This is when killing is justified and this is when it is not,' the army as an institution objects because in the end they want the freedom just to have soldiers obey their orders."

Even in the academic environment of West Point, Kilner's ideas about morality and killing are treated with ambivalence by senior leaders, he said. In 2014 he was allowed to give a presentation to the entire junior class; the following year the command changed the format to one in which combat veterans talked to the juniors about the psychology—but not the morality—of killing in war. Two years earlier Kilner had been invited to help design a series of online training programs as part of the army's Comprehensive Soldier Fitness program intended to toughen soldiers physically and mentally for combat. When I asked about preparing soldiers for killing, Sharyn Saunders, the director of the program, at first told me that Kilner's bubble theory "is not codified" in the training. Several minutes later she corrected herself, saying that four training modules designed by Kilner are in the army's online resiliency training program. In fact, Kilner's ideas about teaching soldiers to see the morality of killing in wartime were cut out of the army's training program. In an e-mail to me, Kilner wrote that the army's "bureaucrats deleted a robust, very helpful way to understand the moral justification for killing (i.e., the bubble theory)." Despite repeated requests, the army refused to allow me to see the training programs it asserts will protect soldiers against PTSD and moral injury.

When Chuck Newton talks about killing in combat, his stories are leavened with humor, as if a straight, sober recounting would be too much to say or hear. "Most kills are like sport, you may as well be hunting a duck or a deer, you know. I'm not a hunter, but I know enough hunters," he told me one evening. "You got twelve guys unloading at somebody running a hundred meters away, and the guy drops, and twelve guys are cheering and claiming they killed him, you know? Now you got twelve so-called confirmed kills, and only one guy was killed. Ya know what I mean? It's like high fives, you know?" We were both laughing at this image. When the laughter died down, I told Chuck about a soldier in Iraq who had looked an insurgent in the eye just before he killed him, and even though he had killed many times before, this particular killing felt awful, evil, immoral, and the soldier was deeply injured by this experience.

Chuck nodded in recognition. Firing at the enemy in a tree line is one thing, he found; up-close killing is different. At a distance, killing the enemy is an easy and justifiable him-or-me calculation. Not so when you look your enemy in the eye. "When it's one-on-one and you see, you take your time even, like I unfortunately did. I thought I was bringing closure. Instead it was just a nightmare." Go on, I said. What do you mean by "closure"? "Let 'em know, like, 'You were trying to kill me, I am trying to kill you, I won.' Ya know? It's over. You continue on." But that didn't happen? "No, because you see a Taliban, a Talib, whatever they call themselves, you see a Talib, and then for a split second you see just a human, a son, a father; it's like—aaagghh! You don't have time to think about it. I can talk about it. I understand the whole one-on-one, close-proximity thing and thinking about, you know, as opposed to the sport shooting, which is what most of it is.

"I had one incident with three guys [Taliban] where, you know, they call 'em spotters; they had a radio and binoculars, whatever, and they ran into a little—they were ducking fire, unloading on us—and they ducked into a little building the size of a garage, and I popped up with a rocket and put it right in the open door, and it was the same thing [from the other marines]. Cheers, yaaaay! I won't brag, but it was a good one."

It's true that in combat some guys hold back. Their training, their weapons, are designed to make it easier to pull the trigger on another human being. Even then, as Jim Gant explained, some don't. "We know guys who did that," Newton said when I asked him once about marines who would shoot into the trees rather than at another human. "Lots of guys." We were lounging around with a couple of beers with Stephen Canty and Xavier Zell and others who'd been marines with Charlie One-Six, and they were listening intently. "Those guys didn't actually wanna try to kill," Newton was saying. "So they just kind of popped off to the side and shot at a tree. We saw it happen all the time. But the thing is, they'd go home and tell their families they're heroes when in fact they put us in danger by showing up, you know, talking the talk but not walking the walk. And we needed everyone focused, we needed guys looking, watching our backs and focusing on the enemy, and these guys are off there having their own personal dilemmas and shooting at a tree and pretending like they're doing something and that's . . .

"I'm sure their brains are worse off than mine because the great thing is that I killed people, I killed people up close and personal, but everybody here, honestly, it's like mutual love. I know these guys will always be there for me," he said, waving a beer bottle at his buddies, "because I proved that I was there for them, when you had other guys wandering around over there and crying on the radio that we're being overrun while I was actually hunting people down and killing them. And guys thanked me for it. And that makes me feel great."

But like other combat veterans I've talked with, Newton felt morally damaged by killing only to the extent that he established a fleeting personal connection with the person he killed. "There's a split second, it's just him and me and . . . two guys with parents and brothers and sisters and . . . you know, families that care about them, walking around on the earth under the same sun, nothing to do with the war and . . . You know, I'm not a psychopath, because I understand there are people who just relish that, and I am not one of them."

In the video that Canty has made, interviewing the marines of Charlie One-Six about their experiences at war and afterward, Chuck Newton talks again about the time he killed someone after looking him right in the eye. "I drew up on him and I shot him in the face and I watched the bullet go in between his eyes and I watched it come out behind his ear, I watched the life go out of his face and he fell on the ground, and that's an image I can't get out of my head, you know. And I know why executioners wear a mask and why the condemned always faces away from the executioner. Because the image of someone dying as you look him in the eyes is nightmarish. It's something no one should ever do. And I would tell someone, 'If you're in that situation, don't look 'em in the eye, you will not go one day without thinking about it, you will not go to sleep without thinking about it.'

"I've decided to move on with my life," Newton says in the video. "But the fact that this still haunts me shows that beyond the military, on a human level, there's..." Searching for words, he trails off. "Other than the nightmares about how I killed people and stuff, other than that, there's really no adverse effect."

Canty, behind the camera, interrupts. "Wouldn't you say that's a pretty big adverse effect?"

"Yeah," says Newton. "As a member of the animal kingdom, you probably shouldn't be killing your own species."

But guilt, remorse, sorrow, and grief can descend on anyone, even those who are not trigger pullers. Stacy Pearsall taught me that.

CHAPTER 9

Vulnerable

I saw battle-corpses, myriad of them,
And the white skeletons of young men—I saw them;
I saw the debris and debris of all dead soldiers;
But I saw they were not as was thought;
They themselves were fully at rest—they suffer'd not;
The living remain'd and suffer'd—the mother suffer'd
And the wife and the child, and the musing comrade
* suffer'd*
And the armies that remain'd suffer'd.
—Walt Whitman, "When Lilacs Last
in the Dooryard Bloom'd"

A couple of hours into our conversation, Stacy Pearsall mentioned in passing that during her second combat tour, in Iraq, three of her friends had been killed in the explosion and collapse of a house that had been rigged with hidden bombs that detonated when the soldiers entered. It was part of a story about why, as a military photographer, she had started making a portrait of each soldier she accompanied on patrol. "In case they didn't come home," she explained. At that point she had lost many friends who were killed in combat and was herself deeply wounded. "You don't know how long they're going to be around," she added, speaking of the living.

Medically retired now as an air force staff sergeant, Stacy was nursing a dark beer, her black boots hooked around a barstool, absentmindedly toying with the folded handkerchief I'd given her earlier when she came to a difficult part of her story and had to mop up drenching tears. The bomb-rigged house incident was a small patch of the tapestry of death, loss, heartache, and physical and emotional pain that has dominated her life for a dozen years and more. When I asked her what she saw in the faces of the soldiers she photographed, she said one word. Vulnerability.

"When someone says 'American soldier' or 'combat soldier,' people think of brawn, strength, invincibility, and immortality. But what I saw in front of me was a bunch of kids, eighteen, nineteen, twenty years old. Some of them hadn't drunk alcohol in their lives. Or felt the touch of a woman. Or maybe never heard gunfire. Now they're thrust into this foreign country with all these expectations, maybe expectations they've put on themselves, unrealistic sometimes, that they'll perform heroically when the first rounds go downrange. I wanted people to see the reality, the vulnerability. That's what makes them human beings."

Stacy was thirty-five when we spoke, eight years after her final exposure to a string of IED blasts that left her with traumatic brain injury, a diagnosis of PTSD, cervical spine trauma, a faulty memory, near-constant pain, night terrors, and occasional seizures. She wears her dark brown hair chopped and tied back in a hasty ponytail, and her large brown eyes and tight smile said to me: *Stubborn, tough. And vulnerable.*

She was born into a family with a military tradition dating to the Revolutionary War. Her parents divorced when Stacy was an infant, and she and her mother "bounced around a lot, she got remarried and we moved and then that [marriage] dissolved and we moved again." She enlisted in the air force at seventeen, signing up as a photographer. In the military, the job title "combat camera" designates both the tool and the person. You could be an infantryman, a naval petty officer, a C-130 pilot, or a combat camera. Stacy was a combat camera. The job is to document combat operations—raids, assaults, firefights, IED ambushes, the wounded, and the dead—for analysis within the military, although some images are selected for public viewing. It's a demanding and dangerous assignment requiring quick reflexes and steady nerves. Combat cameras carried weapons along with their other gear. Stacy loved the work; the military provided the stability, structure, and consistency that her childhood had lacked.

Assigned to Iraq in 2003, she worked out of the tent city at Camp Sather, a U.S. military facility at Baghdad International Airport. She accompanied troops on patrols and on manhunts for former regime and Iraqi army officials, traversing Baghdad's dangerous streets and the neighborhoods known for suicide bombings. After a few months she got her footing and began capturing images not only to document what happened but to explain how it felt. She looked to capture the impact of war on people for folks back home. "The public provided my paycheck," she explained. "They were relying on me to provide imagery of the war in which their country was involved."

She began "focusing more on the military as human beings, with all these things that happened in front of my camera that they are going to live with for the rest of their lives. Yes, watching pornography on their iPhones or joking around about silly things back home, chain-smoking cigarettes, talking about shitting their pants, or making fun of each other. The small intimate details." She also documented the wounded and the Iraqi civilian dead, often capturing images of bodies that had been carved up. Corpses missing limbs, and heads without bodies. "Seeing a mutilated body did not affect me," Stacy told me. "There wasn't life in it and it was tragic that it happened. Please don't misunderstand what I am saying. We needed evidence that the enemy was mistreating local people. I was not emotionally affected by seeing it or photographing it. But seeing the wives of those killed and mutilated and the emotional impact the war had on them, that... carries with me."

Just before she completed her first deployment, in 2004, Stacy was riding in an unarmored Humvee that was wrecked in an IED blast. She was "shaken up quite a bit" but insisted she was okay. When she got home, however, she experienced a cascade of symptoms: insomnia and then nightmares when she did fall asleep, constant fatigue, anxiety, not eating well. Some of it was undiagnosed PTSD; some of it was moral injury that would never be diagnosed. Whatever it was, she felt she was falling apart. A Vietnam veteran she met persuaded her to check in with the mental health unit at Charleston Air Force Base, South Carolina, her home station. "I walked in, and it was weird: there were people there for couple's therapy. I went to the counter and said that I needed a little help, I was not sleeping, and the person told me to see my primary-care doctor and get sleeping pills. I said, 'Really? So I can overdose and kill myself?'" Stacy turned and stomped out, but a counselor ran after her and suggested that she see the chaplain. "I said fine. I showed up at his office fifteen minutes early. The office was locked and dark. I waited until fifteen minutes after my appointment, and he never showed up. Turned out he was at a golfing tournament and totally blew me off."

Eventually she did get help from a VA-operated vet center at Syracuse University, where she had won a spot in a military-photojournalism course. The vet-center therapists taught her to recognize those sights and sounds that would trigger her emotional reactions and how to deal with them. Driving past what looked like potential IED sites, for instance, on safe American streets. Feeling more in control, she got married in 2006 to Andrew Dunaway, also a combat camera, and she immediately went off on other military assignments.

Back in Iraq on her second deployment in January 2007, she felt more emotionally stable. "I felt if I was stressed, I could stop in the moment and stop my brain from getting away from me, and understand that I'm in control and can change the outcome if I want to by presence of mind," she said.

It was a brave attempt. But in Iraq the killing had accelerated. President Bush had ordered a troop surge, and insurgents were stepping up the resistance. Twenty-five Americans were killed in battle on a single day, January 20; in all, 904 American troops would be killed in Operation Iraqi Freedom that year. The danger and stress rose to extreme levels and played out in some unexpected ways. When I asked Stacy about the time she pulled a gun on a child, she sighed and stared into her beer for a minute or two.

At that point, at the height of the war, she said, many Iraqi men had been detained or killed or simply fled, often leaving wives and children to panhandle or find some other way to survive, and some of the kids were taken in by insurgents and paid to pickpocket U.S. troops or dig a hole for an IED or carry a grenade into a crowd. Everywhere she went, kids would swarm around, trying to get into her pockets, and she'd have to strong-arm them away, and she began to feel utter disdain for the gangs of children. "Repugnance" is the word she used.

One day, she was out photographing an operation to hunt down insurgents thought to be hiding in an apartment building, a painstaking and dangerous job of examining stairwells and rooms and shadows from floor to floor. "We had encountered heavy fighting, and I hadn't slept in several days, and it was taking a really long time," she said. At one point she came down out of the building to one of the waiting vehicles. "The driver was sitting there, and the turret gunner was up there, and I had the door open, it was sweltering hot, and a young kid came running at us full speed…" Stacy yanked out her 9-millimeter semiautomatic pistol and the other soldiers swiveled with their weapons and everyone froze, and it turned out the kid only wanted a soccer ball, sometimes handed out by American soldiers.

"At that moment, even though none of us acted precipitously and fired our weapons, we took the time to make sure he wasn't a threat, and thank God nothing negative happened, but…it definitely made me look inward at myself, like, What kind of woman am I? Women are made to make life, not take it. It was a moral thing. It definitely tested me, and it changed how I think of myself," she said. "Now if I see a group of kids, I'm walking the other way."

In an earlier conversation, Stacy had told me, "I have many reasons for not having children of my own. But in the long run that [incident] has persuaded me not to."

Stacy Pearsall was not physically hurt in the situation where she almost gunned down a child; nor did that incident contribute to her old PTSD. Instead, her injury was a moral one, and like other combat veterans I've known, she recognized the difference immediately. "I feel differently in situations where there was a moral problem versus what triggers my PTSD," she had told me in our first conversation several weeks earlier. "Moral injury is more deep-seated. Any human being has difficulty justifying things that happen, and a lot of things happened that don't sit well with me, some that I don't really want to get deeply into. I'm just not ready for that."

But now she was ready and wanted me to know.

Not long into her second deployment, she was assigned to cover the operations of a U.S. Army team working with Iraqi soldiers. The American soldiers at the forward operating base were clearly not eager to have her there. That kind of reception was always emotionally difficult, because combat cameras bounced around from one unit to another, rarely having time to develop friendships, and they came to rely on the instant camaraderie that is usually possible among men and women at war.

Not this time. "They were bastards, cold and unwelcoming was the general feeling I got, and I loathed the idea of working with this team," she said. The prospect of entrusting her life to a group of men indifferent to her existence who excluded her from their intimate circle was daunting. But the unit's commanding officer, the captain, was "a ray of sunshine in these dark clouds. He was always joking around, always had a smile. A family guy, married with kids...I loved him."

Under orders, she worked with the unit for a few days, then was assigned elsewhere, and then came back, and she came to value her time with the captain. (She asked me not to use his name.) They ran into each other occasionally "for a couple of months," Stacy said. "No! Gosh, wow, it was really fast actually, like maybe six weeks." One day, as the soldiers gathered for a mission briefing, she felt there was "a really, really bad vibe, kind of funky, but it was a critical mission. Everybody was hanging around with little rain clouds over their heads acting all down, and the captain was there on his computer, Skyping home, and he was a little out of sorts and actually kind of abrupt with me, a little short in some ways. I was like '*Aaaaaggghhh!* I hate this place!' I was so mad and angry with him because he was supposed to be my breath of fresh air."

The rest of the story came in short gasps between sobs and long silences as she worked to form the words. "So my feelings were hurt and we were riding in two separate vehicles, we were getting ready to leave and I didn't say...anything...so we left the FOB and we hit heavy resistance right away, like we couldn't even get into the village and mortar rounds were coming in and small-arms fire ricocheting off our vehicle and mortar rounds were, you know, homing in, we were getting targeted a little closer and closer and we were feeling the pucker factor after a while...and then guys from the other vehicle radioed over that the captain had been hit and he was...he was...down...And the medic was the driver in my vehicle, so we pulled up alongside their vehicle and opened the doors, and there was gunfire and cross fire, but it was weird, in this moment it was really quiet, and I had the medic's medical case and I passed that off to him and we didn't know the extent of, what severity, his injuries were, but it was pretty bad and the commander made the decision to get back to the FOB for a helicopter medevac.

"My vehicle pulled in first. We got out and I had my camera in my hand and I stood there debating what to do. Because the journalist in me has to document what is happening, because people need to know, and it doesn't matter that...he is my... friend...So I started taking pictures of the soldiers taking the body out of the vehicle, and I found it just repulsive physically to do it, like the act of having the camera to my face and taking the pictures just made me feel less than human. Like I had no...feelings...I was a voyeur. That I had no morals. And I was judging myself harshly, thinking about what Uncle Sam was having me there to do in the first place, and I felt this sense of obligation. And in that moment the soldiers turned to me and called me every name in the book, they were screaming at me for doing what I did, and I felt bad enough already...and the last picture I took he was unconscious, but his eyes were open, and I remember thinking..." She stopped to try to compose herself, and after a while she was able to go on.

"The helicopter landed, and I put my cameras down feeling disgusted with myself, feeling awful about what the soldiers thought of me, and I watched them put him in and everybody went and took cover, but I just, I couldn't move, I felt cemented there, and the rotor wash sprayed gravel everywhere, rocks and sand just pelted me, and I felt it was retribution, I guess...or my penance?

"He died fifteen minutes later."

Soldiers on the FOB had adopted a stray puppy they named Crockett, and Stacy found Crockett and took him to a quiet dark corner and curled up and held him and sobbed, and after a while an officer found her and squatted down and apologized for the way soldiers had yelled at her. And he said, I am sorry, but the mission is critical, and we really, really need to go back out there and get this image, and we need to leave shortly, but I understand if you don't want to go. Stacy said, I'm here for a reason and I have to work, so that's fine.

And while they were walking out to the vehicles, a medic came running with the news that Stacy's battle buddy, a young female combat camera, had been shot on a mission. Usually they had worked in pairs. But this time they were assigned different missions, and as the older of the two, Stacy felt responsible for watching over her.

"Shot? She's been shot? 'Shot' means a lot of different things; the last shot I witnessed ended in death," she told the medic. It was hours before news came that her friend was wounded but alive. "I carried the guilt from that for a very long time," Stacy said.

But the death of the captain, and her struggle to accommodate the competing demands of job and heart, tore a hole in her soul that is unrepaired. She paused for a long time when I asked her if she had come to accept that whatever she'd done would always feel half right and terribly wrong. "I still don't know what to think of it," she said finally. "I would have given my life for him. You know? If I could I would have traded places with him. I felt devastated for the loss of my friend. And I feel like I didn't maybe uphold myself to the same standards as any other journalist would have in that situation."

Stacy was medevaced from Camp Warhorse in Iraq in April 2007 after the second time an IED blew up her vehicle, and eventually she came home to Charleston, where she underwent treatment for her neck injury. That required twice-weekly hospital visits under anesthesia, which meant she couldn't drive. With her husband still deployed in Iraq, members of her air force unit were assigned to drive her. That didn't work out well. "There would be mornings they just wouldn't show up, and I had to take a taxi, and I couldn't help but think, You guys were really cool when I was able-bodied and I could do everything you wanted me to do, and now that I'm broken you don't want to have anything to do with me."

In truth, she probably was more than a little irritable, and she acknowledged that "I probably did myself a disservice by not letting them in on my emotional state. I was not ready to talk."

One day not long after, she was sitting in the waiting room at the Charleston VA. Probably glowering at the other patients, mostly elderly men who, she felt, were staring at her. At the VA, guys were either mistaking her for a nurse—"Miss? Where's room one forty-three B?"—or undressing her with their eyes. None of them, she felt, saw her as a fellow veteran. This time, one guy in particular was staring at her. She could see him out of the corner of her eye, looking at her as a sex object or sex toy, thinking about her in "unnatural ways." She couldn't decide whether to speak to him or get really angry. Speaking to him won out. "Can I help you?" she asked, summoning her most charming southern belle voice. He brightened. Grinned. Soon he was relating his experiences in World War II, the fighting, the death and camaraderie, the liberation of concentration camps.

Stacy was enthralled, listening hard and thinking to herself, These are good stories. This is a valuable human being whom I almost didn't get to know because of my own prejudices. Like the soldiers whose portraits she had captured in Iraq, she thought, this guy might not be around much longer. And that's how the Veterans Portrait Project was born, giving her a renewed purpose as she travels the country capturing images of veterans young and old, men and women who served in World War II and Korea, Vietnam, Afghanistan, Iraq, and countless places and missions in between.

On the black-and-white images of their faces, the lines and creases of war, the depths of their eyes.

The vulnerability of human beings.

CHAPTER 10

Betrayed

Any army, ancient or modern, is a moral construction
defined by shared expectations and values.
                    —Jonathan Shay, *Achilles in Vietnam*

The moral injury of Sarah Plummer didn't begin with the killing, although that came to be a part of it. It began when she
suffered a violent assault, a personal betrayal that grew into an
institutional betrayal, jarring experiences in which Plummer felt
her fellow warriors and superiors profoundly violated the moral
codes of honor, loyalty, respect, and professionalism she had
believed were the very embodiment of the United States Marine
Corps.

Betrayal is a violation of trust, and trust is the bone and sinew
of the military. Daily military life is sustained by trust embodied
in the common phrase "Got your six," "six" referring to the blind
spot immediately behind a fighter pilot's helmet. Six o'clock on a
clockface as you face twelve. A pilot's wingman watches his buddy's six so nobody sneaks up behind him. More broadly, it means

"I'm protecting you. Depend on it no matter what." Those who volunteer for military service live daily with the responsibility for someone's six and trust that somebody's got theirs. Trusting and being trustworthy are learned skills not deliberately practiced in civilian life, but in the military trust is bedrock, taught from a recruit's first day. In army basic training, I have watched new soldiers instructed to topple over backward from a five-foot-high platform, trusting that fellow recruits gathered below will catch them. After more weeks of training, recruits are required to complete a buddy team live-fire event, in which a soldier low-crawls while her buddy is laying down suppressive fire with live bullets, from behind. The exercise, drill sergeants say, teaches new soldiers to put their lives in the hands of other soldiers.

Beyond that immediate moral covenant, the men and women we send to war trust that the physical preparation and other training they've been given will enable them to survive and prevail in combat; that their weapons and equipment work and are better than those of the enemy; and that their superiors, up to the commander in chief, are competent and act in their best interests. They have to trust that their friends and allies won't shoot them in error or in anger; that they won't be left behind; that medics will save them if wounded; that their lives will not be squandered by politicians back home. That the war they are fighting is moral and just, and that their service will be seen as honorable.

In war, betrayal of that trust is inevitable. That's a truth that runs through military history and the literature of war. Betrayal forms the basis of the Greek classics—Homer's *Iliad* and Sophocles's *Ajax* among many others—and appears in such classics as Erich Maria Remarque's *All Quiet on the Western Front* and Karl Marlantes's Vietnam memoir, *What It Is Like to Go to War.*

In the wars of Iraq and Afghanistan, betrayal seemed to come from all directions. Some Americans joined the military eager to participate in the noble work of building peaceful, prosperous democracies as the White House promised, and individuals did good work in mentoring judicial and municipal officials, building bridges and schools, and working with farmers to increase crop yields and exports. Yet much of that progress was thwarted or undone by a lack of consistent long-term support from Washington and by bureaucratic rules that delayed or strangled innovation in the field. A common belief among those who served in Iraq and Afghanistan is that the politicians in Washington never gave them enough manpower, time, and other resources to do the job right. Grunts in Iraq and Afghanistan, for instance, at first traveled in unarmored vehicles until casualties from IEDs skyrocketed; then soldiers and marines began devising and installing their own makeshift armor plates, often at their own expense. Finally, after years of prodding from parents, journalists, and politicians, including the late senator Edward Kennedy, help from Washington arrived in the form of heavily armored Humvees and blast-resistant armored trucks.

At home, people turned against the war even as military families braced for second and third deployments, sending their own loved ones back into wars the public had decided were lost causes. In the war zones, civilians that the troops were there to help sometimes turned out to be the enemy, planting IEDs and targeting American patrols for insurgent snipers. Americans assigned to work with Iraqi and Afghan security forces sometimes were shot by the soldiers they were mentoring, in what the military came to label "green-on-blue" violence.

This betrayal of trust is the most basic violation of our sense of right and wrong and can carve a jagged moral wound deep in the soul. Betrayal sours into cold fury and a bitterness that veterans know civilians find hard to understand. Betrayal corrodes their ability to trust again, extending the moral injury through families and colleagues and impairing participation in civic life.

Brandon Friedman was a young lieutenant with a combat tour

in Afghanistan behind him when he and the platoon of 101st Airborne infantrymen he commanded took part in the 2003 invasion and occupation of Iraq. The premise of the entire war, Saddam's alleged weapons of mass destruction, had been exposed as a falsehood, and the U.S. invasion had unleashed a bloodbath of violence and killing. The night that two of the unit's sergeants were killed, Friedman lay on his cot and simmered with pent-up fury. Recalling that night in his 2007 book, *The War I Always Wanted,* he wrote,

> I had always wanted to fight. But I never wanted any part of something like this. I was a professional soldier. I wanted to believe in my work. Instead I was watching as politicians with no military experience hijacked the army . . . Two guys in our battalion were dead, two families ruined. And try as I might, I couldn't figure out what the purpose of that was. Things that had been welling up inside me all summer suddenly exploded in my head like a dozen roman candles. I hated the president for his ignorance. I hated [then defense secretary] Donald Rumsfeld for his appalling arrogance and his lack of judgment. I hated their agenda. I hated Colin Powell for abandoning the army—for not taking care of his soldiers—when he could have done something to stop these people . . . I hated them because now, it meant that my guys could be next . . . I felt like we had been taken advantage of. We were professionals sent on a wild goose chase using a half-baked plan for political reasons.

Recently, I asked Friedman if he still felt that way. Oh, yeah, he said. Brandon is tall and rangy with a thatch of brown hair, deep blue eyes, an informal style, and a pleasant grin. He had completed his army obligation in late 2003 and later gone to work for the Obama administration in Washington, D.C., advocating for veterans. Married with a family, he was settled, but the war was still with him.

"The moral imperative for me is to stay away from anybody who served on President Bush's national security team. I won't socialize with them. I don't trust them as equals. I pulled out of being considered for a job when I found out who I'd be working for. To me, it's not like 'Well, all that happened a long time ago, we're all good.' That's not how it works. I was at Walter Reed a few years ago and saw a guy in a motorized wheelchair, which he operated with his mouth. Because he had no arms or legs. It's one thing to hear stories like that on the news. But go to Walter Reed and see for yourself. That's the cost of war—in this case, a war that never should've happened. And I won't sit here and say that's okay. The Iraq War was bullshit. And I'm not gonna shake hands with the guys responsible for it."

That same bitterness gripped Stephen Canty when he and other marines of Charlie One-Six were on their second tour in Afghanistan, where they'd been assigned to train, mentor, and fight alongside Afghan National Army soldiers. "You go out there and at first you want to do the best thing you can, be the nicest you can, you really believe in the hearts-and-minds stuff," he said. "You really want to help these guys. Then you realize, it doesn't work like that. We got guys sleeping next to us in the ANA who are Taliban, and we're supposed to be guarding these fucks, supposed to be training them? And we're supposed to count on them during missions to watch our backs? You have Washington saying, 'Hey—hearts and minds! Hey! Partner with the Afghans!' And these motherfuckers are shooting your own buddies, soldiers and marines, in the back? And you're gonna sit here and keep telling us to partner?"

Canty said it got to where "you couldn't trust a single person except the guys next to you." Five years after he returned from Afghanistan, Canty told me, "That's why we have trouble trusting people."

Sarah Plummer was a bright twenty-four-year-old marine lieutenant who went to war in 2005, in charge of an intelligence unit based in western Iraq that operated small, unmanned surveillance drones. Working out of Al-Taqaddum Air Base, she and her enlisted marines flew Pioneer and ScanEagle drones equipped with video cameras and monitored and analyzed the live video feeds to hunt for insurgents planting IEDs or setting ambushes of friendly troops. Often they were asked to track individual insurgent leaders, so-called high-value targets. They'd guide an attack by hunter-killer teams of commandos or by air strikes or artillery, then advise the U.S. command of the outcome, called a battle damage assessment, or BDA: number of bodies, number of vehicles or houses destroyed.

It was a painfully close-up view of the ugliness of war, the drones' powerful video cameras drawing Plummer and her operators and analysts into an intimate communion with death. As in any war, the violence sometimes was inflicted on innocents. "We were seeing some of the murders and beheadings, and we were not pulling the trigger, but we'd do target recon beforehand for marines or soldiers," she said. Often, she and her marines were not told who the target was or why it was being hit but were just given map coordinates and told to keep an eye on that location. "Then we'd see pretty much an entire family get murdered on the roof of their house, even though we'd be told to go off target [that is, look away] before we could see what was happening. But we knew...we did a lot of BDA during or immediately after the bombs had been dropped or artillery fired."

That was years before the U.S. military noticed that many of its drone operators, whether they were based overseas or in the

United States, were becoming emotionally sickened by watching people being killed. By 2013, for instance, when I visited a highly classified drone operations and intelligence center at Langley Air Force Base in southern Virginia, the rates of trauma had risen so sharply that the air force had begun helping its people cope by adding to the staff a full-time psychologist and a chaplain. They'd walk the floor, stopping to check in with the operators and analysts bent over their screens on twelve-hour shifts monitoring video transmitted from drones soaring high over Afghanistan.

But in Iraq between 2005 and 2007, even though the carnage Plummer saw up close was horrific, she never sought out a chaplain or mental health counselor to talk it through. "All that actually made a pretty big impact on me and on my marines, but we didn't have a context to talk about it," she told me. "When you're in a trigger-puller environment" of hard-core warfighters "and you're just the support person, you feel you don't have the space to say how that affects you."

At the start of her career, Plummer was determined to become a marine aviator, a highly competitive and sought-after assignment for which she was well positioned after graduating from the University of Virginia on a navy scholarship and completing four years of Reserve Officers' Training Corps (ROTC). She'd done her civilian flight training, excelled at athletics, and gotten top grades. Her dad had been an air force navigator. Now she was officially accepted in the naval aviation program. "Flying was what I always wanted to do," she said.

Then, she said, she was raped, by a fellow ROTC midshipman.

It was two weeks before graduation and her commissioning as an officer. "It was someone I knew and cared about. I was screaming and punching, it was pretty black and white, I fought him off me, but that's not how it was interpreted later when I did report what happened." She went the next day to her marine instructor, intending to tell him exactly what had happened. But like many rape victims, she found herself unable. "I felt shame, I felt bad and dirty, that somehow it was my fault, that I could have prevented it," she said. Because it had happened within the university's small military family, she felt as if she had been raped by her brother and now had to tell her father. At the last minute, she couldn't do it. Instead, she just told the officer that she was having a hard time with things, and let it go at that.

After graduation she went to the Basic School, the tough Marine Corps officer-training course, and during orientation week she and her fellow fledgling officers were given a briefing on sexual assault. The briefer, a female officer and lawyer, gave several examples of sexual assault. One of the stories was similar to what had happened to Plummer. She and a friend talked after class; her friend urged her to report her rape. If she didn't, Plummer thought, he might rape again, "and I wouldn't be able to live with myself. I knew this wouldn't turn out well, but it was the beginning of getting some agency over what had happened."

It went badly. An investigation went nowhere. Like other victims of military sexual assault, she was questioned and then requestioned in a way she felt was hostile. One day the military lawyer handling her rape case passed her in the hallway. "We put a note in his record," the officer said. No further action would be taken. Case closed.

Sarah sought out a mental health counselor. She told the story of her rape and discussed other concerns, acknowledging that after the rape she had experienced periodic depression. Emotionally drained but undaunted, she showed up at Naval Air Station Pensacola to begin formal military flight training. But after her first flight physical, she received a shock: the corps had disqualified her from ever flying.

She had been told that seeing a mental health counselor would not affect her chances of being selected as an aviator. "They told me this was the new Marine Corps and counseling wouldn't affect my career," she said. "I was never on medication, I was not suicidal, I was a top performer with great grades and physical-fitness scores." But it turned out that attitudes in the corps weren't so modern, after all.

"I was deeply disappointed with and utterly wounded by the institution which not only let me down but continued to punish me in one way or another for years afterward for having reported the rape," she later wrote in her blog, *Semper Sarah*.

Eventually, she took an assignment with marine intelligence and ended up deploying twice to Iraq. There, on her second deployment, the story of her rape surfaced among some of the unit's officers and she started seeing a mental health counselor. "I felt I had done well seeking therapy," she told me, "but then it was thrown back in my face. It felt even worse than the immediate aftermath [of the rape], because being deployed and dealing with the retraumatization of telling my story, being shuffled around from chaplain to commanding officer to therapist and having to tell my story about thirty more times and meantime working fourteen-hour days, seven days a week... for me it felt like basically every area of my life was touched by trauma or stress or drama."

Finally, a navy psychologist and a senior officer rescued her and found her a new assignment, and after a few months she rotated back to the United States where she finished her six years in the Marine Corps.

Sarah found healing from her moral injuries not so much through formal therapy dedicated to relieving the shame and bitterness and depression but through her own personal faith and drive. She's found meaning in working as a life coach, yoga instructor, speaker, and nutritionist and by developing a habit of positive thinking. Her healing began during her second deployment in Iraq, when she discovered yoga. "Those days I got on the mat, I could actually breathe," she wrote in her blog. "Even if it was only for a few minutes at a time it was a life-saver, because the rest of the time I literally felt suffocated." Yoga helped bring her to the recognition that healing from her trauma was up to her, that she had the power to take control of her life and move on. "To me, choosing to live out of love instead of fear or anger is not due to an absence of trauma, but in spite of it . . .

"No one is going to do it for you, even if you have an amazingly supportive spouse, family, or friends. I spent years wishing people would do something more for me, believing they should be doing more for me, until it clicked that, in some ways, it almost did not matter what anyone did for me because ultimately true healing would only come from within me."

But she cautions that healing from the moral injury of betrayal doesn't come quickly or easily or even completely. "We don't heal never to be in pain again; we heal so that we're strong enough to take that hill, persistent enough, courageous enough," she says in a video she recorded in the mountains of Colorado, where she sounds like the soccer athlete she once was.

"On bad days you push yourself—it still hurts . . . if you're one of those people, and we've all been there, and you're feeling that pain, pick up the phone and talk to somebody and let yourself feel the pain . . . being strong enough to ride the tide."

She makes it sound easy. But from the combat veterans I've spent time with, I know it's not easy. Some, like John Lee, keep it locked up for almost a lifetime.

CHAPTER 11

War Crime

If we do not prepare them adequately, their moral failing is ours, though they are the ones left to suffer the consequences.

> —Rebecca Johnson, Dean, U.S. Marine
> Corps War College

In the waning days of World War II, Private First Class John Lee and other American GIs assembled about sixty German soldiers, lined them up against a brick wall, and, as the Germans stood with their hands raised in surrender, shot them down in fusillades of fire.

These were no ordinary Wehrmacht troops; they were fanatical Nazi SS soldiers. The Americans had just broken into the notorious death camp at Dachau, where the SS served as guards. Gaping at boxcars full of corpses, the Americans were beginning to comprehend the ghastly reality that the SS had tortured, beaten, starved, mutilated, and murdered untold numbers of Jews and others. The German SS troopers were grinning and taunting the Americans. It seemed unlikely, in those chaotic last days of the war, that the SS men would ever be brought to real justice for the crimes they had committed. Nevertheless, gunning down surrendering soldiers was itself a war crime.

At least technically a war crime. Punishable by hanging. But was it immoral? Unjust?

John Lee was a frail and astonished seventy-five years old when I knocked on his door after tracking him down in a Cleveland suburb in 2001, fifty-six years after that incident. I was curious how he thought about his actions and whether he ever felt twinges of moral remorse. He invited me in, and after we'd talked for a while, he acknowledged that killing the German prisoners had been wrong. He readily acknowledged the guilt and regret of moral injury and the pain of having held his secret for so long. But for me to judge what he'd done as an exhausted and anguished twenty-year-old, he said, "You had to have been there."

I continue to be troubled by that reproachful remark, his admonishment that the acute moral dilemmas of war cannot be understood by outsiders; that the moral injuries of wartime should be left for the individual to bear alone. Certainly Dachau was a morally treacherous situation for John Lee, a dilemma with no obvious right answer, one that would be familiar to veterans of other wars and, most recently, to the young Americans who fought in Afghanistan and Iraq. I think John Lee was wrong. We must see and identify those wartime actions that clearly violate our own moral and legal standards. But we must also acknowledge the pain of those who struggle at these crossroads and make a fateful choice. Whether or not we ourselves would have made the same decision, whether we would have pulled the trigger at Dachau or stood apart from our combat buddies in that moment, we must accept moral responsibility for the decisions of those we send to war on our behalf.

Otherwise, like John Lee, they do bear their moral injuries alone.

How do you define "morality" in wartime? More precisely, how do those young Americans we send to war sort through the emotional and legal thickets in the crashing immediacy of battle? How can they think clearly about moral issues that remain muddied despite debates by learned theologians, legal scholars, and philosophers down through the ages? Sanctified killing, or murder? When the deadly erupting blast of an IED has just torn off the legs of your best buddy and steel fragments sliced through his brain, and you find cowering in a gully an unarmed teenager holding one end of the detonating wire, should you kill him? Or detain him for questioning that may result in his release? For the rest of your life, to whose version of morality do you answer: Your own? Your dead buddy's? The version understood by the battalion commander? The one presented to a court-martial jury? The morality of the God who let your buddy die? The moral beliefs of your buddy's widow? If you refrained from shooting at the SS guards at Dachau and they went free, would that weigh on you the rest of your life?

In any of the confusing but common moral crossroads in war, how should our young troops avoid sustaining a moral wound? In cases where a moral choice can lead to a war crime, who should bear the weight of a legal judgment and the pain of the moral injury?

The U.S. military has spent years and fortunes perfecting the most realistic and thorough combat training in the world. But in preparing young Americans for war, it has failed in one glaring aspect. Those we send to war are never trained to anticipate the moral quandaries of killing that they will face; they are given no opportunity or encouragement to think about or to discuss what makes some killings moral and others a sin or even illegal. We send them into a situation that puts me in mind of jungle-warfare training in Panama, where I once accompanied an army platoon on a daytime patrol. The dense, tangled jungle is notorious for spookily swallowing whole groups of men. Sure enough: fifty meters into the green murk, the vegetation was so thick I lost sight of the soldier directly ahead. Fifty meters more and the path disappeared in the darkening gloom, and we stepped into thigh-deep water. Compass needles swung uselessly. Then the radios went dead.

In a very real sense, men and women go unarmed into the moral swamp of war from which many return bearing lifelong injury.

Often, you can get lost in what seems a simple, binary choice. Kill the guilty Germans, or let them go without penalty while the skeletal death-camp survivors howl from behind the fences. It may be more a complex choice between two evils: Kill to protect yourself and your buddies and to accomplish the mission—and risk a life sentence for murder. Or do nothing and jeopardize the lives of your buddies, those whom you love most and on whom you depend for your life.

That was the choice a young American made in our most recent wars, a choice that haunts him years after he left the war. It was a choice he made deliberately, one that he still feels was morally and ethically correct. Yet it was a choice for which he would be liable to a murder charge and perhaps a life sentence were his actions more widely known by the authorities. The person I'll call John Doe agreed to allow me to tell his story if I protected his identity. "I want the story told," he said, "so that people know."

Terrible things happen in wartime. Terrible things are done by bad people, and by good people making choices that might cause us to shudder. Here at home we have constructed an image of war in which its vileness is airbrushed away. We insist that we act on a higher moral plane than the enemy. We don't shoot prisoners. Marines who are caught urinating on an enemy corpse are punished. To a large extent the conviction that we hold the moral high ground in war is true, often obtained at high cost.

Jim Gant, the former Special Forces officer, told me of a desperate battle in eastern Afghanistan's Pech Valley. "One of the most brutal firefights I've ever been into. We were taking gunfire on entry into this compound. We were exchanging gunfire from, I mean, like here to there," he said, gesturing at the ten-foot distance from my dining room table into the kitchen. "Two women were shot. Who shot them? I don't know. But in this gunfire between these fuckin' al-Qaeda guys and us, these women and a child ran between us, and [a Special Forces trooper named] Scott Gross, about six-three, two hundred forty pounds, put his weapon system down as gunfire is exchanging, picked up the small child, turned his back to the gunfire, crashed in this door, put the baby on the floor, turned around, and came back out," and here Gant mimicked raising a weapon, "gun up." How to explain the impulse to save a baby's life at the peril of your own? Gant sighed and blinked. "Where do you get a guy like that?"

I knew a helicopter gunship pilot, on a combined air-ground operation, hovering over a medical clinic that had been seized by militants in eastern Afghanistan's Paktika Province. Ground troops were waiting for him to fire a missile into the building and destroy the Taliban. But the pilot and ground commanders couldn't be certain there were no civilian hostages inside; in a missile strike they would be killed along with the Taliban. Instead, a decision was made for the American soldiers to storm the building. As the lead trooper rushed into a hallway, he was killed in a fusillade of enemy fire. His buddies pulled the body aside and continued the assault. Eventually the insurgents were killed, and the building secured. There had been no civilians present.

We accept such risks to take the morally higher ground. We do not bomb mosques. Risking the lives of civilians is wrong. We instruct military recruits on the rules and insist that our service-men and -women act with untarnished moral integrity. From afar, the moral choices we ourselves would make in their situa-tions seem clear and uncomplicated, perhaps even obvious. Shoot-ing surrendering prisoners is wrong.

In reality, of course, those decisions are more complicated, the right choice less obvious: it would be morally repugnant if the SS guards escaped justice. Or perhaps there is no "right" choice. Yet for reasons of military hierarchy, responsibility for making these choices almost always falls on the most-junior soldiers of the working-class military. People like twenty-year-old WWII infan-tryman John Lee. In those freighted moments when a choice hangs in the balance, higher authority is usually too distant, too busy, or simply disinclined to help. These intimate battlefield decisions about killing do not fall to the ranking officers on the other end of the radio miles away (or, worse, circling high over-head in a command helicopter). Nor are those decisions the bur-den of the distant generals who guide the course of the war. Politicians in Congress and the White House, who authorize and fund the war and cheer from the sidelines, likewise are excused from that responsibility. And it never falls on those in the military legal system who would judge and perhaps condemn John Lee and others for what would be determined, in retrospect and with-out context, the wrong choice.

Nor do those of us at home ever have to scramble to find the line that divides "just" killing in wartime from murder. We send young Americans into the moral jungle of war while we absent ourselves from those awful calculations. But like the Roman spec-tators who passed verdicts on gladiatorial contests from the upper tiers of the amphitheater, we seem quick to judge how our troops have behaved. If they come home silent but uneasy about the choices they've made, we avert our attention. Or we simply thank them for their service and move on.

To place someone in that circumstance, in which a momentous moral choice demands to be made, is to expose them to a lasting sense of betrayal by higher authorities who didn't have to make the decision. To a lifetime of having to keep the secret—or of bitterness at being judged. Guilt, perhaps for having violated the rules. Shame for taking a life in an act that could be murder. In short, a deep moral injury.

This is why the ancients devised complex rituals of cleansing and forgiveness for their returning warriors, recognizing that the moral damage of war was inevitable and allowing for the healing, of both warrior and his society, to take place.

We have abandoned that practice. Instead, we have sought to define and regulate moral practice in war by law. The U.S. military spends an enormous amount of time and effort trying to ensure that it conducts its military operations in strict conformance with international and domestic law. In the army alone, forty-six hundred lawyers are assigned as staff judge advocates. Military lawyers are called JAGs for short, because they are assigned to the Judge Advocate General's Corps. Senior JAGs I have known work at the top levels of the Joint Chiefs of Staff and in places like the headquarters of the Joint Special Operations Command, the highly classified operations center of the U.S. special mission forces. Less senior JAGs work at almost every staff level in the military, including in the tactical operations centers of warfighting units. When the Second Brigade of the Eighty-Second Airborne Division made a mass jump at night not long ago, a slim, thirty-seven-year-old woman in full battle gear, wearing dark-frame glasses and a ponytail tucked under her helmet, jumped with them: Major Megan Wakefield. Paratrooper, lawyer, staff judge advocate. I have many times watched JAGs like Major

Wakefield advise battalion staffs on how to shape a planned operation so that it falls within the narrow and specific laws of war. I have seen them advise against a proposed attack because it would unnecessarily expose civilians to harm or because using air strikes to "soften up" the target area would be a use of force disproportionate to the expected military benefit of the operation. Their judgments are sometimes met with groans of frustration and then grudging respect from warfighters. But I have also seen a general overrule his JAG when he felt military necessity trumped the law.

The laws of war are a loose accumulation of treaties, declarations, precedents, and understandings of how war is to be declared, conducted, and concluded. They represent an earnest international effort over more than a century to make war less brutal, more humane, and, in at least one extreme case, downright illegal. The U.S. military historically has issued its own set of rules for war, including George Washington's Five Rules for Honorable War ("Don't abuse prisoners") and President Lincoln's 1863 General Order 100 ("the unarmed citizen is to be spared"). Today the laws of war include the Hague Conventions of 1899 and 1907, which, among other prohibitions, outlawed the practice of dropping bombs from a balloon and "any other new methods" of air warfare.

A more comprehensive effort came with the Geneva Conventions of 1949. This assemblage of treaties and agreements was amended as recently as 2007 when its overseeing body, the International Committee of the Red Cross, ruled that individuals wearing the Israeli Red Shield, as well as those wearing a Red Cross or Red Crescent, are protected as medical or religious persons involved in humanitarian work. (Anyone engaged in fighting while wearing one of these symbols is guilty, under the Geneva Conventions, of "perfidy.")

Collectively, the laws of war have prohibited the use of exploding bullets (1868), distinguished between combatants and civilians

(1907), and banned chemical (1899) and biological (1925) weapons and land mines (1998). While these agreements are still on the books, others have faded in memory and usefulness. In 1928, diplomats of the United States, France, and Germany solemnly affixed their signatures on an agreement never to go to war. The Kellogg–Briand Pact was ratified soon after by most other nations, even as they rearmed and slid toward World War II. (The pact is technically still in force. Barbados was the most recent signatory, in 1971.)

On the books or not, each of these well-intentioned admonitions about behavior in wartime had been broken by the opening of the twenty-first century, although some internationalists argue they remain important safeguards against the mistreatment of prisoners and noncombatants. The Pentagon, officially and formally, insists that its personnel adhere to the laws of war. But any expectation now that all warring parties will abide by these rules seems dangerously naive. They were, after all, designed for an era when uniformed armies fought pitched battles face-to-face in declared wars over terrain designated as a war zone. None of those conditions was met in either Iraq or Afghanistan. Instead, American troops faced off against insurgents who shunned uniforms and for the most part avoided pitched battles; who nullified the concept of fixed war zones by flowing freely across borders, between Pakistan and Afghanistan, for instance, and from Syria and Iran in and out of Iraq. (The United States, for its part, conducted air strikes with bombers and missile-firing drones on alleged terrorists in Yemen, Pakistan, and Somalia, stretching the original battle zones and authorizations for the wars.)

Even the term "combatant" used in the Geneva Conventions now gives off an odor of ancient mildew. Is a kid who is hired to dig a hole for a deadly IED a combatant? What about the farmer driving a battered pickup truck piled with bags of ammonium nitrate from Pakistan into eastern Afghanistan, material that could be used for fertilizer or suicide bombs? How about the unarmed civilian idling outside the gate of a U.S. Marine outpost in Iraq's Anbar Province, who signals to unseen assailants every time an American foot patrol heads out?

The Geneva Conventions' thoughtfully crafted rules for treating and ultimately releasing prisoners didn't seem to apply, either. In 2001, the administration of President George W. Bush famously declared that detainees and prisoners in its War on Terror were "unlawful combatants." It thus avoided having to accord them the legal rights and protections of prisoners dictated by the Geneva Conventions, although the Bush White House promised to treat its prisoners humanely as if they were legitimate POWs. In the old days, that meant that prisoners of war were to be held under humane conditions until the end of hostilities and then released. In the unending War on Terror, however, there *is* no end of hostilities. In January 2002, I stood outside the then temporary detainee facility at Bagram air base in Afghanistan, chatting about the ultimate fate of the prisoners with the U.S. military police officer in charge. Under the terms set by Bush, I wondered, how could they ever be released in a way that is both safe and humane? His shrug was eloquent, and the question stands unanswered today, as does the detention center, in a new facility at Bagram. Still full of prisoners.

After 2014, when Islamist militants began executing prisoners in Iraq and beheading and burning alive hostages in Syria, it seemed unlikely that future conflicts would see a return to the humane aspirations of generations past. Nevertheless, in 2015, the Defense Department gamely released a 1,176-page *Law of War Manual* detailing the legally permissible battlefield behavior for U.S. troops and the expected behavior of the enemy. Seeming to ignore the insurgencies of Iraq and Afghanistan that took the lives of more than five thousand Americans, the Pentagon's official rules demand that "honor forbids resort to means, expedients, or conduct that would constitute a breach of trust with the enemy" and "combatants must take certain measures to distinguish themselves from the civilian population." And in a section that strains credulity, the manual advises that adherence to these laws by Americans in combat "can encourage an adversary also to comply with those law of war rules."

But the wars in Iraq and Afghanistan required more explicit rules to enforce moral behavior, and deploying troops were expected to comply with the rules of engagement. The intent was to embrace the evolving strategy of counterinsurgency, in which the main effort was not to destroy the enemy but to protect the civilian population. Thus the ROE sought, for instance, to curtail the accidental killing or wounding of civilians, a faint echo of the hearts-and-minds campaigns of the Vietnam War. But the effect of the ROE, in Vietnam as in Iraq and Afghanistan, often was to push decision-making down to the lowest level, the individual trigger puller.

The rules weren't easy to apply to real-world situations. For instance, the ROE for American troops in Iraq and Afghanistan insisted that force could be used against a potential or possible enemy only if he or she threatened an imminent use of force. As the 2005 standing ROE put it, "The determination of whether the use of force against U.S. forces is imminent will be based on an assessment of all facts and circumstances known to U.S. forces at the time and may be made at any level. Imminent does not necessarily mean immediate or instantaneous." Imagine a twenty-year-old army infantry squad leader, pinned down after an ambush in a palm grove outside Baghdad, with enemy fire coming at his guys from three sides, trying to figure this one out. Imminent use of force, check. But there is more. He whips out his copy of the standing ROE and reads: "The use of force in self-defense should be sufficient to respond decisively to hostile acts or demonstrations of hostile intent. Such use of force may exceed the means and intensity of the hostile act or hostile intent, but the nature, duration and scope of force used should not exceed what is required. The concept of proportionality in self-defense should not be confused with attempts to minimize collateral damage during offensive operations."

Really? You can imagine our squad leader frozen in indecision, knowing with certainty that his interpretation of this language will be different from the interpretation of a senior officer and lawyer, twice his age, in a solemn court-martial proceeding back at Fort Riley, Kansas. And you can imagine his decision as insurgents close in: *Screw the rules — kill the fuckers!*

These standing ROE were usually supplemented by tactical ROE issued by the combat commander. Grunts carried them on laminated cards, often tucked inside their helmets. These ROE might spell out, for instance, the escalation-of-force steps that must be taken before a soldier could open fire on a vehicle approaching a checkpoint. Such rules undoubtedly saved civilian lives. But the rules sometimes were impossible to follow, because the approaching vehicle would be moving too fast, or the driver might be confused in poor visibility. Or, as in the case of Jake Sexton, a car full of civilians simply didn't stop for reasons no one could figure out at the time or later on.

By the time Charlie One-Six got to Marjah, Afghanistan, in early 2010, so many different sets of ROE had been issued that marines had a difficult time figuring out which ones applied. Some of the marines were carrying ROE cards from the battle of Falluja, Iraq, five years earlier. Others had different ROE cards from the battalion's 2008 operations in Garmsir, and others had been issued new ROE cards. All of them were slightly different.

In the collision between the official rules and the reality of war, moral injury was widespread.

After Smitty and Angus were killed by IEDs on January 24,

the marines probing into Taliban-held neighborhoods in Marjah were battered by so many IEDs—twelve in one four-hour period—that they were ordered to walk behind tanks equipped with anti-mine rollers. And they were told that anyone out ahead of them could be considered hostile. Anyone. "That was the word from our commanders sitting back there in bulletproof MRAPs [armored trucks]," Chuck Newton told me. "Then I guess somebody thought that might not look too good, so it was 'Well, not *quite* anybody.'"

So there were rules, but it was up to soldiers and marines out in the field to figure out whether or how they applied in reality; whether their actions would win a medal or a court-martial and leave them scarred with a moral injury.

In the lexicon of military lawyers and combat commanders, there are "good kills" and "bad kills." The deaths of SS prison guards at Dachau eventually were deemed good kills. Or, at least, not bad kills. When I tracked down John Lee in early 2001, he readily admitted the truth. "Nobody's really proud of doing something like that," Lee told me. He described how he and his unit, India Company of the 3rd Battalion, 157th Infantry Regiment, had fought almost continuously for more than a year, landing at Anzio in Italy and fighting up through France and on into Germany. Ordered to secure what they were told was a local prison, they scaled masonry walls to find thirty-six boxcars of rotting corpses, inmates who'd been starved. It was overcast and chilly, Lee remembered, as he and the others crept forward beneath tall pines, finding more stacks of bodies and atrocities of which some soldiers could not speak even decades later. By the time they began rounding up the prison guards, as the thirty-two thousand gaunt inmates still living cheered and jeered from behind fences, the men of India Company were "boiling mad, half out of our minds," one soldier said later. Lee told me, "I looked at the bodies as we went past—their open eyes seemed to say, *What took you so long?"* As the men walked warily deeper into the camp, some-body muttered, "No prisoners!" Eventually, they rounded up the Germans. As Lee remembered it, there was "a deathly silence. We lined up the SS guards. One of the guys cocked the machine gun. The Germans started moving and somebody shouted 'Fire!'"

In the army investigation that ensued, several similar incidents were documented. A lieutenant had ordered four German soldiers into an empty boxcar and personally shot them. Another American soldier had clubbed and shot wounded SS prisoners who were still moving. Several GIs turned their backs on two inmates beating a German guard to death with a shovel; one of the inmates had been castrated by the German they were killing. A lengthy army JAG investigation report went to General George Patton, the senior regional commander. No action was ever taken. Among the veterans of the 157th Regiment, it was understood that Patton threw the report in his wastebasket, tossed in a match, and barked at the investigators: "Get the hell out of here." But a copy survived and eventually made its way to the National Archives, where I discovered it in a cardboard box.

"Nobody's really proud of doing something like that," Lee told me before he died. But, he added, "The army trained you to fight. It did not train you for psychological shock."

The Americans who fought in Iraq and Afghanistan, similarly untrained for psychological shock, also came up hard against the issue of morally and legally good kills and bad ones. In these wars, the issues often revolved around enemy insurgents who were captured and detained. After the prisoner-abuse scandal at the Abu Ghraib prison in Iraq was disclosed in 2004, U.S. occupation authorities in Iraq and the military command in Afghanistan became more reluctant to hold detainees in prison. The result was that sometimes soldiers suspected or had evidence that an insurgent had attacked American or allied forces; he would be arrested and taken in for interrogation, but a few days later would be free and out on the streets again.

During the Iraq War, high-value enemies—senior officials of Saddam's government, for instance—were either hunted down and killed (no "imminent use of force" judgment was required) or captured and shipped away to the new U.S. permanent prison at Guantánamo Bay, Cuba, or to secret CIA "rendition" sites. Fifty-two high-ranking former regime officials and Iraqi military officers were listed on U.S.-issued playing cards—Saddam Hussein was the ace of spades—distributed to American troops as a kill-or-capture most-wanted list. With a positive identification, or PID, anyone on the list could be killed, regardless of the evidence or lack of evidence against him.

Dealing with less notable enemies could be difficult. Bing West is a marine who fought in Vietnam, served as a Pentagon official, and found a third career as a battlefield journalist living with infantrymen in Iraq and Afghanistan. He detailed the problem in his 2008 book, *The Strongest Tribe: War, Politics, and the Endgame in Iraq*. Low-level insurgents who'd been detained, West wrote, "were routinely turned loose to choose whether they would fight again." By 2006, soldiers arresting suspected insurgents were ordered to collect the kind of evidence required of police for a U.S. court case. Despite minimal training for forensic police work, soldiers found themselves filling out arrest forms, collecting sworn affidavits from witnesses, recording the biometrics (fingerprints, digital facial photos, and iris scans) of detainees, and bagging evidence. "Each arrest package was reviewed at battalion level, then at brigade level, and a third time at Bucca prison in southern Iraq or at Cropper prison in Baghdad," West wrote. Even so, he found that four out of every five suspects detained by soldiers at the battalion level were released. That was the work of JAGs, who were scrutinizing arrests for any irregularity or weakness that could lead to the charge that an arrest was a human rights violation. Approximately fifty-eight thousand Iraqis were imprisoned between 2003 and the end of 2006; forty-three thousand were released.

Inevitably, soldiers and marines fighting insurgents across deadly city neighborhoods and palm-shaded irrigation canals would encounter the same insurgents they'd detained a few days earlier. Army sergeant Michael Leahy later explained to army investigators: "Seems like, even if you do your job and take these guys to the detainee center, they just come right back. The same [expletive] guys shooting at you," he said, according to CNN, which obtained videotapes of the investigation. In 2007, Leahy and other soldiers killed four Iraqis who'd been detained and released and then opened fire on Leahy's unit. Army prosecutors rejected their explanation that the military's arrest regulations made it nearly impossible to complete their missions with insurgents seemingly rotating in and out of detention. Leahy is imprisoned at Fort Leavenworth, serving a twenty-year sentence for premeditated murder and conspiracy. Sergeant John Hatley, who was in charge of the patrol, received a life sentence, later reduced to forty years' imprisonment.

In Afghanistan, during the time that Nik Rudolph and Stephen Canty and others of One-Six were fighting in Marjah, in the early winter of 2010, Special Forces captain Mathew L. Golsteyn, a West Point graduate, was awarded the Silver Star for heroism in combat and was later recommended for an upgrade to the Distinguished Service Cross, the nation's second-highest valor award. After a marine working in Marjah with Golsteyn's soldiers was nearly hit by a Taliban sniper, Golsteyn had quickly organized and led an operation to find the sniper, returning fire with an antitank weapon, repeatedly braving enemy fire to rescue a wounded Afghan soldier, and coordinating air strikes. The action came days after two marines working with Golsteyn were killed and three wounded in the blast of a booby-trapped door. Marines later found a nearby building with bomb-making materials and detained the alleged bomb maker. Golsteyn was convinced that if he let the bomb maker go he would kill more Americans; according to army investigators, Golsteyn said there had been "countless times" when a detainee was let go and days later was shooting again at Golsteyn's men. The investigators reported that Golsteyn took the alleged bomb maker off the base, shot him, and burned the corpse in a trash pit. In 2014, acting on the basis of the investigation, Secretary of the Army John McHugh withdrew the Silver Star award and stripped Golsteyn of his prized Special Forces status. Golsteyn did tell investigators, according to an account in the *Washington Post,* that he felt no remorse over the killing; that he wouldn't have been able to live with himself if the alleged bomb maker had been let go and built another bomb that killed more American service members. The following year, after a four-year investigation, Golsteyn was cleared of almost all the charges and given a general discharge.

But were his actions so different from those of the hunter-killer teams of commandos led by Stanley McChrystal? McChrystal was the lean Special Forces officer who eventually rose to become a four-star general and Afghanistan War commander before being fired in 2010 by President Obama. In Iraq and Afghanistan, secret teams under McChrystal's command tracked and killed men accused, sometimes falsely by their rivals, of being dangerous insurgents. McChrystal often went with his teams. As he recounts in his memoir, *My Share of the Task,* he and his men waged "relentless body blows" against insurgents, and not just against the leaders: they tracked down and killed "leaders, trainers, and mortarmen in order to eliminate their skilled labor" and sought to "disembowel the organization by targeting its midlevel commanders." The teams worked from a Joint Prioritized Effects List, or JPEL, that by 2009 contained more than two thousand names of suspected insurgents. Of those, roughly one thousand had been hunted down and killed.

Around that time, a group of American infantrymen found themselves encountering out on the street the same men they had detained, now released and back in the fight. These were snipers or guys digging IEDs into the paths the Americans used or laying ambushes. Often they were military-age males—MAMs, in GI parlance—signaling with flags or their cell phones when the grunts would set out on patrol. Soldiers or marines would see a guy scanning them with binoculars and putting a cell phone to his ear—and ten minutes later they'd find mortars or a command-detonated IED exploding in their midst. Very often these spotters wouldn't be carrying visible weapons, so they couldn't legally be shot. Sometimes, U.S. troops would be able to capture a spotter and take him into a detention center.

"We'd done it dozens of times, flexi-cuffing guys, collecting evidence, like opening their wallet and finding stuff," said one of the infantrymen, whom I'm calling John Doe. "We'd take 'em to these intel guys, and they'd do this movie-style good-cop, bad-cop kind of thing. I watched 'em do it once. We were up there [at higher headquarters] to deliver something and ate hot food and crapped in half of a barrel, it was like heaven. We heard some yelling and me and another guy went over and watched this [detainee] in a chair getting yelled at. We were laughing, watching this officer in perfectly clean cammies. We sat there for like a couple of hours, and another guy offered [the detainee] a cigarette, untied him; he was speaking English and the guy doesn't speak English, and I said, 'This good-cop, bad-cop routine is the most ridiculous thing I've ever seen in my life.' Then the bad cop comes back and ties him to the chair and starts yelling at him. I'm like this is how it works? Why are these guys getting sent up here just to be flex-cuffed? They should be dead. And then they get released with twenty dollars American, a shower, a meal, basically like the best night of their life, courtesy of taxpayers, after we literally find weapons and radios on these people…it got to the point where all this conversation, like nighttime conversation [in the squad], was like 'Why don't we just kill these people?' You know? It kind of leaves it up to us to be judge and jury and executioner." Several men in the unit had been killed in the past month in IED explosions and from snipers, the kind of unnerving violence that left their buddies dead or dying and nobody to shoot back at. Inside the unit, tempers frayed at the unfairness of it all. They also were terrified that JAGs would nail them for anything that happened without really trying to understand the situation.

The JAGs were often in difficult situations themselves. They'd be told to go investigate a suspicious death—a body would be found, or an Iraqi villager might complain. The JAGs might look into it and think, I might have done the same thing. If the guys in the unit felt it had been a "good kill," the investigation might fizzle out with no finding. That, of course, didn't make it right. But it happened more often than officials have acknowledged.

In one incident where all this came to a boil, the local police had caught a seventeen-year-old with his pockets full of American dollars, not currency ordinary civilians had access to, and two cell phones; one contained contacts known to be insurgent commanders. He'd been overseeing an IED site, waiting until a U.S. or government convoy came by, when he would signal for the device to be detonated. The police, John Doe told me, "wanted to kill him, they wanted our permission to smoke the guy. They were gonna bum rape him and shoot him in the head. But we followed procedure. We had this guy dead to rights." Doe's unit had lost men to IED blasts, men they loved. This kid was probably responsible. But they followed the rules. While they were taking him in for interrogation he was smiling. "It was like *I got it over you*," Doe said.

Out on patrol a week later, "We were getting shot at. We'd set up, move, get shot at. One of the guys was saying, 'Our friend is up there on the roof, waving a blanket every time we move.' We were like *That's the kid we just arrested!* When he came down off the roof we grabbed him by the nape of the neck. We told him, 'You're gonna clear a path for us' [through a possible IED site]. We got to the edge of town so we could see our base. I grabbed him, he had this big smile on his face. I took him into this room and I said, 'You're done.' I put him on his knees, he was still smiling, like *Fuck you guys*. I took my rifle off safe. I said, 'You met the wrong guys, you're not gonna get away with getting my friends killed. It's over.' His face changed. I pulled the trigger. I went out the door. I caught up with the patrol. Nobody said anything. Nobody did anything." No investigation was ever completed.

"The point of it is," he said, "our ROE prevented us from taking care of ourselves and each other. It's an extremely illegal thing. I should be in [the military prison at Fort] Leavenworth right now. But sometimes you have to make decisions, like I have to take a chance with my life to try to save—when you see your friends die, you're like *I can't let that happen again*. It tears your brain apart. Honestly, I'd rather die than to see my buddies die. Or go to jail the rest of my life than to see that guy I had a chance to kill, kill one of my friends." Doe sat unseeing. There was a long silence.

"When things go down," he finally said, "the people in charge aren't there. The people in charge who are supposed to make the decisions are hiding behind walls and behind bulletproof glass because they have a career. They're not there to get shot at. They're not there to risk their lives to help us. They're there to further their career, get a medal, and move on to the next command. Take credit for our good deeds and disown our bad deeds."

When I talk with Doe, I can see in his eyes the pain of the decision he made and the moral injury he carries. At the moment he had to choose, both options in his mind held powerful moral consequences: *Kill to protect my friends but jeopardize my freedom, or not kill and jeopardize their lives.* The face of the man he killed appears in his dreams. And the potential threat of being found guilty hangs over him. The guys in his unit, the sergeants immediately above him, would understand and approve of what he did, he feels. They would see it as a good kill. "But someone [who] didn't know us, some general who sits here in America hears about it? I would be in jail. But I want this to be in the book. I'm not giving specifics, but I feel it's important. It's a subject people don't want to talk about, don't want to touch."

So you think, I said, that what you did carried a higher morality, was more noble, than if you kept turning him in and seeing this catch-and-release cycle, and he kept directing attacks on your guys? Even though killing him was illegal?

"If it hadn't been done," he said, "and the next day we'd have gone on patrol and the same thing had happened, and one of my best friends I ever met in my life had been shot in the face, I'd be scarred for life. And probably in a worse way than I am now. Some scars kind of toughen you. Some scars debilitate."

CHAPTER 12

Atheists in the Foxholes

Praise be to the Lord my Rock,
who trains my hands for war,
my fingers for battle.

—Psalm 144

On his first combat deployment, Army Major Doug Etter had been in Iraq all of two hours when a tall soldier in dusty, frayed fatigues slouched into the chapel and asked for the chaplain. Etter is a Presbyterian minister and as an army chaplain wore a gold cross on the collar of his tan desert uniform, at that time freshly laundered. He gestured to a white plastic chair. The soldier lowered himself and cleared his throat. Etter waited. "I want to talk about the second guy I killed today," the soldier began.

Etter was not exactly unprepared for such an opening conversational gambit. He is a man of deep faith, trained in both military and religious practice. He is one of a cadre of thousands of ministers, imams, rabbis, and priests the military commissions to minister to its men and women, to guide their spiritual and ethical lives, and, as the army puts it, to "strengthen strong personal character and moral well-being" of the troops. If the military offers any aid to those with moral injury, these men and women are among the first responders.

But Etter also was a soldier through and through, from a proud line of warriors dating back to the Revolutionary War. Now it was his turn: 2005 in western Iraq, one of the most perilous times and places of the Iraq War, and Etter had just arrived at Camp Habbaniyah on his first deployment, with Task Force Panther, composed mostly of soldiers from the Pennsylvania National Guard. After a year, when they would complete their twelve-month deployment, they would stand with heads bowed as their scrawled regrets rose in smoke from a stone baptismal font. In the interim, Task Force Panther would be mauled. Fifteen of its soldiers would go home in flag-draped coffins, sixty-one would be wounded, and they would see many atrocities and kill many insurgents in some of the most brutal fighting of the war. Etter's boyish face, benign gaze, and mellifluous voice belied a steel interior. He was an activist chaplain: wearing his body armor and helmet, he often rode into battle with the soldiers of Task Force Panther as they fortified themselves with the black humor of the Molly Hatchet song blasting over the intercoms, "Flirtin' with Disaster." Occasionally Etter would carry a military shotgun, a visible emblem of his belief that war was a sin but sometimes a necessary one and a demonstration of his solidarity with the troops. Chaplains are noncombatants under international law, prohibited from engaging in combat. Under U.S. policy, chaplains may not carry weapons. But Etter, a former high-altitude mountaineer and paramedic, a man with a strong sense of history, is certain of his place on the battlefield as a representative of God. "I am not taking any unnecessary risks," he wrote home, "but I am also not sitting back waiting for soldiers to come to me. I am going to them."

*　　*　　*

There can be few more disorienting places for religious clergy than in the midst of war. Profound cases of moral injury come to them literally through the open door of the chapel. The raw ugliness of violence, the relentless maiming and death of human beings, and the scale of destruction seem to deny the existence of the benevolent God of our childhoods. Existential issues flood the war zone: if there is an Almighty God, why would He allow all this to happen? Then there is the tricky issue of killing. The military is organized, equipped, trained, and deployed to kill, a purpose that transgresses the direct command of God. Even for the most devout, belief can be severely tested in war. In some cases, war has shattered the faith of military chaplains themselves. "There's a saying that there are no atheists in foxholes," Etter once told me. "Untrue. There are lots of atheists in foxholes." There are stories, of course, of miraculous battlefield epiphanies, of soldiers finding God in the midst of mayhem. But for the most part, it may be that the best that can happen is that the warriors grit through it as best they can, that the military chaplains hang tight to their own faith, and that they listen and comfort as they are able, and leave the deeper healing of moral injury until after the war.

But being heard, in a deep nonjudgmental way, can be the beginning of healing. The soldier who walked through the chapel door was just finishing a twelve-month deployment in western Iraq, and Etter assumed he had killed many times. How was "the second guy I killed today" any different? The story came out in a torrent. The soldier was in a unit assigned to assault a house where insurgents were holed up. He was in the second "stick," or group, and as the first stick of soldiers warily stepped into the ground-floor rooms, he crept up the stairs toward the second floor, and near the top, a long hallway stretched into the shadows where an insurgent was raising his weapon. It misfired, and as the soldier brought up his own weapon, it, too, misfired. Desperately, he pulled the charging handle back to clear it, and it misfired again, and at the end of the hallway the insurgent was bent over, beating his rifle on his leg to clear it, and the soldier dropped his weapon and charged, pulling his bayonet from its sheath as he sprinted. In seconds he reached the man and slammed into him, driving the bayonet deep into his heart. The man slumped to the ground and died.

Standard military procedure is to search the body for any usable intelligence, and the soldier found the man's wallet and opened it. Inside, a weathered snapshot of a man posing with several women and children. The man in the picture now lay dead at his feet, and the soldier made the presumption that the photo showed the man's wives and children.

"So he felt very guilty about that," Etter told me later. "Someone who had tried to kill him, someone who had been his target, suddenly became human. Intellectually, he knew he had done the right thing. But emotionally he felt that this taking of a life was in some way morally wrong. And he was unable to synthesize the two in any peaceful way. He came looking for a word of grace, a word of hope, looking for a word of forgiveness. Looking for, I want to say, some way out of the remorse and guilt he was feeling."

In the months ahead Etter would sit with many soldiers he described as "seeking a release from the pressure that was on their soul, their heart, their mind." We were talking late one night in the kitchen of his house in the rural hills of eastern Pennsylvania while a late-spring snowfall frosted the fields outside. How, I kept asking, are you able to give them that release, that grace? Representing a God who unmistakably forbids killing, and the prophet Jesus who taught love, how can you comfort someone with deep remorse over a killing? There was a long pause while Etter reflected. When he began speaking, it was in his slow, soothing voice, the words coming in complete sentences and paragraphs uninterrupted by the "um" and "like" of our modern speech.

For that soldier who killed with his bayonet and for the many others who came seeking comfort, he said, he would remind them that talking to a chaplain in a confessional manner is confidential and protected speech and they could talk freely. He would listen without judgment and ask if they wanted to pray, and maybe half of them would say no, and the others usually wanted Etter to pray for them. "I would remind them that we have all fallen short of our own hopes, aspirations, and dreams for ourselves. That we have all sinned, and that in spite of that God loves us, and in that incredible love God has for us there is freedom, freedom to live boldly, freedom to live happily, freedom to live without guilt and remorse."

Toward the end of their twelve-month combat tour, the soldiers of Task Force Panther were coming to see Etter more often. "There's something I'd like to get off my chest," they'd say. "I'd like to confess. I just want to talk this out." It was an incredible honor to be trusted with such intimate details, Etter felt. "To see them bare their souls . . . after living together for months. I'd seen them naked in the showers, so to see them bare their souls is a whole different level of intimacy. That deserves our respect, our dignity, our highest and best. I think one thing chaplains would agree on, regardless of our religious affiliations, is that you are in a very holy place at that time. It's a place of great vulnerability and must be approached with love and compassion."

But listening can't be all there is to it, I argued. How do you comfort a soldier who just realized he's killed a real human being—and that his country will call him a hero for it? If that soldier feels he has violated some deeply held moral belief, how does he reconcile that with the person he thought he was, before he killed? How can you help him work toward forgiving himself for what he feels was a sin? How does he earn God's forgiveness?

I had recently read a paper by Shira Maguen of the San Francisco VA Medical Center. "Following traumatic events that involve acting in ways that transgress deeply held moral beliefs," she wrote, "veterans may develop views about self, others, and the world that make engaging in self-forgiveness particularly difficult.

"In our experience," she wrote of herself and her clinical research colleagues, "some of the reasons that veterans struggle with self-forgiveness is because they believe (a) self-forgiveness would mean that they are condoning their actions, (b) self-forgiveness would lead to forgetting what happened, (c) they are unworthy or undeserving of forgiveness, and/or (d) they need to be punished to atone for what they did." But there is hope, she continued: "In these situations, helping veterans recognize that although their actions have violated their values, and they may regret their actions, they can work to accept that those actions need not define who they are." *I am an American, a good soldier, a good husband and dad, and also I have killed to protect my buddies, whom I love and honor.* "Moving forward with a focus on values," Maguen wrote, "can be healing for veterans who have killed in combat."

It's not easy, Etter agreed, for anyone to think through the issues relating to killing. "Our society repeatedly tells everyone killing is wrong, killing is wrong. We say it's okay in self-defense, but it should be avoided at all costs. And then we take weapons designed to kill, put them into the hands of our young men and women, and say, 'Go forth with the blessing of our nation and defend it.' And as you know, I think war is sinful but sometimes morally justifiable. And the same is true for killing. I don't know if it is ever *not* a sin. But there are times when I do believe it is the morally right thing to do." He paused. "And holding those two truths, which are almost diametrically opposed and antithetical to one another, is the paradox and complexity of combat that we as warriors experience."

That seemed like a considerable burden to put on people just trying to stay alive in combat. Especially when they are seven or eight months into a life of constant danger and stress and filth and heat that roll on without letup, without ever a day off. But that's what we ask. It seemed to me to virtually guarantee a moral injury, no matter which way an individual soldier or marine chose. I thought of Nik Rudolph and Darren Doss, Joey Schiano and Jake Sexton. Sinners?

What exactly *is* a sin? I asked Etter. And if you sin, don't you require absolution, a formal release from guilt?

"A sin is a violation of God's will, as we understand it," he said.

And you can be forgiven for a sin?

"Yes, absolutely. You must confess; your remorse must be genuine." But forgiveness, absolution, Etter said, likely comes over time, not necessarily in one ritual or one long late-night talk in the chapel at Habbaniyah. It was that understanding, that forgiveness, are more a process than a single act that prompted him at the end of Task Force Panther's twelve-month combat tour to summon soldiers to commit their regrets to index cards to be consumed in flames in the baptismal font. "I wanted to express, as a person of faith, a person of hope, that their sins could be forgiven, that their guilt could be expunged," he said. "My goal was that by the very physical witnessing, the banishing of those cards in fire, they would begin the process of healing. I did not think," he said, standing and stretching, "that they would leave there immediately thinking that everything was great or that all of their sins and troubles had been removed. But I wanted it to be the start of the process where they could find healing and wholeness again."

Finding healing and wholeness back in the civilian world would be a difficult process for Etter himself. In Iraq, he felt strengthened in the presence of other soldiers, comforted in the intimacies shared with those who struggled with the same perils and demons. After several months in Iraq, he felt estranged from the civilian world outside that alternate moral universe of war. Midway through his combat tour, his best friend, Lieutenant Colonel Michael E. McLaughlin, was killed in a nearby IED blast. Etter flew home to Pennsylvania to officiate at the memorial service. When it was over, he turned to his wife and said, I want to go home. She responded, I'll go get the car. No, Etter said. Back home to Iraq, to the battalion. Back to war.

When Etter finally returned to Pennsylvania for good, he found he had absorbed too much of his soldiers' stress and trauma, in addition to his own. He was burned out. Compassion fatigue. "I had nothing left," he explained. "I was spent, emotionally, physically, mentally." The sudden disappearance of danger and stress and camaraderie from his life was disorienting. And he had no one to talk to. The chaplain had no chaplain. His emotions swung violently. He started driving recklessly. Drinking heavily. One day he found himself standing in his driveway, a cigar and glass of scotch in hand. It was 9:00 a.m.

To explain himself, he once told me of one of his warrior ancestors who fought in the Civil War. Wounded and captured, he was sent to the notorious Confederate prison at Andersonville, where some thirteen thousand Union prisoners died of starvation, disease, and exposure. Great-Grandfather survived. When he came home in 1865, he parked himself in the kitchen and never left. He was twenty years old. "I don't know what he did to stay alive at Andersonville," Etter said one evening. "I'm certain he stole food from other prisoners. Was that wrong? Never leaving the kitchen...now I understand." When the fighting is done, when soldiers come home, "some of those spiritual, moral wounds are like an abscess just beneath the surface. Enormous pain, and if left untreated...they can poison the heart and the soul."

Etter eventually sought help and found a caring therapist. But what sustained his moral and spiritual strength during the war, what prevented deeper moral wounds, was not only his religious faith but his unshakable belief in the mission. When soldiers would come to him for comfort, he said, "I always tried to give them my very best, my full attention, all the love and compassion I had—while still maintaining army standards, reminding them of the things we still had to do. For example," he continued, "whenever I did a funeral I always had three goals: to honor the fallen, to comfort their buddies as best I could, and to push them back out the door. Because as we say in a warrior's creed, the mission comes first. I will always place the mission first. That's why we're here. That's my job and I totally support that."

Like many Americans who served in Iraq and Afghanistan, Etter had gone to war filled with moral outrage and an Old Testament desire to strike back at the insurgents who were attacking Americans. "Our enemy has chosen war as his course and we shall fill his plate to overflowing," Etter wrote home one night, shortly after he led a memorial service for one of his soldiers killed in action. "We will dish it out to him in such a way that the very thought of it will nauseate, sicken, and repel him. We will give it to him in such a way that he will never have the stomach for it again."

Some chaplains, though, found it was more of a struggle to absorb the moral realities of war. Steve Dundas, a navy commander and Catholic chaplain, grew up in a military family passionate about the ideals of patriotism, duty, and service. Conservative Republican to the core; a devotee of Rush Limbaugh. After 9/11, Dundas was one of the many people who wanted revenge. Let's go get those bad guys and Saddam, too, he told his military colleagues. But it wasn't until 2007 that he was reassigned from his post at the naval hospital at Camp Lejeune to a mobile training team in Iraq. A year after Doug Etter's soldiers burned their regrets and left

Iraq, Dundas and his team began working out of Al-Taqaddum Air Base, where Marine Lieutenant Sarah Plummer was on duty monitoring drones. Dundas and the team traveled constantly through hostile territory in western Iraq visiting remote U.S. outposts where Dundas would hold worship services and counsel troubled young soldiers and marines.

Steve Dundas is a small man with a polished bald head and an engaging smile; he peers out at the world through wire-rim glasses with a benevolent gaze. A baseball fanatic, he feels most comfortable at a ballpark. ("I know as a Christian that the Bible says to 'cast all of your cares on him [Jesus]' and I do try to do that, but sometimes the ballpark brings me closer to him than a church," Dundas wrote on his blog, *Padre Steve*.) But far out in desolate western Iraq, he was uncomfortably aware that al-Qaeda considered chaplains a high-value target. As the team traveled, he began to realize the immense scale of destruction and misery, beyond what he'd experienced as a trauma chaplain. Back home, he'd ministered to the severely injured. He had seen suffering. He thought of himself as hardened to human pain, untouchable by trauma. But this was devastating: young Americans gruesomely injured or dying; villages and towns turned to rubble; streams of refugees; the few who ventured out to the market or mosque risking being maimed by suicide bombs. And by that time, the rationale for the 2003 U.S. invasion of Iraq had been exposed, Dundas realized, as a fabrication. It all struck him like a physical blow. "I felt lied to. And I felt those lies cost too many thousands of American lives and far too much destruction," Dundas told me over a couple of beers one sunny Sunday afternoon in Virginia Beach. What he had seen from afar as a righteous intervention to unseat a barbaric dictator and bring democracy to Iraq's people now appeared as "one of the most incredibly disastrous foreign policy things we ever got involved in. That aside," Dundas said, "seeing the devastation of those Iraqi cities and towns, some of it caused by us and some of it caused by insurgents and by the civil war that we brought about, that really hit me to the core."

Up until that point, he said, he had always believed that the government would do the right thing, that the country's leaders would tell the truth. That the nation would ask its military volunteers to do only "what's right." Now he was left with the awful knowledge that he distrusted all of them. What's worse, he felt, was that the war had been "a calculated choice by my leaders who all claimed to be Christian. And I didn't see anyone in the churches, at least the type of church I was in at the time, questioning anything. And I wondered where God was, and I began to wonder where God was in *my* life, and for almost two years I was an agnostic, just hoping that maybe God would show up again." A fellow naval officer once asked him, So where do chaplains go for help? "I said, 'Right now, I don't know.'" But he went to see a therapist, who was the first one to ask: So how are you with the Big Guy? "At this point," Dundas replied, "I don't even know if there *is* a Big Guy."

It took what Dundas calls "a Christmas miracle" to bring him back into his faith. He had terrible insomnia when he returned from Iraq, and he flung himself into his work at the Naval Medical Center in Portsmouth, Virginia, as a way to reorient himself. He was on duty one night during Advent, the Christian season of preparation for Christmas, when his emergency pager went off. He grabbed his hospital stole, oil, and Book of Common Prayer and rushed downstairs, where he found an elderly patient, in his nineties, in his last moments. Dundas gave him the sacrament of last rites and a final Prayer of Commendation. Over the man's face passed a sense of tremendous peace, Dundas felt, and the patient took one final breath before he died. "I found out later the guy was a saint, a naval officer, a doctor who would donate his time to take care of prisoners in jail, did pro bono care for pregnant women, deeply active in the Episcopal Church," Dundas said. "I was really in the presence of a saint. I felt . . . God is still around. It became a reawakening of faith."

With his renewed faith—in which he focused less on the details of liturgical ritual and more on living in grace—Dundas began to work closely with marines coming back from Iraq and Afghanistan. "There were a lot of marines who'd come to the hospital because they knew there'd be a chaplain who'd respond any time of the day or night simply because we had a light on, and if you go to the hospital chaplain the guys in your unit don't really know about it." He would see all kinds—believers, agnostics, Wiccans, and questioning Christians. "They came to see me because they knew I wasn't going to run them off, like some chaplains from very conservative congregations," Dundas said. After Iraq, he said, "I became a lot more open to people with questions. And [had more] respect for those who reject faith, because I understand their arguments. I still believe. But I get where they're coming from."

The marines who were most troubled were guys like Nik Rudolph, who was forced from the corps for acting up after his three combat deployments in Afghanistan. Many others were being "med-boarded out," declared by a medical review board to be unfit to serve for physical or behavioral health reasons and dismissed against their will. "These guys with their short careers have been through so much, emotionally and physically," Dundas said. "They would just rend my heart. Because you know they are struggling. And most of them knew what they really wanted to do in life was to continue serving as a marine, and they knew that was not going to happen and that they were being processed out. That was their biggest moral injury, realizing that they could no longer serve."

A waitress brought two more steins of beer. Dundas took an appreciative sip and sneaked a glance at the Orioles game on the wide-screen TV bolted to the wall.

I was curious: Why was being dismissed from the corps a moral injury? Dundas turned back on his stool. "Because their fundamental belief," he said, "was that their service in the Marine Corps or navy or the army was paramount in their lives. That being there for their fellow marines or sailors was an overriding value. Even more than 'I can't serve my country anymore' or 'I can't trust the government' or even 'I lost my faith' is 'I can't be there for my buddies.' And they feel they've let their buddies down. And they feel abandoned by the system. They can no longer do the things that they believe define them as a person."

Eventually that afternoon I asked Dundas what the future held for him, whether he'd retire and go do something else. His long answer was no. He's found a new purpose in ministering to those young marines and sailors who find themselves suddenly out of the service and feeling lost and abandoned, with the depression, anxiety, sleeplessness, distrust of authority, and suspicion of social relationships that often accompany moral injury.

"One of the hardest things to say to them is that even though you can no longer do the things you most value, you can go on. That you can find value in new things. It takes a while for them to process," Dundas said. "And you hope they do, eventually. Because so many of them are such good people. How do we get them to the next part of their lives? That's one of the things we will struggle with in the next ten or fifteen years: how we take all these guys who have been injured, physically and emotionally, who are going to get put out of the military? How do we...help them redeem their loss and turn that into something that helps others?"

He drained his beer just as I was wondering aloud whether the act of forgiving is essential if veterans are to find new life. Dundas waved his hand dismissively. "Forgiveness? I don't know how that works," he said. "I'm still working through a lot of this. It's not like you can say the magic word and forgive." After a pause he added: "I guess forgiveness, whether it's to the people who blew you up, or the people who sent you there, or the people who treated you like dirt when you came back, forgiveness has to be a part of it. But you can't just spring forgiveness on people. It's not a cheap thing. A lot of people, sometimes even in the church, are saying, 'Oh, just forgive them!' Okay, yeah, got that. But what if after you forgive them, something happens and you're still pissed off? Forgiveness is a process. It's not a onetime thing. But I think it is essential to the healing of moral injuries. And I have to confess," he said as he slid off his stool to head home, "sometimes I know I'm not there."

Whether forgiveness is a part of it or not, whether it comes slowly or not at all, there are ways to help heal moral injuries, and the military's multifaith Chaplain Corps should lead the way. That's the conviction of many chaplains with whom I've spoken. Army Colonel Thomas C. Waynick, the senior chaplain at Fort Benning, has helped spur the Defense Department's Chaplain Corps to adopt a new training program on moral injury. "Combat comes at a cost," said Waynick, who rode with the Third Infantry Division in the assault and capture of Baghdad back in early April 2003. "The good news is that in the safety of caring relationships, people can find forgiveness and healing for moral wounds. They don't have to be mortal wounds." It is religious communities, he believes, that can best provide that safe, caring environment. "Religious traditions provide a framework to process moral injury and moral dilemmas," he said. "There are also nonreligious ways to approach the issue, but it is predominantly a spiritual, existential issue." Veterans of any religious belief can speak with their God "as a source of unconditional love without judgment. Chaplains and clergy can support service members by facilitating conversations with God to work through guilt and find forgiveness."

I put that idea to Etter, who virtually burst with enthusiasm. Yes! he said. Healing moral injury "is in our primary lane. It is our work, the work of the church, the synagogue, the mosque. We've been in the business of guilt and confession and pain and suffering for a long, long time. Nobody—nobody!—should know more about it. Nobody should be better prepared to help others through it than us." What chaplains, civilian clergy, and veterans should understand, Etter said, is that there is hope, "ways of finding peace and wholeness and forgiveness."

In fact, clergy and religious groups already are beginning to grapple with veterans and moral injury, looking for ways they can help. In Illinois, Wheat Ridge Ministries has funded outreach to congregations across the country, coaching clergy and parishioners on how to listen to veterans and provide support for healing physical, psychological, and moral wounds. Networks of veterans, therapists, and religious leaders are active in Massachusetts and Pennsylvania. Point Man Ministries of New York links Christian congregations with veterans; the Atlanta-based nonprofit Care for the Troops trains religious congregations to reach out to veterans, involve them in joint service projects, and begin to talk about moral injury. In Fayetteville, North Carolina, Quakers are working with chaplains at Fort Bragg—home of the Army Special Forces and the Eighty-Second Airborne Division—to brief commanders and troops about moral injury. Brite Divinity School's Soul Repair Center in Fort Worth provides education and resources to support faith communities working with veterans.

"We're not trying to tell anyone to ignore their pain or to justify their pain," Etter told me. "We're not trying to tell anybody to ignore it. We are looking it in the eye, squarely facing it. And then we're going to move through it like someone moves through a valley of shadows, to a new place of light and wholeness. This falls right in the chaplain's lane. No one should be more qualified to speak of this than chaplains. It is a matter of the soul and heart. And it's only when the soul and heart are addressed that people can find true healing."

CHAPTER 13

Home

And who is this new me?
> —Lieutenant Colonel Bill Russell Edmonds,
> U.S. Special Forces, following
> twelve months in Iraq, 2005

As they were shaking a year's worth of Iraqi dust out of their gear and crating it all up to ship home, the soldiers of Task Force Panther each got an unusual letter from their senior enlisted leader. That was Command Sergeant Major Paul Walker, a short, well-muscled man responsible for looking after all the battalion's enlisted soldiers. In private life, he is a foreman in the coal mines of southwest Pennsylvania. But in Iraq, Paul Walker was foremost a soldier, the kind of guy who is a stickler for discipline and standards of conduct. Who is passionate about protecting his soldiers— and who would push them forward in combat. He would win a coveted Bronze Star Medal for his performance in Iraq.

His soldiers were exhausted but vibrating with giddy jitters about their imminent flight home. The decibel level of grab-ass around Camp Habbaniyah had risen noticeably. Soldiers going outside the wire were taking extra precautions against snipers and IEDs, reluctant to assume any unnecessary risk on their last missions. In a few hours many of them would gather at the chapel where Chaplain Etter would pass out index cards and stubby pencils. Now, though, they sat and read Walker's letter.

"The life we left eighteen months ago is the life most are hoping to return to," he wrote. But, he warned, each soldier has been forever changed by the war; the person who now returns is not the same one who left, and all you about-to-be veterans will have to absorb the good and bad of your war experiences, figure out who you are now, and how your new selves fit into civilian life. All that, the sergeant major wrote, "is something we will all have to take day by day."

They were about to discover, as many said later, that as they arrived home they would be as vulnerable to sorrow, regret, guilt, grief, and loss as they were in combat. Moral injury often endures long after the WELCOME HOME! banners are faded and torn. More than that, returning troops often suffer additional moral injuries in the bumpy transition back to the civilian world.

No other event in the lives of men and women at war seems to reach a climax as powerful as going home: so hotly anticipated, so quickly accomplished, so unexpectedly difficult. For months it's all you can dream about, spending hours constructing elaborate plans to indulge in every delicious fantasy denied in a war zone. Sleep. Good food. Sex. Finally it's time, and there's the dizzying one-day flight home. Kids and wives and mothers in their holiday finery, many clutching newborns, throng air bases and parking lots to receive the returning troops, and as they arrive, emotions just explode. The first hugs are delicious, the first beers and steaks, the awkward attempts at intimacy—the *newness* of it all that goes by in a flash.

Then comes what can be a crushing sense of loss. First you notice the s-l-o-w-n-e-s-s of home; its flatness. Nothing to jolt the adrenaline. Life seems to have faded from sharp color to fuzzy gray, so different from war, where life marches to an insistent, purposeful drumbeat, where decisions often hold life-or-death consequences: step here and your legs are blown off; step there and you're safe for another minute. At home: Froot Loops or Cheerios? And it's too quiet here: gone is the background rumble of generators, the familiar bellowing of sergeants, the whine and growl of truck engines, rattling gunfire, thudding helicopters. Instead, an empty apartment or a house whose occupants have left for work and school.

Also gone: your stature as a successful warrior. An army sergeant who's taken his squad to war and brought his soldiers back safe? No civilian can understand the field wisdom, the tactical cunning, that accomplishment demanded; the patience required, the hours waiting sleepless and rigid with worry as a team is late returning from night patrol. The pressure-tested leadership it all took. For some, leadership in wartime, responsibility for a few soldiers or hundreds, is the high point of a lifetime. Yet that skill, and the authority it conferred, seem to belong back there in the war; here at home the sergeant is just another guy nursing a late-night beer, or he's the unemployed new father trying to juggle rent and car payments, the electric bill and a wife who's used to operating on her own.

All this can add new bruises to your sense of right and wrong, your image of yourself as a good and deserving person. Being home may reawaken feelings of regret or guilt for having left the family for the adventure of war. Grief for lost friends, deferred while you're at war, can come flooding back. And being suddenly immersed in a society that's either given up on the war or is ignoring it can spark feelings of anger and betrayal.

The jagged emotional transition from war to home is often accompanied by the dull ache of sorrow. At war, you rely on intimate companions for guidance, support, understanding, comic relief, and, literally, your life. And you give it back. *Merry Christmas, Doss!* That's suddenly gone, a loss especially painful for those like Darren Doss who leave military service behind and for the National Guard and reserve troops, like Jake Sexton, who scatter individually to their small towns and urban neighborhoods rather than returning home together to Fort Bragg or Camp Lejeune. The abrupt disappearance of beloved comrades can cause lasting grief whose source, for tough-guy combat veterans, can be hard to identify aloud. Then there's the guilt of explaining why even the most loving and sensitive partner or spouse cannot fill the role of combat buddies. As an army lieutenant, Brandon Friedman commanded infantrymen in Afghanistan and Iraq on long combat tours. When he came home, he found it difficult to sleep when he wasn't in a roomful of men for company. Try explaining that to a girlfriend, he told me with a sheepish grin.

Families mirror these experiences. Homecoming is desperately anticipated, but in the days and weeks afterward, many families struggle to accommodate the new person who's come to live with them, incapable of really understanding what he or she has been through and unable to describe their less dramatic but still difficult and lonely lives at home. The clash of needs can be emotionally painful, and rebuilding relationships an added challenge.

The short distance from dusty battlefield back into the civilian world of clean pavement, unthreatening crowds, green lawns, ATMs, and air-conditioning can be disorienting, which the marines of One-Six learned quickly as they finished their commitment to the Marine Corps after they returned from Afghanistan in the summer of 2010. "You get a sheet of paper and go around and get things checked off, you turn in your weapons and stuff, they print off your DD214 [discharge record]. I came back to the barracks, packed up, and drove home with my sister," Doss told me. "Two weeks before, I'm in Afghanistan. Now I'm at a keg party. Absolutely insane."

But the exhilaration wears off. "I was so happy to be out, to be alive, and then you start to miss it. Little things, how simple it all was. My friends at home had no idea what I did." Doss paused, and the rest came out in a rush. "For me, it was Afghanistan on my mind all the time, and I did want to talk about it, but the few times I tried to tell them stories that happened, it would be really awkward and they wouldn't know what to say. Like my friend getting his legs blown off. What do you say to that? It made me not want to talk about it, ever. And that sucks."

Doss told me that while he was in Afghanistan, all his friends back home in Schenectady got into heroin, and when Doss came home he got into it, too, and did heroin for three years before he was able to quit. "I went to rehab twice and to detox five times and every time I relapsed the first day out," he said. Finally, he said, the VA put him on a heavy regime of Suboxone, an opioid medication designed to treat addiction, and he's been clean for three years. But not out of trouble. In April 2015, almost five years after returning from the war, he hit a bad patch. "I was in bed with a girl and I got up to look at my phone and there on Facebook was a picture of our [Afghan] interpreter who got shot in the face. That pushed me over the edge. I'm just real sensitive about death since losing my dad. I know that pain. I know that ache. There was a little entrance hole in his cheek and I didn't want to see the exit hole, it would be bad...after that I kind of lost it." Doss ended up in an inpatient VA program for PTSD for several weeks. "It was a lockdown," he said. "They take away your shoelaces."

I had seen it over and over again: people who performed not just well but extraordinarily well in wartime military service, who came home, got out of the military—and just floundered. Some were able to find their footing in a new life and move on;

others were not. One of these was Rosendo DeLeon, the marine gunnery sergeant from One-Six who befriended and watched over me in Afghanistan in 2008. DeLeon was a big man, his round face almost always split into a grin, always ready with a word of encouragement when I started to droop after hours on the move. At war he was indefatigable, his good humor and sunny disposition unquenchable. He came back from Afghanistan, got out of the marines, acquired a Harley-Davidson motorcycle, and grew an immense black beard. I didn't know it at the time, but he was carrying a heavy load of guilt and sorrow for marines killed in action, young men he thought of as his sons whom he felt he should somehow have protected.

Gunny DeLeon, which is how I think of him, grew up in Kingsville in South Texas. His family fondly called him Gordie, short for *gordito,* "chubby," but he wasn't fat, just big. He ran cross-country and won scholarships to college but joined the marines instead, thinking he wasn't college material. He did well in the marines; he especially loved training and mentoring young marines. But in 2008 he told me he was getting tired, and in 2011 he retired as a master sergeant. Then things slowly fell apart. He got work as a civilian contractor at Camp Lejeune, but for someone who'd reveled in the position of a senior enlisted leader of marines, it wasn't the same. He felt his experience and talents were being wasted. At one point he got word that a marine buddy had been killed, sending him into a black depression. He felt he was trying to come up for air and kept getting pushed back down. He started running with a motorcycle gang. People close to him noticed the sparkle had gone out of his soul; his eyes looked empty. It looked like he was trying to hide himself behind that big black beard.

It's impossible to untangle the emotional strands of a worsening situation like this. But from what I could piece together, it appears that Gunny DeLeon gradually grew apart from his wife and two teenage children. He had been diagnosed with PTSD and was seeing a counselor once or twice a week, but he hated going and hated taking the medication they gave him. I don't know if Gunny DeLeon had PTSD or not, but the VA's therapy and pills didn't seem to help with the moral injury that wore him down: his grief and guilt over the deaths of his buddies, his deep sense of regret and loss for having quit the corps, and his shame at having to take the medication.

Around Christmas of 2014, something set him off into a violent frenzy that brought the MPs to his house in Jacksonville. But then DeLeon seemed to pull himself together. He got into a program for struggling marine veterans. When he came back, friends showed up to offer help and support. He told a cousin he hadn't realized how many people cared about him and how many people's lives he had touched. He shaved off his beard.

One rainy night in May 2015, he was riding in Jacksonville, just outside Camp Lejeune. According to the Jacksonville police, just after midnight he drove his motorcycle at fifty-five miles per hour through a red light and into an intersection, where he struck an SUV. He died five days later. Whether he crashed on purpose or not can't be known. But one thing is certain. In the end, one family member said, "he was so broken that nobody knew how to help him."

Over dinner one night, the man who commanded the 1st Battalion of the 110th Infantry, Pennsylvania National Guard—Sergeant Major Walker's outfit—tried to explain what it's like to return home. It was five years after the battalion flew back from Iraq, and Loris Lepri was able to step back and look at it dispassionately. For outsiders to understand, he said, you have to know what came before, what you are returning home from.

Loris Lepri takes his names from his English mother, Anne Loris, and his Italian father, Luciano. When Loris took the battalion to western Iraq in June 2005, into the bloody heart of the Sunni insurgency, Anne and Luciano, who owned an Italian restaurant near Scranton, were frantic with worry. Luciano's friend and family doctor always inquired whether Loris was okay out there in all that fighting in Iraq. Each time he asked, Luciano would burst into tears. After a while, the doctor learned to stop asking.

Luciano Lepri was right to worry. His son's battalion, after a year of combat, soon would be burning their regrets and sorrows. From the outset, the sudden violence of Iraq was nightmarish. Loris Lepri lost his first soldier barely two weeks after the battalion commenced combat operations out of Camp Habbaniyah, just off the main road between the hotly contested cities of Falluja and Ramadi. Staff Sergeant Ryan Ostrom, a crewman on an M1A1 tank, was shot and killed by a sniper on that main road, designated Main Supply Route (MSR) Michigan. Ostrom was the son of a highly respected senior Pennsylvania National Guard NCO who had retired a few months earlier. Ryan was twenty-five, a junior in college, a chemistry major. Chaplain Doug Etter held the dying soldier in his arms and administered last rites. The battalion was protected by a marine bomb-disposal team, and in September an IED blast killed one of them, Marine Sergeant Brian Dunlop. In early November the popular and charismatic Marine Gunnery Sergeant Darrell Boatman, also a bomb-disposal tech, died of injuries sustained in a bomb blast two days earlier.

"We were taking two or three IEDs a day," Lepri told me. "Between small-arms fire and IEDs, it was waking up every day and thinking, God, please, don't let anything happen to any of my guys today." Apart from soldiers killed, the battalion's troops collected more than sixty Purple Hearts for battle wounds. Lepri held ultimate responsibility for his soldiers. When he took over from the battalion that Task Force Panther replaced, "It was like *Wow! This is my responsibility now.*" Like most combat commanders, he found he was short of manpower to do the job he was assigned. The previous unit was short of troops, and Lepri had even fewer than that. He had one hundred square miles to cover and not enough soldiers to do it. Not enough to protect local civilians. Not enough to keep his own guys safe.

As battalion commander, Lepri didn't draw up the operations plans; his lieutenants and captains did that. But he scrutinized them and approved them, and he knew which areas were the most dangerous and which soldiers were assigned to patrol down those streets and alleys. "It was difficult watching them go out the gate, difficult when the radios would light up in the tactical operations center and [the patrols] would start calling stuff in, and that was the most hair-raising thing," he said. Casualties were identified by each soldier's identification number, and the numbers would come in over the radios, and Lepri would look up to see who it was, which soldier he'd sent out who wouldn't be coming back. The battalion log recorded the grim details. November 2, Specialist Tim Brown was killed when an IED exploded beneath his Humvee on MSR Michigan. November 10, Michael C. Parrott was killed by a sniper while riding on a tank. The battalion's quick-reaction force (QRF) responded; in the subsequent melee, Sergeant Joshua Terando, twenty-seven, was shot in the mouth and killed instantly. Several weeks later, a convoy of four Humvees was returning to Camp Habbaniyah; there was an argument about the safest route to take, and the lead Humvee mistakenly swung onto a road that hadn't been cleared by the bomb-disposal guys. An IED and fireball erupted beneath the convoy's last Humvee. The turret gunner, Specialist John Dearing, was killed instantly; four others rolled out of the wreckage on fire. Chaplain Etter arrived to administer last rites and comfort the survivors. The four badly burned soldiers were medevaced to the burn unit at Brooke Army Medical Center in San Antonio and, one by one, succumbed to their wounds: Spencer Akers, Joshua Youmans,

Matthew Webber, and, finally, Duane Dreasky, who had lived on for eight months.

As the casualties mounted, Loris Lepri said, "it becomes more difficult because you don't want to be sending missions out where they're likely to have guys killed, so you—there's this balancing of what you really need to do and also how to safeguard your people." Sleep—any kind of rest, really—came hard for Lepri and other commanders. You had to be constantly on alert. "They're always seeding IEDs while you're not watching," he once said of the insurgents.

Then, suddenly, Loris Lepri was home. The battalion flew back to the United States on a Wednesday in June 2006; after paperwork, medical exams, and other chores, they were home the following Tuesday. "It was like 'Okay, here are your papers, grab your stuff and get on the bus and go home,'" he said. "I was sitting there with my duffel bag, thinking that yesterday I was a battalion commander. Now I'm just another joe on the bus."

In late 2007, a year after Loris Lepri's battalion came home, army colonel David Sutherland was finishing up a fifteen-month deployment in Iraq as commander of an army brigade task force of twelve thousand troops. It had been an extremely dangerous and difficult time, and coming home was a gut-wrenching emotional plunge. One day recently he sat over lunch to explain. "What keeps us alive on the battlefield is anger, paranoia, hypervigilance, sleeplessness," he said. "And the sleeplessness, paranoia, hypervigilance, being aggressive, doesn't just turn off when you get off a bus and walk across a parade field and link up with your family. It takes time. That's peanut sauce there for the calamari."

Chewing appreciatively, he went on. "The bonds that exist on the battlefield are unlike any bonds most people can ever imagine, bonds of trust, honesty, candor, humor. Then you come home with those who are closest to you from these horrendous and vile experiences, and those meaningful relationships are ripped apart. Ripped apart. And you no longer have that support network, and your family may not relate to what you've been through."

Once, after he'd been home for a couple of years, Sutherland and his wife, Bonnie, went to an event at a place in downtown Washington, D.C. It was small, packed wall to wall with people. "You couldn't even move," Sutherland said. "Afterward I was so high-strung, it's the first fight she and I had in probably two and a half, three years, and it was all my fault because I was aggressive. I didn't feel comfortable. Because the last time I was in a setting like that a suicide bomber detonated his vest killing twenty-four and wounding thirty-six." His reaction to that stress was powerful and real, but it wasn't PTSD and it wasn't mental illness. It was a normal and understandable, if unfortunate, reaction, a strand of the moral injury Sutherland brought back from combat.

I interrupted: "Who wouldn't have felt that way?" and Sutherland shot back, "Fuck yeah!"

For a few months after he got back home to Pennsylvania, Loris Lepri didn't talk much about the war, the killing and dying, about his inability to protect his own soldiers let alone the local Iraqi civilians who needed protection. Or about his late-night nerves as he sat in the tactical operations center and waited for patrols to call in with casualty reports. He was aloof. Finally his wife got fed up. "I think she was afraid to ask me," he said. "But she finally kind of tore me a new one, and that made me snap out of it. After that I started to open up a little."

But it wasn't until their son, Loris Lepri II, graduated from West Point and went on to serve in Afghanistan that Loris really got it, understood what the wives and families go through and how communicating and sharing really is key to reentry into normal life. Now it was the former battalion commander who worried constantly about his son in combat. In fact he was terrified that one day would come a knock on the door, and there would be Chaplain Etter in his Class As, the army's jacket-and-tie uniform, to deliver the news that his son was a battle casualty.

The role reversal—now he was the one waiting at home with a loved one at war—made him realize he'd been "kind of selfish. I realized I'd been so focused on what I was doing in Iraq that I hadn't given my wife much time. It was a stunning realization... Boy! She was really going through a lot. Now I know what it's like. I needed to be a friend and be more open."

One of Loris Lepri's young captains in Iraq was Brad Ruther. A West Point graduate, class of 1998, he'd become disillusioned with the army and eventually resigned his commission to work in commercial real estate in Ohio. Ruther was a member of the Individual Ready Reserve (IRR), those former soldiers who are unpaid and do not drill or train and are the last category to be summoned back to active duty. But one day his father called to say a letter had come from the army. Read it to me, Brad said, and after listening for a few seconds protested, "Don't be funny!" It was no joke, and he was soon on his way to Iraq with the 1st Battalion, 110th Infantry, Pennsylvania National Guard, where he commanded the battalion's quick-reaction force and the base protection force.

Those were jobs that tested him in every way. Camp Habbaniyah was often under attack by small arms or mortars or rockets, and his teams would leap to the defense in case it was a major assault. The QRF routinely went out with the bomb-disposal guys in response to IEDs and also was the emergency rescue force when troops got in trouble. For the soldiers and for Ruther himself, it was constant stress.

The death of Sergeant Joshua Terando, who served on the QRF, hit him especially hard. Like Ruther, Terando was recalled from the IRR and reported for a war tour when his country needed him. When a loader on one of the battalion's tanks was shot in the head and killed instantly, the battalion launched the QRF to find and kill the sniper. Ruther disagreed sharply with this decision, as his previous training as an infantry officer taught him that the proper tactic in reacting to a sniper was never to break contact—especially in cases like this when the location of the sniper was unknown. The soldiers at the scene should handle it, he thought. Ruther immediately called the battalion headquarters, protesting the decision to send out the QRF and asking for them to be recalled—arguing that searching for a sniper in an unknown location was a bad idea for many reasons. But his protest fell on deaf ears—his guys were already on their way, Terando among them. Ruther deployed with the second QRF platoon and sped to the area of contact. By the time he got there, Terando, who had climbed into the building they called the Old Potato Factory to hunt down the sniper, was shot in the mouth.

That evening at Camp Habbaniyah, Ruther sat down and wrote a letter to Terando's dad. This wasn't something that had been taught at West Point. Ruther did the best he could, praising Terando as a model soldier and leader. But he included his personal e-mail address, and Terando's dad, a retired soldier, wrote back to demand details about how his son had died. "I sent him a lot of stuff that was probably classified," Ruther told me. "But I didn't care. The guy lost his son!" When the battalion returned from Iraq, Ruther called the Terando family and even attended a Terando-family wedding in Chicago—a relationship he nurtured as much for his sake as for theirs. "I had a lot of guilt for a long time," he told me. If he had argued harder against sending out the QRF, he felt, Terando might still be alive. He wondered over and over, Did I screw up?

Ruther had been back from Iraq two years or so when he began jerking awake when his watch alarm mysteriously went off every night around the same time. It was the watch he'd used in

Iraq, but he hadn't set the alarm. "Finally I was like *When did Josh get killed?* And holy shit! Even with the time difference, my watch was going off within fifteen minutes of when Joshua got killed." When he told his wife, she suggested he call and check in with Terando's dad. The next day Ruther called, and they talked. After that the alarm stopped going off.

"But there are some things that just don't go away," Ruther told me. Guilt and sorrow cut deep. And while we might often tell Brad Ruther that he shouldn't feel guilty, that he did nothing wrong, and that death in war is inevitable, his sorrow and guilt are a lasting moral injury.

"My hardest month is November because there are anniversary dates in there," he said. "I tend to be more isolated, I won't really want to work, I tend to drink more, and the demons come back and I'm always in my dreams fighting. Why the fuck am I dealing with this shit ten years later? I have dreams now that I haven't had in a long time, with all this stuff about ISIS."

Even though he hasn't been diagnosed with PTSD, Ruther has done a twelve-week outpatient PTSD program at the VA and found it helped him think more rationally about the war. "I wish I'd gone earlier," he said. "I'd encourage anyone to go get counseling for this stuff."

He still goes to the VA for therapy. "What we did out there was just not normal," he said. "I don't think it will ever get better. You've just got to live with it.

"The good thing is, pretty much everybody I know has issues. The guys that don't have issues are the scary ones."

CHAPTER 14

The Touchy-Feely Tough Guys

It was a rite of passage. It was not a cure. It allowed me to be just a little bit happier. It probably saved my life. But it's not a fairy-tale ending.

— Marine Staff Sergeant, two combat tours,
former patient at the moral injury group,
Naval Medical Center San Diego

The wars in Iraq and Afghanistan had been under way for some time before the mental health community was able to begin grappling seriously with the puzzle of moral injury that was plaguing new veterans like Brad Ruther and Darren Doss. But by 2005 the foundations were being laid for understanding moral injury, for separating it from PTSD. Bill Nash had returned from his tour in Iraq determined to find a better way to deal with combat stress. At the Boston VA Medical Center, Brett Litz was continuing a decade of work, trying to define the varieties of trauma that troops experienced in war and to gain insights into the mechanisms and treatment of these psychological injuries. Eventually they would collaborate on a new kind of therapy designed specifically for moral injury.

At the marine base at Camp Pendleton, meantime, an innovative form of treatment for moral injury was being pioneered by someone who was neither a psychiatrist nor a psychologist.

It was a kid who grew up in a blue-collar family outside Boston, the third of four children of Anna and Carmelo Castellana, a hardworking, hard-drinking World War II veteran. The future therapist was his son Michael, who had been relentlessly bullied in their working-class neighborhood for being smart and sensitive and gay, who had lived through deeply troubling trauma as a young man, who'd discovered that teaching teenagers and gays and lesbians to express themselves through drama could help them deal with their own personal difficulties, and who eventually, after doctoral-level training in psychotherapy, was hired as a therapist for the combat-hardened marines at Camp Pendleton.

Michael Castellana arrived there in 2005, determined to do something to ease the pain and anger of marines returning from combat. A woman staffer at Pendleton heard that Michael was coming. She thought, A gay man? They'll eat him alive! Then she met Michael and thought, He's perfect. Castellana had an intuitive grasp of what marines were feeling and knew from his treatment of other traumatized people how to draw them out and help them. He won the trust of the marines and within a year had written a manual for the treatment of what the Marine Corps called combat stress. In truth, it was a treatment for what would later be recognized as moral injury. After a couple of years working as a therapist at Pendleton, Castellana one day opened his office door to a marine he didn't know. You know I've heard about you, the marine said. People are talking. Castellana said, Yeah? Oh yeah, the marine said. Are you ready for this? They call you the touchy-feely tough guy. You're tough as nails, but you, like, love people. Castellana said, I'm good with that.

Castellana, in his late fifties, has wide penetrating eyes, a neat salt-and-pepper beard, and an open manner that invites easy and thoughtful conversation. He and I were talking over breakfast at an outdoor café in San Diego, enjoying the spring flowers blossoming in the cool early morning air. When he first got to Pendleton, Michael said, he didn't find it easygoing. Marines did come see him and would want to talk in individual therapy sessions, but like Nik Rudolph at Camp Lejeune, many were reluctant to join the group sessions that Michael thought were more effective. Eventually he would persuade them to take part, and once they got used to being in group, they couldn't stop talking. Some of what they had to say, the experiences they wanted to get off their chests, was jolting. "I used to tell my marines, I don't scare easily. Which is a crock of shit, of course, but I would let them tell me anything," Castellana told me. "I've heard the most heinous things that humans can do to other human beings. Stuff to make your toes curl. But in my capacity to love them and to see that, in an effort to do what is right, they sometimes do something so wrong—their goodness seems to be intact and I seem to be able to connect with that. If they were in my office, if they were talking to me, then they were capable of redemption." As the waitress hovered, he broke off. "Two eggs over easy, please." Over light, she corrected. "Right," he said gently. "You turn them over and take them out of the pan."

One key insight that struck Castellana was that the seeds of forgiveness would come not from him or any other outsider. They could only come from a marine's peers. On that he diverged sharply from Chaplain Etter's insistence on the primary role of a spiritual leader. But Castellana built the central role of peers into his model for twelve sessions of moral injury repair. Forgiveness was a critical piece of the therapy, he knew, but a lot of work would have to come first. Combat veterans who feel they have done or seen something awful are often afraid of being shamed or rejected by their peers. Worse, that they'd be made fun of. Those fears would have to be overcome, Michael saw. The opportunity for forgiveness, from the group and from the individual, would come late in the twelve sessions when a marine would feel safe and comfortable and could find the courage to speak of his trauma, to relate something awful he or she had seen or done, and the marine's peers in the room would be ready to accept that without judgment.

I nodded as Michael was describing this moment. Somewhere I had heard the phrase "listening with validation." I understood that to mean what I've often tried to do as a reporter: listening without judgment but accepting the weight of the person's story. Listening to Nik Rudolph, for instance, talking about killing the child, I was tempted to say, *Oh, don't worry about it, you couldn't help it, it was war, he was shooting at you.* All true, of course. But as Nik was struggling toward forgiving himself, not a helpful response. He'd already rejected those flimsy excuses. Killing a child was just wrong; no way around that. As Bill Nash would say, no way to unring that bell. To validate Nik's experience, to recognize it as something hard and real, the best approach was a phrase I'd adopted from the marines: *Yeah, that was fucked up.* Notice that it doesn't affix blame. It doesn't excuse, either. It makes room for other factors *(The kid you shot is partly to blame; he was shooting at you!)*. It allows for acceptance and forgiveness.

In Castellana's group, one staff sergeant kept warning that he had something, that it was coming, that he wanted to tell the story, and Castellana kept saying, Not now, not now, the time will come, and finally around the sixth session the time came and the staff sergeant talked about how he had tortured prisoners. It was bad. *It was fucked up.* He spoke with his head bowed, eyes to the ground. The group sat in silence. When the staff sergeant was finished, Castellana said to him, "You were so concerned about what people would think. Why don't you take a moment and look into the eyes of all the other group members?" And he did that. "He was really trying," Michael said. "A father of three. And I asked him, 'What do you see?' And he said, 'Well, I didn't see anyone look at me differently.' He said, 'I think I'm not the only one here with a story like this.' Imagine the weight lifted off his shoulders.

"I'm getting shivers just telling you this," Castellana said to me as our eggs arrived. His were over light.

Around the time that Castellana was engaging with marines at Camp Pendleton, Brett Litz, who is an energetic man with a close-cropped gray beard, a gravity-defying tangle of red hair, and a perpetual look of doubting skepticism, was bringing the cold eye of science to what had long been the muddled business of treating war trauma. From the outside, Litz seems an unlikely pioneer in wartime trauma. He didn't grow up in a military family or even near a military community. He came of age in the 1970s in Sea Cliff, New York, a prosperous and picturesque village on Long Island Sound. He was drawn into the academic world at North Shore High School, working (and getting high) with teachers who encouraged rigorous intellectual discussions on a first-name basis. Excited by this kind of academic probing, Litz enrolled at nearby Stony Brook University, which happened to be a hotbed of an emerging form of psychotherapy called behavioral therapy.

Behavioral therapy was a sharp change from the Freudian idea that mental illness sprang from unresolved childhood trauma. It was Freud's theory that lay behind the conviction held by many psychologists in World War I that anyone suffering from "shell shock" simply had unresolved childhood issues, and the soldier could be treated briefly and sent back into battle. That approach continued into the 1960s and 1970s, when psychologists began working around the theory that abnormal behavior wasn't a left-over childhood problem after all. It was learned and could be unlearned, through a variety of different therapeutic models. Cognitive behavioral therapy and a variant, cognitive processing therapy (CPT), had the therapist and patient working together to articulate, understand, and challenge distorted and destructive thoughts *(Something bad happened to me, therefore I must be a bad person)* and to replace them with more positive self-concepts. Behavioral therapy was exciting because it promised a more immediate and practical problem-solving approach to mental distress. But what caught Litz's skeptical eye were the dozens of scientific clinical trials that seemed to prove behavioral therapies to be effective.

Litz waded into this work with zeal. He trained as a psychologist in exposure therapy, a form of behavioral therapy in which patients are asked to repeat in detail their most traumatic experience. Unlike critical incident stress debriefing, which relies on one immediate session to share stories, exposure therapy centers on reexperiencing the trauma over and over to the point where it will lose its power, and the anxiety or dread produced by the experience will fade and become extinguished. The problem, Litz soon realized, was that when people were asked to recount a troubling or shameful episode, most of them shaded the truth. It was the same thing Castellana was encountering in his sessions with marines: when they were given an opportunity to talk about what was troubling them, they'd often pick something minor at first; the hard, black stuff would come out later when they'd had a chance to try out a story in group, and it didn't blow up on them. For most people, "It's what they are willing or able to tell you," Litz said. "You have to do some detective work, and you can't assume that what you're being told is all there is to the story. Shame," he said, "often gets in the way."

That got him interested in a phenomenon called emotional numbing or social detachment, now considered a symptom of PTSD and moral injury, a way to bury unpleasant or traumatic emotions by simply avoiding contact with others. "It was very poorly defined. What the hell was it—depression, or something else?" Litz wondered. "I spent two or three years putting a scientific lens on it." By that time, in 1987, he was working at the VA medical center in Boston, engaging with patients. But his real love was the research: figuring out and demonstrating not just what works but why. He found the VA "a great culture for innovation, a lot of creativity."

So nobody objected when in the early 1990s he got interested in the mental health problems experienced by U.S. troops returning from peacekeeping operations in Somalia. He led a team that examined thirty-five hundred recently returned soldiers for signs of PTSD, which at the time was considered the overall explanation for every kind of war trauma. War trauma was thought to be caused solely by fear. Fear dysregulation, psychologists called it. They understood that military personnel exposed to peril often developed acute anxiety, insomnia or nightmares, a startle reflex, all of it caused by fear. You went into harm's way, had a terrifying experience; you got PTSD. The VA knew how to diagnose PTSD and treat it. Litz wanted to know more ("What the hell *was* it?"), and in the course of the research project he found something that would drive decades of his work on moral injury: the rate of diagnosed PTSD among troops who'd served in Somalia was "small but significant." That amount of trauma was understandable, given that the soldiers and marines sent to Somalia had been plunged into the midst of a bloody civil war in which Islamist extremist fighters, the forerunners of al-Qaeda and ISIS, were making their first murderous appearances. Litz and his colleagues found that about 8 percent of the U.S. troops had symptoms of PTSD.

But why? Fear alone couldn't explain it. This had been a peacekeeping mission, and the rate of PTSD was below the contemporary estimates for Vietnam combat veterans (10 percent) and Gulf War veterans (14 percent).

The more Litz thought about it, the more he felt the explanation of PTSD and the therapies designed for it were too thin. Here was a puzzle: if PTSD was fear based as the psychiatry profession declared, if war trauma was caused by one's reaction to a terrifying incident, why was it so prevalent among well-trained American troops engaged in a peacekeeping operation? After all, the military had done its best to inoculate its troops against fear. Service members were preselected for physical and mental acuity: low grades on physical fitness and intelligence tests disqualified many applicants from enlisting. Those who were accepted were relentlessly trained in grueling combat exercises and supported by close intimates who served together over time in small units. That was thanks to a deliberate shift in military personnel policy made in the early 1980s that bolstered unit cohesion by abandoning the Vietnam-era practice of moving soldiers around individually among units instead of keeping them together for years. The peer support that developed, together with the military's effective small-unit leadership, ought to be enough to enable soldiers to recover from dangerous experiences, Litz thought. Then why were the peacekeepers showing up with symptoms of trauma?

In an eerily accurate preview of the wars in Iraq and Afghanistan, in findings published in 1996 he concluded that American troops in Somalia were disoriented and troubled by "ambiguous, inconsistent or unacceptable rules of engagement (ROE); lack of clarity about the goals of the mission itself; a civilian population of combatants; and inherently contradictory experiences of the mission as both humanitarian and dangerous." Somalia, he wrote, seemed to be "the prototype of a new paradigm in military operations," one that "may represent a unique class of potentially traumatizing experiences not sufficiently captured by traditional descriptors of war zone exposure." In other words, the troops were reacting emotionally to morally difficult circumstances; their PTSD symptoms weren't entirely driven by fear. And those circumstances, Litz felt certain, would appear again and again.

Something else began to bug Litz. The treatment offered by the VA for war trauma had come out of the civilian world, and specifically from therapies designed for people who had suffered a onetime trauma or victimization, such as rape. Tested exhaustively in clinical trials, these were known as evidence-based approaches: cognitive behavioral therapies, which Litz had mastered at Stony Brook, were effective in extinguishing the lingering fear in cases of rape, motorcycle accidents, and similar traumas. The label "evidence based" was a kind of marketing seal of approval, like the TV-ad phrase "laboratory tested!" So why were those same therapies less effective in clinical trials with veterans diagnosed with PTSD?

What Litz was learning from the veterans he was seeing at the Boston VA pointed toward part of the answer: the therapies weren't wrong; the diagnoses were incorrect. Their distress wasn't caused only by fear stemming from a life-threatening incident but also from emotionally and morally disturbing incidents in war. Often, Litz found, it was remorse, shame, and guilt from feeling they had failed in some way to act heroically in the face of peril.

Evidence-based therapies using cognitive behavioral techniques, Litz would later write, "do not sufficiently explain, predict, or address the needs of many service members and veterans who are exposed to diverse psychic injuries." He could see the need for a new military-specific form of therapy that would take into account the unique culture and ethos of the military and the unique moral stressors that arise when men and women are sent into the kinds of frustrating, ambiguous conflicts he'd studied in the Somalia peacekeeping operation. Something that would enable combat veterans to voice their deepest concerns and to receive forgiveness.

★ ★ ★

While Brett Litz was puzzling over this, one of his young colleagues, Shira Maguen, was looking for clues in a slightly different direction, linking the moral injury Litz was documenting directly to killing. She found that her PTSD patients frequently mentioned killing as a cause of their distress, killing they had done in combat. Maguen was intrigued but hardly surprised. She had been born in Israel and was familiar with war. Both her parents served in the Israeli Defense Forces; her father had fought in the Yom Kippur War. After college in the United States, she worked with Litz at the Boston VA for four years, using CPT and similar therapies that sought to extinguish fear-based trauma. "But what I was seeing," she told me, "was not so much of the fear-based response but struggles that were related to what they did and what we now think of as moral injury. Crossing certain boundaries, what they defined for themselves as their own moral values." These were issues, she said, "not traditionally captured by treatments of evidence-based therapies."

What was needed, she determined, was an additional specialized therapy that would address the shame, guilt, and feeling of self-contamination that she was seeing in her patients. "If someone is carrying around all those cognitions," she said, "they can't lead a successful life."

Across the country, Michael Castellana had come to the same conclusion, that a new model of therapy for war trauma was needed. Michael wasn't a Ph.D. psychologist. He did not have a medical degree in psychiatry. He had put himself through Brandeis University and earned a master's degree in social work at Boston University. He was the first person in his family to go to college and wasn't able to finally pay off his student loans until he was forty-four years old. He had done doctoral-level training in clinical and pastoral psychotherapy, but his deft touch in working with cases of trauma was intuitive and experiential. What connected him across the worlds of academic, scientific psychology and the gritty reality of people in trauma was his intense personal empathy. It's as if he can see into your soul and understand it.

Over breakfast, he told me that he'd been working in private practice in San Diego when the terrorists struck on 9/11 and the United States lurched into war in Afghanistan and then Iraq. Michael thought, If this doesn't end quickly, I know what's going to happen. It didn't end quickly. He got in touch with everyone he knew in the military, asking how he could get involved and eventually came across a job opening at Camp Pendleton for a trauma therapist. He was anxious, late for the interview, but he got the job.

I stopped him right there. You're a gay guy with no military experience—and it will be years before gays can serve openly. What made you think you could just walk in there and deal with marines' trauma?

He grinned. Approaching Pendleton, "I was really kind of over-whelmed," he admitted. "But I knew trauma." He meant that in a personal way. It turned out to be a long story that unfolded as we dawdled over the remains of our breakfast, and it took us back to Watertown, Massachusetts, where Michael's father, Carmelo, had a barbershop and his mother, Anna, who loved opera and sang in clubs when she was younger, worked in a car-parts factory and sang when she got home at night. In 1951 Anna discovered a tumor in her neck, and doctors cut it out, but the operation left one of her vocal cords paralyzed. She could never sing again. But she kept as happy a home for her four kids as she could, what with money worries and long hours at the factory and Carmelo's heavy drinking.

After Michael was out of college and working as a therapist, she got sick again, and Michael, then twenty-four, moved home to take care of her, living in the basement. They were close, really close. When he had gotten a job in California, they had driven together across the country. She used to tell him, smiling, Michael, you have good taste in men. "She was a wonderful person," Michael told me. "Wonderful."

One night he heard his mother cough in the upstairs bathroom. "It was like someone stuck a knife in my chest. I could feel this presence. Like, my mother needs me. I threw my toothbrush down and ran upstairs, and my father was standing there dazed, white as a ghost, in the kitchen trying to buckle his pants, and he said, 'We have to get to the hospital now!' I ran into the bathroom where my mother was." He paused. "It was like someone had slaughtered a pig. She had a carotid blowout," a rupture of the main artery in her neck, which carries blood from the heart to the brain. She was dying.

Michael bowed his head as he remembered the scene. Birds chirped from a nearby bush, and the waitress collected our plates. It was a few moments before he could go on.

The cops arrived at the Castellana house, carrying a useless little first-aid kit. Michael is holding his mother in his arms, blood all over, pleading with the cops, "Just get us to the hospital," and outside there is no ambulance, only the squad car, so they all cram inside. Carmelo, still somewhat drunk, trying to get the driver in a choke hold, demanding they be taken to Mass General. "But we're racing to Waltham Hospital, it's closer, and my mother is kind of kicking my father and I'm trying to push him down and we're barreling up Main Street and it's like two a.m. and raining."

And from a side street, a girl in a station wagon jumps a red light. She sees the police cruiser bearing down on her and freezes. A second later, the collision. "We T-bone her, I think that is the right word. Push her car sixty feet up the road. I watch this in slow motion. It's the first and only time I have had an out-of-body experience, because I'm standing holding my mother in the rain and there is blood all over me and I see it from up above and behind and I see the flashing light of the gumball machine from the police cruiser that's knocked off into the street…and this ruffian-looking kid in a leather jacket drives by and says 'Man! You need some help?' Hah! And I say, 'Can you get us to the hospital?' And the next day the cops said to me, 'How did you open the car door? Everything was crushed.' And I said, 'I don't know, I just…had to do it.' " Anna had broken her back in the crash. She lived on for a while. But the story wasn't quite done. "When we got to the hospital I got her to the emergency ward and she looked up at me and she said, 'How did you know I called you? I never said a word!' " In the telling now, at breakfast in sunny San Diego, Michael's eyes filled, and he bent his head and whispered, "I heard you, Mama."

Michael Castellana knew trauma.

At Pendleton, Michael worked for a year getting more and more frustrated with the existing treatment models, and in 2006 he was asked to join the Deployment Health Center and given free rein to work with marines returning from combat. It was exhilarating; he felt as if he'd been preparing all his life for this. One weekend he sat down and wrote a detailed curriculum for a brief six-week twelve-session group treatment model, designed to help marines relax in a safe environment and begin to understand their trauma, to learn some coping strategies, and, through the kind of exposure therapy that Brett Litz was studying in Boston, to begin sharing their trauma memories in a validating group. One session was devoted to a discussion about aggression; what happens when marines kill; the "addictive qualities of adrenaline surges"; and how different life is at home, given their experience with the weapons and authorized force and aggression they enjoyed in combat. And, finally, the concept of redemption. In his introduction, Michael wrote a caution to therapists who would follow his model:

The experts in the room are the ones who are there to do the talking, the sharing. We, the therapists, must listen. We are there to insure that the boundaries are kept clear and honored at all costs. We can help the group members to moderate their pain, monitor their progress, and to pace their journey so that they do not falter and lose face. Preserving their integrity is critical. These are remarkable, courageous men and women. We should laugh with them, grieve with them, and, most of all, empathize and inject a human perspective on the terrible experiences these service members have endured. We must bear with them, the distressing and challenging events they have lived through, and accompany them as they make their way to a new, fuller understanding and appreciation of their role in war and as fellow human beings in the world.

It was a sharp break from past therapies: healing would come not from the work done by patient and therapist but would come, in a setting created and monitored by the therapist, through forgiveness from one's peers.

Whenever Michael had a new marine coming in for therapy, he had a ritual. He'd hand the marine two of his business cards. "One card is for you. Put it in your wallet, and if you need to cancel, call me. The other one, put in your pocket because I know damn well you know someone else that needs to be here," Michael said. "People would come and say to me, 'My buddy gave me your card.' I've had people come back and ask for more cards; they'd given all theirs away. And so I built a practice on my credibility. Marines are tribal," Michael told me. "And if you fuck up, it's over. Because word spreads. But conversely when you help someone, it lasts a lifetime."

Michael also had learned techniques to help morally injured

marines understand that they alone don't have to bear all the responsibility for what happened. One method I found easy to understand can be done in individual counseling. As Michael explained it, he would have the patient list and assign a percentage of responsibility to every person or factor that played a role in the injuring incident—say, if a marine had killed a child. The marine might assign himself 20 percent. The kid shooting at him, 15 percent. The Taliban who armed the kid and told him to shoot, 20 percent. God, maybe 30 percent. And so on. The idea is to help the patient see, even while acknowledging his own role, that he doesn't have to bear 100 percent of the responsibility. Life can go on.

One day a marine sergeant came to see Castellana. He admitted he didn't want to come, but his buddy, a guy Michael had treated, had insisted. This sergeant was a tough guy. Hard. His marriage was falling apart. He was angry, punching holes in the walls. When he got into the office, Michael said, Take off your blouse. The sergeant blinked, but he stood up and stripped off his uniform shirt and sat back down in his olive-green T-shirt. And they went at it. It took five individual therapy sessions. The sergeant was a squad leader, and the squad had been under attack by insurgents, including two kids, eleven and fourteen, and one of the kids shot at the marine squad, and the sergeant returned fire and killed them both. It was what the military considers a "good kill." Back home, the sergeant had an eleven-year-old brother, like the boy he'd killed. His guilt was enormous. "He couldn't look at his father," Michael said.

In telling the story, Michael had to raise his voice over the raucous laughter of a trio of college women at the next table. "That was one of his chief complaints when he came in. Didn't want his father to see him. So in the course of my treatment of him he was able not only to confess his 'sin,' and have me still love him, but to hear, as he grieved, how sad he was that the [Iraqi] adults in that situation had made the weapons available to those kids or poisoned them in some way and put them in this untenable situation and that as a marine his job was to ensure the safety of his marines, and he did that. But the cost was a personal one, and he couldn't face his father because in a sense he felt like he had just slaughtered his baby brother." Michael helped the sergeant understand that his pulling the trigger was only a small part in the tragedy; that those who armed the kids were also culpable, that those who set up the ambush were at fault as well. That it was a bad thing that had happened, but the sergeant needn't shoulder all the blame and guilt; he could forgive himself. All this took time.

"Well, that man had one of the most remarkable turnarounds. He went home and he hugged his father and he told his father what had happened and he cried and his father cried and said, 'Oh thank God I have my son back!' Is that not the most beautiful story in the world? That he was able to see that there was no right answer? And that no matter what decision he made, it would have consequences. But his heart was pure, and if I saw him today I would love him just as much...A remarkable man."

When word began to circulate about Michael's trauma model, he was asked to travel around the Marine Corps to talk to groups of marines about trauma and moral injury and to brief other therapists. Soon his model was widely in use. One day at Pendleton, Michael's phone rang. As Michael later remembered it, a voice demanded, "Who the hell *are* you? I read your model. How do you know all this?" Before Michael could answer, the caller said, "Would you be willing to train people across the country on this? Oh yeah — this is Bill Nash."

Nash, the navy captain and combat psychologist, was working on a new concept with Brett Litz. The idea was to modify the previous generations of exposure therapy and cognitive behavioral therapy and construct a new model specifically designed for moral injury in active-duty service members. The demands of the war meant they didn't have much time to work with individuals. The marines and soldiers who needed help needed it fast because they all were on schedule to deploy again. And anyway, Litz and Nash knew that the goal of actually healing a moral injury was unrealistic; what they were aiming for instead was equipping morally injured service members with the knowledge and skills for a lifetime of posttraumatic growth.

Working together, and aided by a half-dozen psychologists who had studied under Litz, they came up with a new definition of "moral injury":

> The lasting psychological, biological, spiritual, and social impact of perpetrating, failing to prevent, or bearing witness to acts that transgress deeply held moral beliefs and expectations.

One key insight underlay their new approach. Cognitive behavioral therapy and cognitive processing therapy sought to help the patient correct distorted thoughts and beliefs. Litz and Nash knew that the thoughts and beliefs held by combat soldiers and marines about their transgressions might be painful but weren't necessarily distorted. Nik Rudolph knew he had killed a child. What needed attention was not distorted beliefs about the act of transgression but the shame, guilt, and anger of having violated your own moral code, one you share with your peers and family. Michael Castellana's sergeant couldn't face his father because he felt he had betrayed his father's moral values and his own. But Litz and Nash understood, as did Castellana, that if service members felt guilt or shame or sorrow or anger, it meant they possessed an intact set of moral values. And they could be listened to and understood and forgiven and eventually healed within a safe and loving community.

For morally injured combat veterans who are earnestly seeking care, they wrote in a 2009 article sketching out their ideas, "forgiveness and repair is possible in all cases." It would require sharing the traumatic experience with a group of peers, the method Castellana was implementing at Pendleton, then guiding the patient toward self-forgiveness and moving forward. The model Litz and Nash had in mind was intended not to complete a healing process but to enable patients to get clear about the event that caused their moral injury and to get the skills and resources they would need for a lifelong process of forgiveness and hopefulness. They called this approach adaptive disclosure.

"In my community there's been this kind of assumption of the equipotentiality of trauma," Litz told me. He meant treating all trauma as the same thing. "Motor accident survivors, one therapy works for them, so let's apply that to service members and veterans. And of course if you just spend time being curious and learn what wars mean for combatants, you can't help but wonder, What are we missing?" Coming up with something new was the obvious next step. "For me," Litz said, "it was a fucking no-brainer."

As part of their work, Nash developed a moral injury events scale to screen veterans for moral injury and to measure the extent and intensity of the wound. It asks for "never," "seldom," "sometimes," or "often" responses to statements such as:

—I saw things that were morally wrong.
—I am troubled by having witnessed others' immoral acts.
—I acted in ways that violated my own moral code or values.
—I am troubled by having acted in ways that violated my own morals or values.
—I feel betrayed by leaders I once trusted.
—I am troubled because I violated my morals by failing to do something I should have done.

As in Michael Castellana's therapeutic model, the Litz–Nash adaptive disclosure approach first establishes a warm, supportive environment in which a marine who is expecting to be condemned for his or her transgression finds instead acceptance and support. Subsequent sessions reflect the idea of behavior extinction, with the therapist encouraging the marine to relate his transgression over and over until it loses its potency. It is helpful to have the patient close his or her eyes during this session, Litz and Nash note. But the goal is to create "a raw and emotional reliving and recounting" to break through whatever avoidance strategies the marine has put in place.

The retelling is repeated often, not to force an extinction of the painful memory but to begin to break down the expectation of shame and rejection. Eventually the therapist introduces the patient to positive "corrective" judgments about himself, and that is followed by sessions in which the patient is asked to imagine himself as a benevolent figure—a priest or senior officer—giving advice and support to a morally injured service member. This encourages the patient to articulate ideas about the capacity to do good, to engage in service, and to accept forgiveness from self and from peers. Finally, the patient begins to "make amends" with actual community service, not to try to offer reparations for past behavior but to reconnect with his positive values.

Further sessions teach the patient to carefully seek out positive and healing relationships beyond the therapy room. "Because many people do not know what to say about such things [the "toe-curling" stories Castellana has heard] and their reactions may be difficult to predict or interpret, guidance will be needed," Litz and Nash warn. The therapy ends with extended conversations with the therapist about the lessons the patient can take on into life. Combat veterans with serious trauma and moral injury should be warned that "there will be challenging times ahead."

In 2009 a group of psychologists working under the direction of Litz and Nash tested out the ideas of adaptive disclosure in six sessions with groups of marines and navy corpsmen recently returned from war and given the umbrella diagnosis of PTSD (the military has no diagnosis of moral injury, then or now). Among the researchers was Amy Amidon, a navy psychologist now working at the Naval Medical Center San Diego. The results were encouraging: the marines reported sharp reductions in the symptoms of moral injury: depression and negative views of themselves.

"We're in a period of discovery," Brett Litz told me on the phone one day. We were talking about next steps, and he was excited—"stunned" was the word he used—that the Defense Department was looking to award research money for work on moral injury repair. Litz had written a long and dense project proposal for a randomized controlled trial of adaptive disclosure for moral injury, one that would extend the therapy from six to twelve sessions.

Their proposed treatment would include a block of therapy specifically related to the moral injury of killing, based on the work that Shira Maguen was doing with her patients in San Francisco, in a program of six to eight sessions she calls "impact of killing" therapy. She explores with patients the emotional and physiological impacts of killing, then deals directly with self-forgiveness. Many veterans are resistant, believing that to forgive is dishonorable, dismissing a wrong they had committed. Eventually they are asked to write a letter to the person they killed, or to their younger self, explaining what they now understand about killing that they did not at an earlier time. "Part of self-forgiveness is understanding the context in which this happened, usually a situation where you are constantly making life-and-death decisions quickly without having all the information," she said.

In 2012, Amy Amidon and Michael Castellana began piecing together all these various strands: the early work Castellana had done, the understanding of PTSD as distinct from the emotions of loss, guilt, and shame that are moral injury, and the new techniques of adaptive disclosure. They started working with patients who had been admitted to a PTSD treatment program at the San Diego Naval Hospital. In a ten-week program they called the Moral Injury and Moral Repair Group, patients learned to talk through their experiences with the group; they were directed to write a letter to themselves asking for forgiveness and were assigned to work in community service projects as a way of rediscovering their altruistic values.

"The healing mechanism of adaptive disclosure is owning your story — 'I've done some bad things' — and having people hear that and accept you," Amidon told me one sunny afternoon as we talked in a courtyard of the hospital. "In the first week we introduce the idea of moral repair, the idea of doing things that in your heart you know are good and kind and bring you closer to the person you want to be."

Disillusionment with the war is a major emotion that marines bring into the sessions: Why did we sacrifice so much, seeing buddies getting hurt and killed? Why did we do so much killing, only to see now that things in Iraq and Afghanistan are actually much worse? "Helping them make their own story to accommodate that — the idea that 'Why am I doing this? What is the point if the world is an evil place?' When you have to do something horrible, the difficulty is making any meaning out of it," Amidon said. "Faith comes up in every session. 'Why did God let this happen?'" She and her small staff do what they can in ten weeks, but it's discouraging, she allowed. "I know the military has to create aggressive, antisocial, callous people, and the younger ones have this attitude that they're going on one deployment and will come back the same person that left — but they won't. Should we harden them?" she asked, repeating a question I had asked. "No, we should not! But we should be doing a better job of mentally preparing them for things like kids shooting at them and the woman with the bomb under her burka. That's something the military misses in preparing them for war: 'Why am I doing this?'"

The San Diego program is the only government initiative I could find that specifically addresses moral injury. There is nothing like it in all of the Defense Department's medical facilities or at the VA, beyond the kinds of research that Shira Maguen and a few others are doing and some individual VA therapists who provide moral injury therapy. In fact, the world of those working with war-related moral injury is exceedingly small. Many of the published research on moral injury, for instance, lists the same people: Bill Nash and Brett Litz; Amy Amidon; Matt Gray of the University of Wyoming; NYU clinical psychologist Maria Steenkamp; Matthew Friedman of the VA's National Center for PTSD; Richard Westphal, a former navy psychiatric nurse; and a few others. "It's only us," Litz told me. It's a small world."

In December 2014, the Department of Veterans Affairs signed a $16 million contract with IBM to install software at the VA's data center in Austin, Texas, that the VA said would assist its doctors and therapists confused about how to treat patients diagnosed with PTSD. VA staff can plug in clinical data and electronic medical records, and the computer will spit out the appropriate treatment plan.

Despite this step toward the mechanization of war trauma therapy, I was impressed that even the small group of researchers was doing such innovative work on healing strategies for moral injury and mildly pleased that the VA and even the Pentagon were willing to fund research and clinical trials of the most promising approaches.

Still, I couldn't help noticing an almost-complete disconnect between the enthusiasm of researchers like Brett Litz and Bill

Nash and the many soldiers and marines I have talked to who came back after their combat tours and got no help whatsoever. One who did get help was Darren Doss, the marine from Charlie One-Six. In the spring of 2015, several months before I took him to lunch in Schenectady, Doss was arrested after a traffic altercation; in court he was offered a choice: jail or the VA's PTSD clinic. He chose the latter. "I know a ton of dudes who should be here," he told me at the time. "The reason they aren't is—pride."

I related this to Bill Nash one day, saying that it seemed to me that, despite all the research being done, not much of it was reaching the people who needed it the most. And something else that had been nagging at me: some people I knew, like Nik Rudolph and Stephen Canty and Stacy Pearsall, came back from war with deep moral injuries, and they seemed to be doing okay, perhaps healing slowly and perhaps just stuffing all that pain deep down inside. Canty said once that he tries to "distance" himself from the war. "I meditate, do yoga, to try to find peace with what happened in the war and who I am as a human being. I try not to be defined by that four-year period in my life and the fifteen months I spent in Afghanistan," he said. "I can't let that guilt consume me."

It occurred to me, though, that even guys like Canty who seem to be doing okay would benefit from the best healing techniques that the mental health professions have learned about moral injury since 2001. But there appeared to be no connection between therapists and veterans to enable that to happen.

Nash sighed deeply. "It's more than that, it's something else," he said. "We don't have good treatments. We simply don't."

We'd met on a summer Sunday at an Asian restaurant in McLean, Virginia, and were waiting for his Mongolian beef and fried rice. Nash had just read a disturbing paper by Brett Litz and his colleague Maria Steenkamp. They had studied thirty-six major clinical trials of therapy for PTSD among active-duty troops and veterans, conducted between 1980 and 2015. They concluded that the most widely used therapies for PTSD—cognitive processing therapy and prolonged exposure (PE)—were only marginally effective. Their paper, published in the *Journal of the American Medical Association (JAMA)* in the summer of 2015, reported that "between one-third and one-half of patients receiving CPT or prolonged exposure did not demonstrate clinically meaningful symptom change." Two-thirds of those receiving therapy still had symptoms of PTSD afterward. Contrary to earlier assurances of its effectiveness, prolonged exposure therapy tested in one large clinical trial "did not lead to meaningful PTSD symptom reduction," they reported. In other cases, alternative therapies such as acupuncture or "healing touch," which involves tapping specific points on the body while being guided through positive imagery, were just as effective.

I found this outrageous: the only therapies widely available from the United States government for combat veterans were ineffective. We sent people into war, and when they came home with moral injury, either they were ignored, or they were diagnosed with PTSD and given therapy that didn't help. How could this happen?

The VA had officially endorsed both CPT and PE for treatment of PTSD back in 2008, based largely on studies of traumatized civilians, suggesting these therapies were effective. But they weren't. Why? Perhaps, Litz and Steenkamp wrote, because war trauma is fundamentally unlike civilian trauma. Among those differences, they noted, were "the extended, repeated and intense nature of deployment trauma, and the fact that service members are exposed not only to life threats but to traumatic losses and morally compromising experiences that may require different treatment approaches." They also noted that veterans dropped out of the therapy sessions at a higher rate than civilians.

Bill Nash also found all this eye-opening. "So with no treatment at all, some people are going to get better; some will stay the same; some will get worse," he concluded. Those who got therapy fared about the same.

Nash paused to tuck hungrily into his beef, then went on. "What I look at to make sense of all this is, for those who get better, what is the effect size of the treatment? How much better do they get?" Effect size, he explained, is measured statistically by how far the results of a clinical trial deviate from the expected outcome, expressed as a standard deviation. The mean result might be, for instance, a control group that got no therapy, and a good result would be to achieve several standard deviations beyond that mean. "So an effect size of 1.0 means you have lowered the mean by exactly one standard deviation," Nash said. "So 1.0 is really a small change. In the rest of medicine that would be considered failure. In the rest of medicine, you would not spend money on blood pressure medicine if in a population it lowered blood pressure by 1.0 standard deviations. Right?

"So the effect sizes for cognitive behavioral therapies, prolonged exposure, cognitive processing therapy, the ones that are most studied, in rape populations is about 1.3. And in combat veterans 1.0." In the 2011 pilot study that Litz and Nash did using adaptive disclosure, "we had a 1.3, you know, which is better than 1.0, but how much better do we make the world? And then how much better is that than they would have gotten if we had done yoga or taken them fishing or horseback riding or…anything else in the world? It's not compelling!"

And the risk of adverse outcomes is not known, Nash said. Prolonged exposure therapy can cause people to react violently, for instance, but there is no data on adverse outcomes for exposure therapy. "Over the years, working in inpatient units in psychiatry I have had many people who just lost it, gone crazy in exposure treatment for some trauma," he said. "People know this at a gut level, or they hear of someone who had a bad experience. But what the rates are we have no freakin' idea—we've never looked!"

There's also a shortage of data, of understanding, about people who get better naturally, without treatment: "What are the predictors of getting better? Was it a spouse that could tolerate hearing the stories? These are the anecdotes that I hear all the time, guys say, 'What saved my life was my wife hearing all the things that I did and telling me *I love you anyway.*' And convincing them that they deserve to be loved. How many [got better] because they found God and forgiveness in church? How many because of peer support? How much of it was because they just did the things we all do to heal from moral injuries? I mean moral injuries have been around for as long as humans, right? What are the cultural ways of responding to that? You make amends? You seek amends. You try, if you have created evil, to create good!"

Nash paused as our server cleared away the plates. While adaptive disclosure and Maguen's impact of killing therapy hold great promise, he said he thought the ultimate answers may lie elsewhere. "You have these treatments that are really not hugely better than nothing at all—and because of the side effects, there's a chance they might make you worse." For combat veterans who are badly broken, he added, "you do need mental health intervention to get them to sleep, to reduce the arousal level, manage suicide risk. But if you ask my totally shoot-from-the-hip opinion, I don't think psychotherapists will ever be the solution for moral injury."

Dr. Harold Kudler, the VA's chief mental health consultant, sighed deeply when I called to ask him about all this. "Science tells us that prolonged exposure and cognitive processing therapy are treatments that work for PTSD," he said, and added quickly, "when they are the right treatment for that person. What we're less good at is deciding who's the right person for which type of treatment. It's not the therapy that's wrong; it's the goodness of the fit. I think the VA has a lot of work to do, and it'll take a lot of years to do it well, to establish a sound method of determining the goodness of fit for any of our therapies. We need science behind that." When I asked if that kind of research is under way, he sighed again. "Unfortunately, many people are so invested in their models that they have trouble stepping back to also consider the individual they are working with."

None of these therapies, he added, is designed to fit moral injury. "I do think we don't consider the moral injury aspect of this as much as we could or should. Some would argue that it's not the place of clinical people, that we're not chaplains or oracles. That's an unsatisfactory answer in the twenty-first century. It's in our province to do something about it, or at least to recognize it and have an approach to it."

That confirmed a conviction that had been growing since I began studying moral injury: true healing of veterans with war-related moral injuries will only come from community, however we and they define community—peers, neighborhoods, faith congregations, service organizations, individuals.

That means it's up to us.

CHAPTER 15

Listen

The "truth" of combat is walking all around us, right
under our noses, so we had better start listening to the
truth about what happens to our sons and daughters in war.
—Karen Wall, Major, U.S. Army (Ret.),
and Psychiatric Nurse, U.S. Department
of Veterans Affairs

Moral injury is real. There is no turning away now. We know
that the men and women we send to war can feel strengthened by their experiences, and also damaged. We know that living through combat endows veterans with awful knowledge that
we ourselves have avoided. And we have abandoned the rituals of
cleansing and forgiveness and healing that welcomed returning
combat veterans in past eras and other cultures.

Major American military operations in Iraq and Afghanistan are
over, but we have unfinished business with those wars. As we honor
the stories of Nik Rudolph and Darren Doss and so many others, it's
becoming clear that their healing will come only as they're able to

tell their stories, to share their knowledge with us. Asking and listening is not easy. "Most people, for good reasons, don't want to hear the truth about the battlefield," Jonathan Shay once told me. "You see good kids doing terrible things. Who wants to hear that stuff? And so the truth of war is constantly being submerged." But it's our responsibility to reach for ways to deeply understand these stories, these veterans, before their moral injuries harden into isolation and despair. And for us to understand and weigh the human costs of the new wars that are coming. Time is slipping away.

I think what Karen Wall said, that the truth of war is all around us if we'd only listen, is right, but only half right. Yes, we do need to start listening to veterans and their families, listening in careful and validating ways. But what I have in mind goes beyond listening.

The healing of moral injury demands participation. The long years of war have left us with unshared stories and emotions, unexamined issues and unanswered questions. What did we feel during those years of warfare in Iraq and Afghanistan? Some at home felt apprehension and the dull ache of sorrow knowing that young Americans were in peril and that the morning news would bring portraits of the battle dead. Some sought a connection by sending care packages to troops. Some didn't know what to do. Many of us did nothing. What does that feel like to us? To those who were away at war?

For those few who persevered through long deployments, what was it like to do good in a conflict America had decided was wrong? To lose buddies in a cause that seemed to have been casually abandoned at home? What pride, what guilt, sorrow, and regret linger from the roles each of us played during the war years? How do we feel now about the weight of military service falling on so few of us? About the way the White House and Congress treat the decision to send troops into combat, lurching between partisan rancor and casual hubris? What promises can we make to the next generation we will send, those wide-eyed teenagers now self-consciously trying on their new combat fatigues at marine boot camp and army recruit training?

We should demand that the Department of Defense acknowledge that moral injury is real and that the military services find ways to prepare our troops to meet the moral challenges of war. We should push the Department of Veterans Affairs to better understand moral injury and develop new ways to help veterans find their own paths to cleansing and healing.

We must start by listening to one another. How to begin?

First, let's stop defining veterans in terms of PTSD and twenty-two suicides a day. That's wrong and offensive. Some veterans do have post-traumatic stress. And too many come to feel they can't continue living, a decision that's often an indication of moral injury too painful to bear. Every suicide is tragic, and we can do something to help. But suicide and PTSD do not define the generation newly returned from war. Where healing is needed, it cannot begin with pity.

Next, let's acknowledge that as much as we'd like to absolve ourselves of responsibility and let the government do it, the fact is that the Department of Veterans Affairs alone cannot remedy these veterans' moral injuries. No government agency, no matter how thoroughly reformed or creatively managed, can do that, even with more money. And we've seen that the mental health profession, despite impressive gains in understanding moral injury, isn't making helpful connections with many veterans. "Right now," Bill Nash told me, "the situation for the most part is that individuals who are morally injured use their chaplains, use their friends, they pray, just ignore it—whatever!"

Yet it is not only those who served in our longest wars who suffer moral injuries. It is all of us. We made it possible for Darren Doss to be recruited, armed, and sent to Afghanistan; our attention was elsewhere while he was struggling through gunfire to help save Kruger and during the Christmas-tree-theft caper. We sent Gunny DeLeon to war twice, but we weren't watching as he came home haunted and broken. We recruited and trained Sendio Martz, but we weren't aware that he needed forgiveness. We enlisted Jake Sexton and sent him into the fight, but we didn't listen to the stories that troubled him until it was too late.

Like it or not, fair or unfair, we are all connected by the wars. Now what?

Let's set aside the question of war itself. Like many others, I have considered the idea that killing and destruction are something we should never under any circumstances impose on others. Nor should we send our youngest generations into wars in which we ourselves are too squeamish, or too wise, to engage. My earlier life as a Quaker and conscientious objector and my experience in war strongly tempt me in this direction. Yes, for a long time I found war captivating. But the man who writhed and bled and died in front of me long ago in a dusty village in Ethiopia has shadowed me to many Pentagon briefings and presidential speeches and stirring patriotic ceremonies where, in the urgency of that moment, war seems thrilling and meaningful. It is not, he reminds me. It is also true that in war I have seen individual acts of breathtaking generosity and quiet nobility. But from a larger perspective, it's clear that good rarely comes of war. The human misery and the wreckage are hard to overstate.

I was astonished, walking through my first battlefield after the smoke cleared, at the scale of ruin: burned carcasses of trucks, miles of fine wire from antitank guided missiles, and brass shell casings littered the ground along with rags, shattered glass, a puddle of blood and an empty boot, abandoned rifles and used rocket-launcher tubes, a few crumpled bodies, torn cardboard boxes, an empty bag of IV solution, and cast-off broken helmets. And scampering among the deadly land mines whose rims protruded from the sand, children scavenging for precious metal and food scraps.

Beyond this criminal waste, the inevitable strategic miscalculation and wildly unpredictable consequences of war far overbalance the glorious benefits of armed conflict touted by politicians.

In that conviction I have found harmony with those who have fought in combat, for they have the keenest appreciation of the ugly depravity of mass state-justified bloodletting. I once lived for much of a year with a marine battalion whose senior enlisted marine, a towering, tattooed, broken-nosed sergeant major, had served in Vietnam. I felt instinctively that he detested liberals and especially the "liberal media"—I'd sometimes notice him seeming to glare at me. A Quaker liberal journalist probably was at his outer limits of tolerance. I tried to avoid him, but one day during a pause in a long combat operation he cornered me.

"You were a conscientious objector during Vietnam," he said. It sounded like an accusation.

Glancing around for an escape route, I admitted, Yes, Sergeant Major, I was.

"You know I lost a lot of good people in that war." The word came out *whoa-ah* in his syrupy Tidewater Virginia accent.

Yes, I am sorry, Sergeant Major.

"And you were out on the streets protestin' while I was out there fightin'."

Yes, I was.

Long pause. Then he said with unexpected bitterness, "Well, that's where I should have been, out there on the streets protesting that damn woah-ah 'stead of fightin' it."

And yet.

I once stepped onto a field of tall grass near the town of Chimoio in western Mozambique, and when the wind shifted I staggered against the stench of putrefying flesh. It was a time of bitter fighting; a nearby guerrilla camp had drawn an attack, and there was a massacre, mostly women and children whose bodies were strewn everywhere. In my helpless revulsion, I wanted justice, a battalion of marines to hunt down and kill whoever had committed the atrocity.

I felt the same blind impulse when I stood in the street outside the mayor's office in Srebrenica, a mountain town in Bosnia. There, in July 1995, Serb militiamen swept in and massacred more than eight thousand Bosnian civilians, mostly Muslim men and boys. Eight months later I was being jostled there by Serb thugs laughing away what they'd done and jeering at me and the unwillingness of the United States and its allies to bring them to justice. I wanted a company of Army Rangers to come set things very straight. I wanted revenge. I wanted a killer like Jim Gant. And I didn't stop to think about the effect of that killing on young marines or rangers or even seasoned killers like Gant.

In that I am like most of us.

But when there is casual talk in Washington about putting "boots on the ground," I want to bellow a furious correction: Americans on the ground! Let's name it — humans! *Our kids.* I want us to be more careful with them. While we're figuring out whether and how to end war, I want us to be more skeptical of lofty claims of what military force can achieve and more mindful of the costs that will be borne by the people we send to fight.

For that, we need the insights gained by those who have come back.

It's not easy to initiate and carry forward a conversation with a combat veteran. Often there's awkwardness on both sides, even suspicion. I've found a good icebreaker is to ask about the veteran's job in the service. I know what it means if the answer is "Eleven bravo," but don't pretend to know if you don't. It's okay to ask; in fact, that's the whole point. "Eleven bravo," or 11B, is a military occupational specialty — MOS — or job title, in this case for an infantryman. There are hundreds of MOSs, and only a few personnel experts know them all; even seasoned troopers might be stumped by a 21L, a lithographer. Next question might be "Can you tell me about that?" Veterans like to talk about their military jobs; from there, guided by questions like "Tell me more," "How did that feel," or "What was that like," the conversation can go deeper.

David Sutherland, whose familiarity with combat and moral injury was gained over fifteen months as a troop commander in Iraq, now campaigns for Americans to pick up where the VA falls short. "The VA and [the Pentagon] don't solve all problems. This whole thing needs to be about listening, understanding. Asking and not thanking." Bumper stickers and parades are appreciated, he said. "But no one sits there and goes, 'How ya doin'? I can't imagine what you've been through, but I'd love to listen to you, if you want to talk about it. And I'm not gonna compare my cat peeing on the carpet to your fifteen months in Iraq.'"

Still, grunts like Chuck Newton are skeptical. He was reluctant at first even to meet with me, and he scoffed at the idea that civilians should listen carefully to marine veterans. But seeing that I was interested, he talked for hours over several days. Even then, he was doubtful about what I was doing. "Who's gonna read your book?" he demanded one day as we sat admiring the view of Manhattan from across the East River in Brooklyn. "Only people who already agree," he answered himself.

To help with the awkwardness that can exist between veteran and civilian, a structured approach was developed by the clinical psychologist Paula Joan Caplan. Her idea was to match veterans with volunteer civilian listeners for a long session of uninterrupted, intentional listening.

In an experiment at Harvard's Kennedy School of Government, she arranged for veterans to talk without interference for as long as three hours. The listeners were coached to begin by saying,

"As an American whose government sent you to war, I take some responsibility for listening to your story, so *if* you want to talk about your experiences at war and since coming home, I will listen for as long as you want to talk, and I will not judge you." And they were instructed to listen silently but with total attention, smiling where appropriate but not responding verbally. This is to avoid the understandable temptation to interrupt with a comforting "Oh, I understand," when it's likely that a civilian listener cannot understand the full breadth and depth of a combat veteran's experience. Based on the positive response from veterans and listeners, Caplan has sought to make this model available nationwide.

For a more interactive experience, I went back and reread Michael Castellana's directions for therapists dealing with morally injured marines. It's good advice for all of us who approach veterans in a spirit of close listening:

> These are remarkable, courageous men and women. We should laugh with them, grieve with them, and, most of all, empathize and inject a human perspective on the terrible experiences these service members have endured. We must bear with them, the distressing and challenging events they have lived through, and accompany them as they make their way to a new, fuller understanding and appreciation of their role in war and as fellow human beings in the world.

In short, listening with validation. *Yeah, that was fucked up.*

But also, an integral part of what Castellana teaches: *I honor your service.*

"When I came home, people were afraid to ask me about the experience. Because they were afraid it would disturb me. But I found it more disturbing to have that significant part of my life ignored." This is Robert Certain, an unstinting advocate for listening as a way of helping veterans heal their moral injuries. Certain is an Episcopal priest and longtime military chaplain who began his military career as a young, redheaded air force captain, a B-52 navigator. His experience in war came four decades ago, but his own enduring moral injury can teach us about connecting with today's new generation of veterans. During Linebacker II, the so-called Christmas bombing of North Vietnam in 1972, Bob Certain's aircraft was shot down; three of the crew were killed. Certain was captured and held prisoner until all POWs were released in March 1973. Those searing experiences led him, on his return, to the seminary and into a new life in ministry.

Several weeks before his last flight over North Vietnam, Certain had been assigned to a mission on a B-52 bomber code-named *Purple Two;* the crew was told the targets had been carefully selected, like previous missions, as strictly industrial sites. "People targets were rarely discussed," he told me. "Rarely would we be told we were going after troop concentrations, a North Vietnam battalion or something." They returned safely from the mission, but later they learned that friendly ground troops had gone into the area after a B-52 strike and reported finding 156 bodies beneath the flight path of *Purple Two.* "Well, that was my airplane," Certain said in a soft voice. "Those were people down there."

His moral injuries, from the death of his close buddies and the deaths of Vietnamese from the American bombing, were devastating. But because no one asked, no one listened, it took Certain thirty years to break out of his protective shell of grief, loss, and guilt and to ask for and receive professional help. Central to his continuing recovery is sharing his story. Veterans, he said, "don't want advice, unless they ask for it. I think they want to be able to talk, to sort out what is going on in their soul and mind. And a lot of us do that verbally."

Certain is a gentle man with a kindly, grandfatherly demeanor. Moral injury, he said, "is not a psychological problem. It's a problem of conscience, of spirituality. Of the soul." We were talking in his comfortably modern riverside home in northern Georgia. When I asked whether the VA could play a constructive role in helping veterans verbalize their experiences, even helping heal moral injury, he visibly recoiled. "I don't want the government to do it," he said firmly. "They screw everything up. They got us into this! No, from my perspective it is a moral obligation for the population to take this responsibility, and it takes a lot more than applauding returning soldiers at the airport. It takes listening to them very carefully."

The technique he described is simple. " 'What can you tell me about your experience over there?' You'll never get the whole story," he said. "But over time you might learn more and more. It takes time to build that trust. You might get nothing. But be prepared. You might get a dump."

The idea may be simple, but I think it's not so easy. I know former marines who don't *want* to talk to anybody except other marines. And the deep divide between military and civilians, one of ignorance and perhaps suspicion, hostility, and guilt, becomes harder and harder to cross. And yet I believe there is a reservoir of goodwill on both sides, perhaps even a desire to step over the military-civilian divide. It seems clear that encounters between veteran and civilian most easily can happen in a community context where there is already social engagement. By "community" I mean religious gathering, neighborhood association, sports team, book club, service project—however we each define "community."

There are dozens, perhaps hundreds, of nongovernmental projects under way across the country, providing ways for civilians to get involved with veterans. The Mission Continues, a national nonprofit, has launched fifty-three service platoons with more than five thousand members, including active-duty and reserve servicemen and -women, veterans, and civilians; the teams undertake local service projects. Another nonprofit, Team Red White and Blue, involves eighty-one thousand members, including twenty-four thousand civilians, in sporting and social events, in an effort to close the military-civilian divide. Many of these veteran-oriented nonprofits welcome civilian volunteers; no experience necessary.

Similar efforts are under way in the faith community. An organization called Care for the Troops, led by Robert Certain, trains community leaders, therapists, religious congregations, and social-service providers to understand how to receive and relate to veterans. Retired army chaplain Dave Smith, who served in both Iraq and Afghanistan, runs a program called the Soul Care Initiative to help connect church congregations with veterans.

"What has worked for me is when people are unabashed, not afraid to ask tough questions," Stacy Pearsall said to me as we nursed our beers. She's the combat camera who worked two tours in Iraq, and while her physical problems have eased, her moral injuries are still painful and the temptation of suicide lurks. "It's taken a lot of work to stay on the right side of the dirt," she said.

I had been telling her of all the opportunities for civilians and veterans to start talking and listening. But I confessed that I didn't see it actually happening much. She nodded. "I think a lot of what society does now is dance around the cancer. You can't do that. We keep it in hushed tones because it may be painful and maybe the people asking the questions are afraid of what answers they may get; the answers may not be the ones they really want to hear. But it's important to make sure these things are out in the open."

She paused, dabbing absentmindedly with a napkin at the dark circles of condensation the beer bottles were leaving on the bar.

"You don't have to talk military language to really understand the emotions of it. You should never say, 'Oh, I understand,' because you can never understand unless you've been there. However, you *can* say, 'I can't imagine what that must be like, can you just explain to me a little more why you feel that way, or what draws you to the conclusion you feel guilty?' You don't have to sympathize—I don't want your sympathy," she said. "But your understanding would be nice." She stopped to chuckle. "And empathy maybe?"

To what end? I asked. Why is it so important to you that people listen, and understand and respond?

Long pause, while she folded and refolded the napkin, pressing it into smaller and smaller squares.

"I would hope we would think a lot more deeply about sending people to war, given the impact it's had on our society and community and nation with the whole ripple effect that war has," she said. "We went there and fought on behalf of our nation. That's what we signed up to do. That's the job we raised our hands for and said we would give our lives to do. So I don't regret that. And I cannot say—and I've battled with the morality of this—that Iraq was not worth it, because then I would be diminishing the sacrifices my friends made on the battlefield, and I cannot do that."

She turned to see if I understood and then went on, "Not every war is favorable, not every war is popular, and the outcome is not always what we had hoped it would be. But then again, that's the cost of war.

"I would hope that, given this length of combat in Afghanistan and the impact that Iraq had on all of us, we would think a little bit more smartly before jumping headlong into another one.

"Gotta run," she said, slipping off her stool and shouldering her camera bags, and off she went to capture in haunting photographs the pride, vulnerability, and moral injury etched on the faces of combat veterans.

Acknowledgments

This book could not have been written without the steady support and encouragement of Arianna Huffington, president and editor in chief of the *Huffington Post*. Over the years she has provided me with unprecedented time and resources for deep reporting. She was enthusiastic about my idea of exploring wartime moral injury and generously allowed me time away from the busy news cycles to think and write.

Gail Ross, my agent, was instrumental in helping me focus what I have learned about war into a more coherent form. I am grateful to Gail for her friendship and her tireless efforts to make this book a reality. Nor would this book have been possible without the enthusiasm and guidance of Tracy Behar, my editor at Little, Brown.

I have focused mainly on army soldiers and marines for reasons of simple logistics. While I have flown with military air crews and lived on warships, the ground-force grunts are the men and women with whom I have most easily spent time. Those in the U.S. Navy and U.S. Air Force also serve honorably and in difficult situations and face equally challenging moral dilemmas at war. I am grateful to all of them for their grace under pressure and for their willingness to share their lives.

The extraordinary professionals who work with the military and veterans in mental health research and therapy were patient and generous with their time in helping me understand the complexities of moral injury and moral healing. Jonathan Shay has been a friend and mentor for many years, and I am deeply indebted to him for his gentle tutoring and warm encouragement. Deepest thanks to Bill Nash, Michael Castellana, Brett Litz, and Shira Maguen for sharing their insights and wisdom with me.

Over the years of covering the military at war I have been lucky to work with other visionary editors, especially my former editors at the *Huffington Post,* Tim O'Brien and John Montorio. I deeply miss the late Deborah Howell, who was my editor for two decades at Newhouse News Service and from whom I absorbed much about the profession and craft of journalism. I gained from the guidance and friendship of Linda Fibich at Newhouse News Service and Melinda Henneberger at AOL's *Politics Daily* (and now editor in chief of *Roll Call*). I am grateful to all of them for their guidance and trust.

Some of the material in this book was reported and written for the AOL website *Politics Daily* and for the *Huffington Post.* I have used it here with the gracious permission of AOL and the *Huffington Post.* Steven O. Newhouse likewise granted me permission to use some material I had written for Newhouse News Service.

I am indebted to Anne-Marie Slaughter, Peter Bergen, and others at New America for their encouragement and support while I was a fellow at the Future of War project.

Almost all of the reporting for this book was done away from home, often on long trips into foreign war zones. The weeks and months I spent there imposed burdens on my wife, journalist Beth Frerking, and on my children, Seth, Peter, and Samantha, and my stepsons, Matthew and Evan. It was on them to pick up my share of household chores and to endure the uncertainties and worries concerning my whereabouts and my safety. I am grateful for their unconditional love and support.

Acknowledgments

In short, many people have contributed to this work, most prominently my wife, Beth, whose ear for storytelling and resolute sense of professionalism have energized my work. Many others, including active-duty military and veterans and family members, are unnamed here but have enriched my life and earned my appreciation for their service. Any errors or shortcomings of this book, however, are mine.

Notes

vii.   General Ray Odierno: Remarks at the New America Foundation Future of
       War Conference, Washington, DC, Feb. 25, 2015.

Chapter 1: It's Wrong, but You Have No Choice

7.   Paul D. Fritts: "Adaptive Disclosure: Critique of a Descriptive Inter-
       vention Modified for the Normative Problem of Moral Injury in Combat Veter-
       ans" (paper presented at Yale Divinity School, New Haven, CT, Sept. 12, 2013).
14.   In her study of Afghanistan and Iraq veterans: Shira Maguen, "Killing and
       Latent Classes of PTSD Symptoms in Iraq and Afghanistan Veterans," *Jour-
       nal of Affective Disorders* (2012): 344–48.
16.   the VA has hired IBM: http://www.ibm.com/press/us/en/pressrelease/
       45701.wss.
16.   Major Paul D. Fritts wrote: "Adaptive Disclosure."
17.   as psychologist Aaron Antonovsky has written: Quoted by Ronnie
       Janoff-Bulman, *Shattered Assumptions,* 18.
29.   As Eric T. Dean Jr. writes: *Shook Over Hell.*
32.   diagnosed with traumatic brain injury (TBI): Traumatic brain injury is
       damage to the brain caused in wartime mainly by exposure to a concussive
       blast. The symptoms experienced by some forty-five thousand U.S. troops
       diagnosed with combat-related TBI range from temporary and mild to
       severe and disabling. For more information see the Defense and Veterans
       Brain Injury Center, http://dvbic.dcoe.mil/about/tbi-military.
34.   Rebecca Johnson . . . has pointed out: "Moral Formation of the Strategic
       Corporal," in *New Wars and New Soldiers: Military Ethics in the Contemporary
       World,* Tripodi and Wolfendale, eds.

Chapter 2: Regardless of the Cost

36.   Henry James: "The Moral Equivalent of War" (lecture, Stanford University,
       Stanford, CA, 1906), http://www.uky.edu/~eushe2/Pajares/moral.html.

Chapter 3: The Rules: Made to Be Broken

53. Clint Van Winkle: Personal interview. Van Winkle is the author of *Soft Spots.*

59. chaplain Paul D. Fritts explains: Paul D. Fritts, research paper, Yale Divinity School, April 29, 2013, accessed at http://www.cgscfoundation.org/wp -content/uploads/2014/03/Fritts-AdaptiveDisclosure.pdf.

69. detailed by the Pentagon's inspector general: *Report of Investigation: General William E. Ward, U.S. Army Commander, U.S. AFRICOM* (Washington, DC: Inspector General, United States Department of Defense, June 26, 2012), accessed at http://www.dodig.mil/fo/foia/pdfs/wardroi_redacted.pdf.

69. was sentenced to seventy-five months in prison: FBI press release, http:// www.fbi.gov/sandiego/press-releases/2010/sd041410.htm.

70. a study by the U.S. Army War College: Leonard Wong and Stephen J. Gerras, *Lying to Ourselves: Dishonesty in the Army Profession* (Carlisle, PA: U.S. Army War College, Strategic Studies Institute, February 2015), http:// www.strategicstudiesinstitute.army.mil/pubs/display.cfm?pubID=1250.

70. wrote in *Military Review:* "The Myths We Soldiers Tell Ourselves," *Military Review* (Sept.–Oct. 2013), http://usacac.army.mil/CAC2/MilitaryReview /Archives/English/MilitaryReview_20131031_art010.pdf.

Chapter 4: A Friend Was Liquefied

77. A report prepared for VA clinicians in 2004: *Iraq War Clinician Guide* (Washington, DC: U.S. Department of Veterans Affairs, 2004), 22, 23, http://www.ptsd.va.gov/professional/manuals/manual-pdf/iwcg/iraq _clinician_guide_v2.pdf.

78. the army's Mental Health Advisory Team (MHAT) reported: *Operation Iraqi Freedom (OIF) Mental Health Advisory Team Report* (Dec. 16, 2003), http:// www-tc.pbs.org/wgbh/pages/frontline/shows/heart/readings/mhat.pdf.

81. A study by the Institute of Medicine: *Returning Home from Iraq and Afghanistan: Assessment of Readjustment Needs of Veterans, Service Members and Their Families* (Washington, DC: Institute of Medicine of the National Academies, March 2013).

81. An alarmed army report: *Army 2020: Generating Health and Discipline in the Force,* United States Army (2012).

92. she wrote in 2013: Shira Maguen and Kristine Burkman, "Combat-Related Killing: Expanding Evidence-Based Treatments for PTSD" (San Francisco: VA Medical Center and University of California). *Cognitive and Behavioral Practice,* Oct. 2013. 476–79.

94. a Defense Department task force: *An Achievable Vision: Report of the Department of Defense Task Force on Mental Health,* U.S. Department of Defense (June 2007).

Notes

Chapter 5: Just War

100. Michael Walzer: "The Triumph of Just War Theory (and the Dangers of Success)," *Social Research* 69, no. 4, International Justice, War Crimes and Terrorism: The U.S. Record (Winter 2002).
105. As Princeton's Michael Walzer wrote: "Triumph of Just War Theory."

Chapter 6: Trotting Heart, Shell Shock, Moral Injury

116. George Loeffler: "Moral Injury: An Emerging Concept in Combat Trauma," *Residents' Journal* (April 2013).
120. As Freud once wrote: "Thoughts for the Times on War and Death" (1915).
121. his doctors noted with some puzzlement: Dean, *Shook Over Hell.*
123. "an invention of the Jews": Rick Atkinson, *The Day of Battle: The War in Sicily and Italy* (New York: Henry Holt, 2007).
125. "get a medical board": A military medical board is a team of physicians who determine whether a service member can fulfill the requirements of his or her job. A negative decision can result in a job change or even lead to dismissal.

Chapter 7: Grief Is a Combat Injury

133. Dan Levin: *From the Battlefield: Dispatches of a World War II Marine* (Annapolis, MD: Naval Institute Press, 1995).
136. What she found was stunning: Ilona Pivar, "Unresolved Grief in Combat Veterans with PTSD," *Journal of Anxiety Disorders* 18, no. 6 (2004).

Chapter 8: It's Really About Killing

142. Timothy Kudo: "I Killed People in Afghanistan. Was I Right or Wrong?," *Washington Post,* Jan. 25, 2013.
145. Samurai warriors used Zen meditation: Winston L. King, *Zen and the Way of the Sword: Arming the Samurai Psyche* (New York: Oxford University Press, 1993).
145. Athanasius wrote: Letter to Amun, retrieved at http://www.newadvent.org/fathers/2806048.htm.
146. "anyone who knows he killed a man": Bernard Verkamp, *The Moral Treatment of Returning Warriors in Early Medieval and Modern Times.*
147. He found deep trauma: Brett Litz, "A Randomized Controlled Trial of Adaptive Disclosure for Moral Injury" (grant proposal, project narrative, 2012).
154. In 2010 she published the results: Shira Maguen, "The Impact of Reported Direct and Indirect Killing on Mental Health Symptoms in Iraq War Veterans," *Journal of Traumatic Stress* (Feb. 2010): 86–90.
156. *Thoughts of a Soldier-Ethicist*: http://soldier-ethicist.blogspot.com.

Notes

Chapter 9: Vulnerable

170. "feeling the pucker factor": A common military term meaning "scared," referring to tightening the sphincter muscles in fear.

Chapter 10: Betrayed

182. her blog, *Semper Sarah:* http://www.sempersarah.com/1962#sthash.oAW PfXAc.dpuf.

Chapter 11: War Crime

184. Rebecca Johnson: "Moral Formation of the Strategic Corporal."
193. *Law of War Manual:* http://www.dod.mil/dodgc/images/law_war_manual15.pdf.
194. As the 2005 standing ROE put it: *Chairman Joint Chiefs of Staff Instruction 3121.01B, Standing Rules of Engagement/Standing Rules for the Use of Force for U.S. Forces* (June 13, 2005), accessed at https://navytribe.files.wordpress .com/2015/11/cjcsi-3121-01b-enclosure-l.pdf.
199. explained to army investigators: Interrogation tape obtained by CNN, http://www.cnn.com/2009/US/11/17/army.tapes.canal.killings.
200. he felt no remorse: Dan Lamothe, "Inside the Stunning Fall and War-Crimes Investigation of an Army Green Beret War Hero," *Washington Post,* May 19, 2015, accessed at https://www.washingtonpost.com/news/checkpoint/wp/ 2015/05/19/inside-the-stunning-fall-and-war-crimes-investigation -of-an-army-green-beret-war-hero.
201. hunted down and killed: Sean Naylor, *Army Times,* Sept. 12, 2010, http:// archive.armytimes.com/article/20100913/NEWS/9130311/JSOC -task-force-battles-Haqqani-militants.

Chapter 12: Atheists in the Foxholes

210. a paper by Shira Maguen: "Combat-Related Killing: Expanding Evidence-Based Treatments for PTSD," *Cognitive and Behavioral Practice* (November 2013).

Chapter 13: Home

220. Lieutenant Colonel Bill Russell Edmonds: *God Is Not Here.*

Chapter 14: The Touchy-Feely Tough Guys

251. in a 2009 article: Brett T. Litz et al., "Moral Injury and Moral Repair in War Veterans: A Preliminary Model and Intervention Strategy," *Clinical Psychology Review* 29 (2009).

Chapter 15: Listen

261. Karen Wall: Communication with author.

Select Bibliography

Armstrong, Karen. *Fields of Blood: Religion and the History of Violence.* New York: Anchor Books, 2014.

Boudreau, Tyler E. *Packing Inferno: The Unmaking of a Marine.* Port Townsend, WA: Feral House, 2008.

Brock, Rita Nakashima, and Gabriella Lettini. *Soul Repair: Recovering from Moral Injury After War.* Boston: Beacon Press, 2012.

Certain, Robert. *Unchained Eagle.* Marietta, GA: Deeds Publishing, 2003.

Dean, Eric T., Jr. *Shook Over Hell: Post-Traumatic Stress, Vietnam, and the Civil War.* Cambridge, MA: Harvard University Press, 1997.

Doerries, Bryan. *The Theater of War: What Ancient Greek Tragedies Can Teach Us Today.* New York: Alfred A. Knopf, 2015.

Edmonds, Bill Russell. *God Is Not Here: A Soldier's Struggle with Torture, Trauma and the Moral Injuries of War.* New York: Pegasus Books, 2015.

Friedman, Brandon. *The War I Always Wanted: The Illusion of Glory and the Reality of War.* Saint Paul, MN: Zenith Press, 2007.

Grossman, David A. *On Killing: The Psychological Cost of Learning to Kill in War and Society.* New York: Little, Brown, 1995.

Herman, Judith. *Trauma and Recovery: The Aftermath of Violence—From Domestic Abuse to Political Terror.* New York: Basic Books, 1992.

Janoff-Bulman, Ronnie. *Shattered Assumptions: Towards a New Psychology of Trauma.* New York: Free Press, 1992.

Keegan, John. *The Face of Battle.* New York: Penguin Books, 1978.

Levin, Dan. *From the Battlefield: Dispatches of a World War II Marine.* Annapolis, MD: Naval Institute Press, 1995.

Lieberman, Jeffrey A. *Shrinks: The Untold Story of Psychiatry.* New York: Little, Brown, 2015.

McChrystal, Gen. Stanley. *My Share of the Task.* New York: Portfolio, 2013.

Marshall, S. L. A. *Men Against Fire: The Problem of Battle Command in Future War.* Alexandria, VA: Byrrd Enterprises, 1947.

Meagher, Robert Emmet. *Killing from the Inside Out: Moral Injury and Just War.* Eugene, OR: Cascade Books, 2014.

Plummer, Sarah. *Just Roll with It: The 7 Battle-Tested Traits for Creating a Ridiculously Happy, Healthy and Successful Life.* Newport Beach, CA: Bandera Publishing, 2012.

Shay, Jonathan. *Achilles in Vietnam: Combat Trauma and the Undoing of Character.* New York: Scribner, 1994.

———. *Odysseus in America: Combat Trauma and the Trials of Homecoming.* New York: Scribner, 2002.

Tick, Edward. *Warrior's Return: Restoring the Soul After War.* Boulder, CO: Sounds True, 2014.

Tripodi, Paolo, and Jessica Wolfendale, eds. *New Wars and New Soldiers: Military Ethics in the Contemporary World.* Burlington, VT: Ashgate, 2012.

Tyson, Ann Scott. *American Spartan: The Promise, the Mission, and the Betrayal of Special Forces Major Jim Gant.* New York: William Morrow, 2014.

Van Winkle, Clint. *Soft Spots: A Marine's Memoir of Combat and Post-Traumatic Stress Disorder.* New York: St. Martin's Griffin, 2009.

Verkamp, Bernard J. *The Moral Treatment of Returning Warriors in Early Medieval and Modern Times.* Scranton, PA: University of Scranton Press, 2006.

Walzer, Michael. *Just and Unjust Wars: A Moral Argument with Historical Illustrations.* New York: Basic Books, 1977.

West, Bing. *The Strongest Tribe: War, Politics, and the Endgame in Iraq.* New York: Random House, 2008.

Whitman, Walt. *Drum-Taps: The Complete 1865 Edition.* New York: New York Review Books, 2015.

Wilson, Timothy D. *Redirect: Changing the Stories We Live By.* New York: Back Bay Books, 2015.

Index

Index

Brite Divinity School, Soul Repair
  Center, 219
Brown, Tim, 228
"bubble theory," 158, 159
Bush, George W.
  Iraq War and, 33, 66, 77, 78, 167, 177
  just war doctrine of, 106, 107
  national security team of, 178
  on prisoners, 193

Campbell, Rob, 85–86
Canty, Micheline, 24
Canty, Stephen, 23–25, 31–32, 41, 78
  on betrayal, 178–79
  boot camp and, 54
  combat stories of, 25–28, 34, 43–44,
    49–50, 61, 103, 137, 138–39, 140,
    141, 160–61
  documentaries by, 141, 161–62
  enlistment of, 29
  on mental effects of war, 43
  moral injury in, 256
  moral values and, 66, 67, 68, 72
Caplan, Paula Joan, 267–68
Care for the Troops, 219, 271
Casey, George, 32, 96
Castellana, Anna, 235, 244–46
Castellana, Carmelo, 235, 244, 245
Castellana, Michael
  on listening, 247, 268
  personal trauma of, 244–46
  treatment model of, 132, 235–38,
    239, 243–44, 246–49, 250, 251,
    252, 253–54
Catholic Church, 106, 118–19
CBT (cognitive behavioral therapy),
  239, 242, 249–50, 258
Certain, Robert G., 147, 268–70, 271
Chaplain Corps, 218
chaplains, 205, 206, 213
Charlie Company, One-Six, 44–46
  boot camp and, 54
  casualties in, 44, 114, 133–35,
    136, 195
  combat mission of, 66, 100, 101–3,
    109–11, 136–41

counterinsurgency mission of, 178–79
  interviewing members of, 24–25, 141
  just war doctrine and, 112–13
  relationships in, 31–32, 135–36
  rules of engagement for, 195–96
children
  betrayal by, 63–65
  encounters with, 167–68, 188
  as human shields, 102–3
  killing of, 7–8, 13–14, 16–17, 23, 26,
    64–65, 110, 113, 125, 145, 237, 248
  rape of, 66
CISD (critical incident stress
  debriefing), 124–25, 126–27, 239
City of God (St. Augustine), 104
Civil War (American), 29, 105, 121
Clark, Philip, 74
cleansing rituals, 3–5, 9, 118–19,
  190, 211
Coggins, Bryan, 21–22
cognitive behavioral therapy (CBT),
  239, 242, 249–50, 258
cognitive processing therapy (CPT),
  239, 243, 250, 257–60
COIN (counterinsurgency), 33–34,
  85, 105, 152, 178–79, 194
combat camera, 163–64, 165, 167, 271
combat stress, 48, 78, 125, 129, 235
  See also moral injury; posttraumatic
    stress disorder
Combat Stress Injury (Nash), 130
community involvement, 260, 270–71
Company of Heroes, A, 30
compassion fatigue, 212
Comprehensive Soldier and Family
  Fitness (CSF2), 96–98, 159
conscientious objector, 38, 39,
  264, 265
Cornum, Rhonda, 96
counterinsurgency (COIN), 33–34,
  85, 105, 152, 178–79, 194
CPT (cognitive processing therapy),
  239, 243, 250, 257–60
critical incident stress debriefing
  (CISD), 124–25, 126–27, 239
Cutright, Kevin, 70

284

Index

Index

Index

Index

Index

Index

Walter Reed Army Medical Center,
80, 100, 178
Walzer, Michael, 100, 103,
105, 114
war
cost of, 43, 48, 264–65, 272
emotional transition from, 221–23
laws of, 12, 84–89, 190–96, 203
moral dimension of, 11–12, 17–18,
20–21, 58, 91, 145–47, 185,
186–90
new kind of, 12, 82–83
rationales for, 103–4
See also Afghanistan War; Iraq War;
just war doctrine; Vietnam War
war crimes, 83–84
morality of killing and, 186–87,
197–201
against prisoners, 66–68, 71–72,
197, 237
World War II, 83, 184–86, 187,
196–97
Ward, William "Kip," 68–69
War I Always Wanted, The
(Friedman), 177
War on Terror, 193
war trauma
civilian trauma vs., 257
defining nature of, 89–92
doctrine for treating, 119, 120–27
moral dimension of, 91
physical, 80, 82–83
preexisting weakness and, 120, 128
prevention of, 96–98
psychological, 80–82
in World War II, 29–30, 80, 123
wound concept of, 129–32

See also moral injury; posttraumatic
stress disorder
Washington, George, 191
Waynick, Thomas C., 218
Webber, Matthew, 229
West, Bing, 198
Westphal, Richard, 255
Wheat Ridge Ministries, 219
Whitman, Walt, 163
Wicker, Roger, 99
Wilks, Kye, 51
Wilson, Timothy D., 124
Wilson, Woodrow, 105
Wiltsee, David, 121
Wong, Leonard, 70
Wood, David
in Afghanistan, 12–13, 40–43,
45–46
early life of, 37–38
as *Time* correspondent, 36–40,
265–66
and Vietnam War, 264–65
Wood, Elizabeth Smedley, 37–38,
40, 47
World War I, 105, 119, 120–23,
124, 238
World War II
fear of killing in, 156–57
return from, 87
trauma in, 29–30, 80, 123
war crimes in, 83, 184–86, 187,
196–97

Youmans, Joshua, 228

Zell, Xavier, 44, 49–50, 136–37,
160–61

About the Author

DAVID WOOD has reported on wars and conflict around the world for more than thirty-five years. His series on severely wounded American veterans of Iraq and Afghanistan won the 2012 Pulitzer Prize for national reporting. Wood grew up as a Quaker and in the 1960s spent two years in national civilian service as a conscientious objector. Since then he has covered conflicts in Europe and Central America and across Africa, the Middle East, and Southwest Asia. He has embedded with U.S. troops many times in war zones and in domestic training. At home, outside Washington, D.C., he bicycles for sport while waiting for cold weather and ice climbing.